with my best wish

Daphne Gerlis

Dear Linn and Steve,
We will ever remember
the wonderful day
    July 26, 1997
You gave us, your nice
  family and you, dear friends
  With much love,
Yours Vera, Victor
  and George
    Samoilovich

North Bergen, September 10,
    1997

THOSE WONDERFUL WOMEN IN BLACK

The Story of the Women's Campaign for Soviet Jewry

Daphne Gerlis

MINERVA PRESS
MONTREUX   LONDON   WASHINGTON

THOSE WONDERFUL WOMEN IN BLACK
Copyright © Daphne Gerlis 1996

ISBN 1 86106 321 0

First Published 1996 by
MINERVA PRESS
195 Knightbridge
London SW7 1RE

Printed in Great Britain by
Antony Rowe Ltd, Chippenham, Wiltshire

THOSE WONDERFUL
WOMEN IN BLACK

*This book is dedicated to the memory
of Raiza Palatnik – our inspiration.*

In February 1976, Golda Meir, the Prime Minister of Israel, addressed the Brussels II Conference of American Soviet Jewry activists, British, French, and Israeli organisations working for Soviet Jewry. She drew attention to "the ladies in black" who were present in the hall, and referred to their sweeping the streets saying that she would be proud to sweep alongside the 35s...

Acknowledgements

The following list of those who have helped me with this book by no means reflects the order of the degree of assistance. I was helped by so many people, but those mentioned here gave me of their time and their advice, some so unstintingly and generously that I shall be forever in their debt.

I trust that I shall be forgiven for any omissions and errors, unwittingly made. Many documents were missing, many photographs impossible to reproduce, and some information was not forthcoming.

I must single out the name of my husband, Leon, without whom this book would not have been written.

Michael Alge, Joanna Aron, Jonathan Arkush, Sylvia Becker, Rita Bensusan, Sir Rhodes Boyson, Joan Dale, Rochelle Duke, Rita Eker, Dora and Sydney Gabrel, Doreen Gainsford, Roz Gemal, Jeremy Gerlis, Sir Martin Gilbert, Simone Goldfarb, Naomi Goldwater, Linda Greenlick, Peter Halban, Zelda Harris, Susan Hayman, Myra and Greville Janner, Delysia Jason, Rachele Kalman, Bernard Levin, Sylvia Lukeman, David Massel, Professor Aubrey Newman, Evelyn Nohr, Ida Nudel, Barbara Oberman-Katz, Ijo Rager, Margaret Rigal, Gish Robbins, Professor David Ruben, Susie Sainsbury, George Samoilovich, Sylvia Sheff, Michael Sherbourne, Colin Shindler, Joyce Simson, John Simpson, Carole Spiers, Cicely Woolf, and all the 35ers who responded to my requests.

Foreword

I

This book is about the Women's Campaign for Soviet Jewry, affectionately known as the 35s, who will celebrate their 25th anniversary in May 1996.

It was born out of an urgent need to help Raiza Palatnik, a Russian Jewish woman, imprisoned on a trumped-up charge of 'Slandering the Soviet Union'.

The group rapidly became a powerful force in the Soviet Jewry movement in this country with a network of branches and affiliates in the British Isles, Europe and overseas.

The women, most of whom were NW London, middle-class Jewish housewives and who had led somewhat circumscribed lives, achieved undisputed recognition for their novel and sometimes outrageous demonstrations. For many years they were at odds, not only with the Anglo-Jewish establishment, but also with the Israeli Government, who objected to their form of campaigning. But it will be seen that their approach was justified.

II

The story of the struggle to liberate the Jews of the Soviet Union is an uplifting one. In its day, it seemed an uphill, and at times a hopeless struggle, against a determined tyranny. But the women whose stories are told in these pages did not allow themselves to be cowed or deterred. If they were downhearted at times, they tried not to show it. They held out a hand (indeed, many hundreds of hands) of sustenance and hope to the Jews who were trapped, whose liberation they played such a major part in securing, and whose needs, to this day, they refuse to neglect. I can think of no more impressive group, battlers for truth, openers of the gates, and marvellous people in themselves, drawn together in a common cause. This book is a tribute to their persistent and remarkable efforts.

Sir Martin Gilbert

Prologue

"...It's really awful, I miss her so much, and now who knows when we shall see each other again? When she goes I trust that she will take us with her (in spirit). I can hardly believe that some day the time will come when I too will be able to leave. I'm carrying the photograph about with me and often look at everyone on it and I recollect our meetings and conversations and again I feel jealous. For they are all now free and I must stay here and wait in vain for my freedom.

"Daddy, I was very surprised by your suggestion of applying for a pardon. Under no circumstances should you do so; don't even think about it; don't humiliate me. It's bad enough that they sentenced me for no reason at all and then on top of it do I have to ask to be forgiven? And for what? Cast the thought out of your mind. And tell Lenka that I'll give him what for, for helping you with this notion. Has he got nothing else to do? I beg you not to have anything to do with this idea..."

Extract of a letter[1] from Raiza Palatnik to her father during her imprisonment in Russia for the crime of having applied for an exit visa. This referred to the impending emigration of her young sister Katya, to Israel, November 1971.

[1]   Translated from the original Russian

By the same author:

The Story of the Grimsby Jewish Community,
(co-author L M Gerlis), Humberside Leisure Services, 1986

Contents

Introduction

Many groups and individuals have been part of the Soviet Jewry campaign in Britain and elsewhere, but as a virtually exclusively female Jewish group, the 35s are unique in this country.

I have been fortunate in that many of the founder members of the Women's Campaign for Soviet Jewry have been able to contribute much authentic source material. It has proved impossible to contact the hundreds of women who worked with the 35s, nor did I find it necessary to interview all the known participants, as after a number of interviews it was apparent that many of the stories were being repeated. A letter published in *The Jewish Chronicle* in March 1993 asking for information, etc. resulted in only three replies. If any major contributor to the campaign has been omitted, it was inadvertent and I apologise.

Unless otherwise stated the sources are either oral, or from the 35s newsletters, files and press cuttings. Sadly, due to hasty office moves, much documentation has been lost over the years; hence there are gaps in the narrative.

From the 1970s background of typical Jewish housewives these volunteers developed a professional expertise; hard-headed yet compassionate, they wept tears of sorrow and tears of joy. Their effectiveness was due to their total dedication to the cause of Soviet Jewry, passionately motivated by the 'never again' rationale.

When I came to live in London in 1986, I wished to resume the Soviet Jewry work which I had been doing throughout the 1970s in my home town of Grimsby. I contacted the 35s and have acted in the humble capacity of 'filing clerk' ever since. The hive of activity was an inspiration to me and as I worked among the files I began to sense that here was a remarkable story waiting to be told. I hope that my efforts as an amateur historian will do justice to it.

Chapter One

Jewish Emigration From Russia
– The Historical Background

> For not one man only has risen against us, but in
> every generation do men rise up against us to
> annihilate us.

Each Passover Jews recite these words in narrating the story of the sufferings of their people in Egypt over three thousand years ago. For more than two and a half thousand years, since the Assyrian and Babylonian conquests, Jews have been on the move, settling, suffering persecution and moving on again to another land, sometimes illegally and sometimes by forcible expulsions.

Jews have lived in Russia and its neighbouring countries since the sixteenth century. The growth of their current desire to emigrate echoed the events of one hundred years earlier when, fuelled by a repressive regime of poverty and persecution, pogroms and punitive conscription, a great tide of Russian Jews sought refuge in Britain and America.

Following the assassination of Tsar Alexander the Second in 1881, and although emigration was even then illegal, over 2¾ million Jews made their way from Eastern Europe to the West.

The British Aliens Immigration Acts of 1905 and 1907 together with the 1914-1918 war in Europe stemmed the tide to this country, and the advent of the Bolshevik Revolution in 1917 slowed it to a trickle. Some Jews of Russia eagerly embraced Bolshevism in the hope that the Revolution would bring the promised freedom and equality, ease the burden of their lives and, for all time, stamp out the anti-Semitism which was endemic there. They were to be proven horribly wrong. During the civil war which followed the Revolution approximately 150,000 Jews were massacred, by both the Red and White armies. Close on the heels of the civil war came Lenin's "Use of Terror" policy, which led to the murder of the leaders of the religious, educational, cultural and Zionist organisations that together had woven the rich tapestry of Russian Jewish life.

The Lenin Terror was replaced from 1934–1953 by the Stalin Terror, and the annexation of the Baltic States of Latvia, Estonia and Lithuania enabled him to extend his brutal policies to the once great Jewish communities of Riga, Kovno and Vilna, which had been virtually destroyed by the Nazis during their occupation of 1941–1944. Stalin was determined to eradicate what remained of Jewish life within the Soviet Union. From 1948 onwards his purges against Jewish writers and artists succeeded in wiping out the cream of their intelligentsia and it was only his timely death in 1953 which prevented the murder of those arrested in the notorious "Doctors Plot".

Yet again, after Stalin's death the Jews entertained hopes of parity with their fellow countrymen, but the much-vaunted principle of equality turned out to be a myth. Although his death may have lessened the excesses of the secret police (later the KGB), nonetheless their persecution continued unabated, sometimes by subtle means but more often quite blatantly. The official stance that there was no anti-Semitism was shown to be false. Jews met with discrimination on all sides. There was great difficulty in obtaining places in institutes of higher learning, particularly in the faculties of mathematics. Most institutions and organisations had their 'token' Jews, in order to counteract accusations of discrimination. "Tokenism" was evident also in the sphere of religion. Officially there was no place for religion under Communism, nevertheless a few synagogues and other places of worship were allowed to function. Some of the officials of these institutions were known to be collaborators with the authorities but this was a necessary pre-requisite for their continued existence.

If a Jew took the courageous step of applying for an exit visa, life became even more intolerable. Branded as traitors to Mother Russia they were invariably dismissed from their employment and were fortunate if they could find menial occupations such as caretakers, cleaners, or stokers. If they were unable to find work this led to accusations of 'parasitism'[2], and KGB harassment, resulting in mysterious attacks in the street, arrests and false imprisonment.

Small wonder then that Jews in the USSR called themselves "invalids of the fifth category". The first four entries in the internal passport dealt with names (patronymic, etc.) and address; the fifth line was for nationality. Whereas other Soviet citizens had their birth State entered in this document, e.g. Georgia, Ukraine, Jews had the word JEW entered into the space for nationality.

Thus, through a gradual process of elimination, all Jewish religious and secular institutions were disappearing together with their leaders, apparently silencing forever the Jews of the USSR.

But the Six Day War of 1967 was to stir the dormant emotions of these Jews of Silence. The euphoria which followed the Israeli victory, together with resurgent anti-Semitism and its co-evil anti-Zionism, were the catalysts for an overwhelming desire, not only to learn about their religion and historic heritage, but indeed to leave the land of their persecution and to find new roots in Israel, the land of their forebears.

> All their lives they had remained hidden as Jews: they wanted to come out into the streets and dance and talk with other Jews about this miraculous Israeli victory. They wanted to be JEWISH. They were intellectuals who needed to learn what it meant to be Jewish. They applied to leave the USSR in order to live as Jews; and they were refused. This time they would not be silenced. They realised that if they continued to make a noise and be supported by the West, they would be let out.

> Margaret Rigal, co-chairman of the 35s

Mark Dymshitz, a Jewish air-pilot, was frustrated, not only in his desire to emigrate to Israel but also by his inability to obtain a job commensurate with his experience, because of his application for an exit visa. He and ten others (including one woman, Sylva Zalmanson, and two non-Jews) bought all twelve tickets on a small aircraft, intending to tie up the pilot, leave him at Leningrad airport and fly the

---

[2]   It was illegal to be without employment in the USSR, hence the unemployed became "parasites".

plane to Sweden, in order to get to Israel. However, they were betrayed, captured, and charged with attempting to leave the country illegally.[3] Two of them were sentenced to death and the rest received long prison sentences. These harsh sentences even further aroused Jewish consciousness both inside and outside the USSR. Led by Mrs Amelie Jakobovits, the wife of the Chief Rabbi, a march by members of the Association of Jewish Women's Organisations to the Soviet Embassy in London, on behalf of the condemned, was an early intimation of the hitherto unsuspected activist potential of Jewish women. Margaret Rigal remembers taking part in this march together with a number of other women who subsequently also became members of the 35 group. After worldwide protests, organised virtually overnight, the death sentences were commuted. Undoubtedly, the pressure from the outside world had induced this change of heart. Encouraged by this, the campaign on behalf of Soviet Jewry gained momentum which in turn encouraged the activists in the Soviet Union who doubled their efforts, despite being harassed, assaulted and arrested. They knew that they were now being supported by the outside world.

[3] This was often wrongly reported as an attempted 'hi-jack'. Technically, it was not a hi-jack because there was no such crime in Soviet penal law at that time.

Chapter Two
Soviet Jewry –
The British Awakening

The stirrings of support for Soviet Jewry in Britain began to be felt by the mid 60s. The students, the Board of Deputies of British Jews, and a number of individuals were then contributing to what was to develop into a dynamic and influential movement.

Prominent early individual activists included Emmanuel Litvinoff, a noted journalist and author[4], Eric Graus, a leading Zionist Revisionist[5], and Michael Sherbourne, who was to become a valued member of the Women's Campaign for Soviet Jewry.

It was much to the students' credit that the earliest organisation actively involved in support of Soviet Jewry, in this country, was started by them in 1966. The Universities Committee for Soviet Jewry (UCSJ) played a positive role in organising demonstrations, petitions and letter-writing campaigns.

In May 1966 under the leadership of their first joint-chairmen, Gordon Hausmann and the late Malcolm Lewis, they marched one thousand strong to the Soviet Embassy in London. In February 1969 a crowd of ten thousand marched from Speakers Corner, Hyde Park, to the Soviet Embassy. They then continued on to the Iraqi Embassy to register an additional protest at the outrageous public hanging of Jews in the centre of Baghdad.

---

[4] Emmanual Litvinoff, Editor 'Jews in Eastern Europe'.
[5] Eric Graus, President of "Herut" movement in Great Britain. This is a right-wing Zionist organisation.

These 'up-front' activities were deplored by the Board of Deputies, which had tried to prevent their first march from taking place. Colin Shindler, who was joint chairman of the UCSJ with Jonathan Lewis in 1969, commented:

> by about 1970 the community was becoming aware of the Soviet Jewish situation, due to the work of the students. The Israeli Embassy was frustrated by the lack of action by the Board of Deputies and worked through the students instead.

With the passage of time the work of the UCSJ gradually diminished and was largely replaced by that of the 35s. However, throughout the years that followed, the students continued to work for Soviet Jewry under the banners of various organisations. The Students and Academics Committee for Soviet Jewry, the leader in the field, has continued to work closely with the 35s.

Further active participation came from B'nai Akiva, a Jewish religious youth organisation. Colin Shindler recalls that:

> a constant stream of young people was sent into the USSR by B'nai Akiva. The Israeli Embassy and associated bodies considered them to be excellent emissaries since they were well versed in Judaism and Jewishness and could therefore really 'give' something to the Soviet Jews other than purely material goods.

B'nai Akiva has maintained a continuing interest in Soviet Jewry and in 1990, in conjunction with the 35s, they organised a youth-camp in Helsinki for Jewish youngsters from Leningrad.

Michael Sherbourne was one of the first people in this country to recognise the need for a vociferous campaign of support for Soviet Jewry. He began his one-man battle in 1969 and has never been afraid to show his head above the parapet. For over twenty-five years he has at times berated the Board of Deputies, the Israeli Government and their Soviet Jewry representative Nehemia Levanon, and any person or organisation that he felt was not pursuing the cause with sufficient zeal. He commented: "if we had listened to the Israeli Government how many would have come out?" From his fertile pen there has flowed a host of articles, pamphlets and letters.

Before his involvement with the 35s he worked with the Soviet Jewry Committee of the Southgate branch of the Association of Jewish Ex-Servicemen (AJEX). He had previously visited the Soviet Union in 1962, 1963 and 1964 as a leader and organiser of school journeys, but from 1970 he was blacklisted by the Soviet authorities because of his activities.

In January 1972 he attended a public meeting called by the Chief Rabbi and was disgusted, not only by the sparse attendance but also at the lack of resolve displayed by the participants.

> I couldn't contain myself any longer. I stood up and asked the Chief Rabbi to tell his Ministers and Honorary Officers to get their fingers out! I sat down again, and to tell you the truth I was appalled at my own temerity. To my amazement I heard someone clapping; it was Myra Janner[6]. She came up to me after the meeting and said 'you sound like one of us' and when she learnt that I spoke Russian[7] she invited me to meet Katya Palatnik, who would shortly be arriving in England campaigning for her sister Raiza.

So it was that Michael Sherbourne became one of the earliest and longest serving male members of the Women's Campaign for Soviet Jewry.

In the 1970s and 1980s, while still working full time as a teacher, he was spending an average of 35–40 hours a week telephoning "refuseniks" in Russia, a time-consuming but immensely valuable and rewarding task. The personal contacts and the access to up-to-date information from inside the Soviet Union gave great encouragement to all the campaigners.

> In 1971 I was on the telephone to Russia and my contact, Gabriel Shapiro, used the word OTKAZNIK, a word unknown to me. He translated this into the Hebrew word SIRUVNIK (from the verb "to refuse"). Ah, said I, a REFUSENIK.

And thus the word 'refusenik' came into being.

---

[6] An early 35er.
[7] Michael Sherbourne had taught himself to speak and read Russian.

Sherbourne started telephone conversations with Sharansky in 1973 after Sharansky had been refused an exit visa and spoke to him several times a week until his arrest. "I started to talk to Ida Nudel[8] in 1972. She was the contact for the Jewish Prisoners of Conscience so I was able to pass on all the news I received from her".

Sherbourne calculates that during a period of twelve years he made about five thousand phone calls. This very costly activity was financed by Cyril Stein[9]. Details of these telephone conversations were circulated in his self-produced newsletter until this became too costly and then, for some years, the 35s included his information with their own newsletter.

An article in *The Guardian* newspaper (1st May 1972), "Putting Hope on the Line" by John Windsor, described the work of the 35s and detailed these telephone activities.

In 1972 Sherbourne contacted twenty of the leading journalists of all the broadsheet and many of the tabloid newspapers in this country, hoping to enlist their support for refuseniks Valentin and Ludmilla Prusakov. Bernard Levin, *The Times* columnist, was the only one who responded. He invited Sherbourne to his home to learn about their situation[10]. It was an all-too-common refusenik story: applications for exit visas to Israel, dismissal from workplace, KGB harassment and assault, and the added hazard of Ludmilla's precarious state of health due to toxaemia of pregnancy. But to Bernard Levin this was all shockingly new and he asked Sherbourne to telephone the Prusakovs there and then. He recalls Levin saying to him "just ask one more question, what do his neighbours think of his situation?"

Sherbourne: "I remember Prusakov's bitterness as he said – 'neighbours! You don't tell neighbours anything, they are all anti-Semites". I had to explain Russian anti-Semitism to Levin as he appeared to be surprised at the level of the virulence experienced by Jews in the USSR".

The first annual award of the All-Party Parliamentary Committee for the Release of Soviet Jewry was presented to Michael Sherbourne in 1980, a fitting tribute to a man whose whole life has been dedicated

---

[8] A prominent activist, imprisoned in 1978.
[9] Cyril Stein, a prominent businessman and philanthropist who financed the work of the 35s for many years.
[10] See chapter 8 for the far-reaching effects of this incalculably valuable meeting between Sherbourne and Levin.

to the fight against tyranny. Ironically the description by the Soviet News Agency, TASS, in 1977 of "the British Lord (sic) Sherbourne" as being a fascist, underlines the effectiveness of his work.

Now in his late 70s he still devotes many hours daily to the translation of letters and publications from Russian and Hebrew. In all this work he had the constant support of his late wife Muriel. Until prevented by ill-health, she was, for many years, an active 35er, working mainly on gathering material for the newsletter.

The Board of Deputies of British Jews is the elected representative body of Anglo-Jewry. Initially the Board's involvement in Soviet Jewish affairs came within the scope of its Foreign Affairs committee, which, in 1967, sent a letter to Prime Minister Kosygin, on the occasion of his visit to this country, expressing concern at the continued anti-Jewish discrimination in the USSR.

In April of that year a delegation from the Board saw Ambassador Smirnovsky and reiterated their concern about the deteriorating situation of Russian Jews.

Prior to his departure for Moscow in January 1968, the Prime Minister, Harold Wilson, received the Chairman of the Foreign Affairs Committee, Sir Barnett Janner, MP, who apprised him of the serious position of Jews in the USSR. The Prime Minister wrote to the Board, on his return, stating that he had discussed matters appertaining to discrimination with Prime Minister Kosygin, but that there was no change in the Soviet attitude.

During this period the Foreign Affairs Committee was also deliberating on Jewish affairs in Aden, Austria, Germany, Poland, the Arab countries, and at the United Nations. It was felt by the Board's critics that this broad agenda was detracting from the urgency of the Soviet Jewry situation. Those already active in Soviet Jewry affairs (such as the students and Michael Sherbourne) claimed that there appeared to be more deliberation than action by the Board, and that little had been done to alleviate the distressing plight of Jews in the Soviet Union.

The Board's reply to their critics was that there were 'behind the scenes activities' (e.g. meetings with government representatives) of which they, the critics, could not be aware.

A Conference on Soviet Jewry was convened by the Board in June 1969, to focus attention on the current situation.

Throughout 1970 and the early part of 1971 the Foreign Affairs Committee devoted special attention to the situation of all Jews in the Soviet Union. A number of press conferences and emergency meetings were convened, calling for public action. The situation became urgent following the so-called Leningrad hijack incident and the subsequent death sentence in December 1970. The following month a ten thousand strong protest march, of Jews and non-Jews was led by the President of the Board of Deputies, Alderman Michael Fidler. The participants included the Chief Rabbi, Dr I. Jakobovits and the Dean of St Paul's, the Very Reverend Martin Sullivan.

In March 1971 Soviet Jewry matters were removed from the Foreign Affairs Committee to be dealt with by a newly formed Soviet-Jewry Action Committee. Joan Dale, one of the founder members of the 35s, was an early member of this committee. At about this time, Colin Shindler was editing the Newsletter *Jews in the USSR* under the auspices of the Board of Deputies. He, together with Sylvia Becker and Deborah Lloyd (who were soon to become early 35ers), was asked by the Board to start a "link-up" scheme, whereby Soviet Jews who wished to receive messages were twinned with families in the UK. This subsequently was taken over by the 35s and developed into their Adoption and Twinning Programme.

In his book *The American Movement to Save Russian Jewry*[11] William Orbach described the work of the Soviet Jewry Action Committee as consisting of innumerable meetings and minuscule activity which later activists dubbed "The Inaction Committee".

However, mounting criticism of this Committee led to the creation of a three-man exploratory committee comprising the Hon. Greville Janner, QC, MP, Dr Stephen Roth, and Mr Eric Nabarro. The President of the Board, Lord Fisher, said that they represented "the beginnings of a complete change" in an area of work which was growing more important year by year[12]. This resulted in the convening, in December 1975, of the first National Conference on Soviet Jewry, bringing together all the organisations involved in work for Soviet Jewry.

Following this, and amidst a certain amount of dissension, the National Council for Soviet Jewry came into being. This was intended to be the co-ordinating body for Soviet Jewry work in this

[11] University of Massachusetts, Amhurst, USA 1979.
[12] *The Jewish Observer and Middle East Review*, 25th July 1975.

country. Opponents to this move were apprehensive that such an organisation would abrogate the authority of the Board of Deputies as Anglo-Jewry's representative organisation and that it could be taken over by the militant activists whose "hoodlum methods" the community would never endorse or support.[13]

A year after its inception Doreen Gainsford, then chairman of the 35s, resigned as vice-chairman of the National Council. She disagreed with the Council on outlook and policy:

> while I did not feel that I was doing justice to the job, the other members of the Council also were not. They are just sitting around and talking... The 35s agree with the Russian activists who say that we have to tell the Russian Government, in every possible way, what you feel, and forget delicacy. We are unconcerned with what people in Britain think about us. Many people in the National Council are too concerned about the image of Anglo Jewry.[14]

Rita Eker, co-chairman of the 35s, commented that:

> the National Council for Soviet Jewry hated our guts because we didn't hold committee meetings and forums and deliberations. We just got on with the job. As far as we were concerned there were only two reasons for not taking action – if it hurt the refuseniks or if it hurt Israel; otherwise we went ahead.

The Board of Deputies strongly disapproved of the high-profile activities of groups such as the students, Herut, and the 35s, and on occasions tried to prevent them. By its very nature an establishment organisation, with its executive committees and sub-committees, the Board moved ponderously and was often overtaken by fast moving autonomous activist groups.

Doreen Gainsford recalls:

> after our first demonstration, a twenty-four-hour hunger strike, dressed in black, on a hot day – and we had swept the street to clean up our litter – I walked into a

---

[13] *The Jewish Chronicle*, December 1975.
[14] *The Jewish Observer and Middle East Review*, December 1976.

Board of Deputies meeting. I was hot, sticky and not very clean, and one of the women Deputies said to me 'my dear, you will just cause anti-Semitism; what are you doing?' This was the general attitude of the establishment.

However, a gradual change in attitude became apparent in 1973 when an executive vote was carried by a majority of four to three. Lord Janner, together with his wife, Elsie and their son, Greville, joined by Victor Mishcon favoured demonstrations for Soviet Jewry and support for the 35s in their work. Doreen Gainsford commented:

remember the Board had to work within the Anglo-Jewish establishment. They are what they are and therefore any expectations from their leadership was not what they *could* do, but what they *would* do. They agreed to start a Soviet Jewry Committee (The National Council for Soviet Jewry) but I had to be a *vice*-chairman. That was the way they would control us. The act of allowing a 'wilde chaye'[15] to be part of them was terrific. They were a pain; so inactive and inflexible. They couldn't look ahead; but they were decent. I didn't expect any more; I realised that they were incapable of doing things. To expect more than they could give was ridiculous.

Myra Janner felt that "the Board's heart was in the right place" but the critics questioned whether or not this had produced any results. Cyril Stein was of the opinion that the Establishment had never changed and never would.

It is interesting to note that this dichotomy between the establishment and the activists was mirrored in the United States of America. A crucial factor in both countries was the influence of the Israeli Government. Following the Six Day War in 1967, diplomatic relations with the Soviet Union were severed, and the Israeli Government had to tread very warily in its endeavours to help Soviet Jews.

Ijo Rager, who was Counsellor in charge of Soviet Jewish Affairs at the Israeli Embassy in London from 1971-1973 said that:

---

[15] Yiddish. Literally 'wild animal', maverick.

the official Israeli policy until the 1970s was – don't make the Soviets angry by over-activism because they might take revenge on the Russian Jews. But by 1971 Israel was already behind the Brussels International Conference on Soviet Jewry.

Directives from the Israeli Government to the American and British Jewish establishments conflicted with the approach of the activists, who complained of sabotage of a number of their efforts. As an example of this, Michael Sherbourne remembers that, after Colin Shindler's editorship, the information he submitted to *Jews in the USSR* (a Board of Deputies publication), from translations of his nightly telephone conversations with refuseniks, was suppressed or delayed, often leading to lack of liaison with those in need of immediate help. In the prevailing climate of persecution and imprisonment, delay could be disastrous, and it was important for the Soviet authorities to know that if a certain refusenik was interrogated or imprisoned, the activists would move immediately. George Vins, a Russian Baptist leader who was expelled from Russia after imprisonment, said that "whenever there was support-action in the West I was treated better by the warders and prison administrators. When there was no support the conditions immediately became worse".[16]

In his book *Refusenik*[17], Professor Mark Azbel wrote:

> once, at the end of an interview, a KGB chief said to me sourly – 'well, we know that before you leave this room, the news of your detention and everything we said here will be broadcast'. And it was almost true. When you have supporters everywhere, all over the world; when a whole people sympathises with you, when your friends never relax their vigilance – nothing is impossible... In the depths of my soul there was always an almost subtle, sub-conscious awareness of this constant defence and, in a very real sense, that is what kept me alive throughout those very hard years.

---

[16] *Daily Telegraph*, May 1979.
[17] Published by Hamish Hamilton, London 1982, p 404.

Chapter Three

The Birth of the 35s.
Raiza Palatnik – Prisoner of Zion

Raiza Palatnik had always been conscious of her Jewishness. Despite the erosion of Jewish life in the USSR and the consequent reluctance of parents to raise their children as Jews, she constantly looked for opportunities to identify herself with her Jewish roots. Whilst still at school her courage, which was later to become so apparent during her imprisonment, was demonstrated by her refusal to learn the Ukrainian language as she insisted that her mother tongue was Yiddish.

Raiza's father had been a political prisoner when the Stalin terror was at its height in the early 1950s, so he and his family were more aware than most of the gravity of the situation in which Jews found themselves.

But Stalin died, the doctors were released, and Raiza rejoiced, in the naïve belief that justice had triumphed and that anti-Semitism would become a thing of the past.

These hopes were soon to be dashed when, following her graduation from the Moscow Institute of Librarians, she found it impossible to find work commensurate with her high qualifications. It was only with difficulty that she eventually managed to obtain a post in a small library in Odessa.

It was this, together with the continuous anti-Semitic campaigns and trumped-up charges by the KGB, that first turned her thoughts towards emigration to Israel. These ideas were further fuelled by the outcome of the Six Day War, which strengthened her determination to leave the Soviet Union. She began to take an active interest in everything connected with Israel and applied to locate her relations in Israel. From then on the KGB began to take a special interest in her. They searched her apartment and that of her parents, her books and papers were confiscated, and she was repeatedly summoned for questioning, as were her relations, friends and colleagues.

In December 1970 Raiza was arrested. Every few days she was interrogated, with all the psychological pressures and threats beloved of the KGB. True to her uncompromising nature, she would answer only in Yiddish, reiterating that it was her mother-tongue. At one time she was subjected to a psychiatric examination, a favourite ploy of the authorities, in an attempt to have her certified and committed to a mental institution.

At her trial in June 1971, she pleaded not guilty to the charge of "Slandering the Soviet Union" but she was found guilty and sentenced to two years imprisonment. Her life in prison was one of brutality and neglect. Anti-Semitism was rife. She was held in ignominious and unsanitary conditions, with prostitutes and bed-bugs for cellmates. She was kept in handcuffs and was not allowed to wash herself regularly. Her incoming and outgoing mail was often confiscated, and she was subjected to periods of isolation. She wrote to her parents:

> ...I am in very low spirits – this one's an informer, that one's a sneak, another one persecutes (me)... I am suffering from dizziness, headaches and heartburn. I have lost weight. I look older and I am going grey... there is no one I can talk to here, they only talk about food, about drinking and getting drunk and they talk only in foul, four-letter language.

She went on a hunger strike in December 1971 and again, at great risk to her health, in April 1972. Prior to her sister Katya's departure for Israel in 1972, she visited Raiza in prison and discovered that she had suffered a heart attack for which she had received no medical attention. Katya told her friends that Raiza looked so ill she scarcely recognised her.

Raiza was moved from Odessa to a labour camp in Dnieprodzerjensk, a thirteen-hour journey from her home. Throughout her incarceration there, under distasteful and disgusting conditions, her hope lay in the knowledge which filtered through to her intermittently, that the 35s and other Western organisations were working on her behalf.

Katya had vowed that she would not rest until Raiza was released, and following her arrival in Israel the campaign gained momentum in Britain and the USA.

In Kensington Palace Green, London, Ijo Rager[18] had the inspired notion that he would find valuable allies amongst the Jewish housewives of Britain, not only in the fight for Raiza but also in wider issues.

> I felt that it was the women in the community who had the time to devote to the cause. The students, who up to then were the only active force for Soviet Jewry, were busy with their studies. The men in the community had little free time and the Jewish Establishment was very cool about the movement.
>
> I saw that women activists could be a good gimmick so I started to address women's organisations. There were three women who stood out and who appeared to be willing to do something; Joan Dale, Doreen Gainsford and Barbara Oberman. They were the fore-runners and we held meetings in their homes. In fact, the very first meeting of the 35s was held in Joan's home when Colin Shindler spoke as I was unable to be there.
>
> One day I had a call from my office in Israel about Raiza Palatnik. I sat thinking – how can I bring this issue to the public? I called in the three women and told them – here is a thirty-five year old woman, about your age, who is in trouble in Odessa. If thirty-five of you demonstrate on her behalf the message might come across.

They decided to deliver a letter about Raiza to Madame Smirnovskaya, the wife of the Ambassador at the Soviet Embassy. Joan Dale suggested that they should copy the example of the Black

[18] Current Mayor of Beersheba, Israel (1995).

Sash women of South Africa and demonstrate silently dressed in black.

A new movement was about to be born.

London, May Day 1971, a warm spring day. A group of Jewish housewives, dressed in black, intend to hold a twenty-four-hour fast. They hope to deliver a petition to Madame Lyudmilla Smirnovskaya, wife of the Soviet Ambassador at the Soviet Embassy, signed on behalf of all thirty-five-year-old Jewish women in Britain and calling on her to use her good office to stop the KGB torturing Raiza Palatnik.

Doreen Gainsford recalled:

> we were so lucky because they had no gates or security fences in those days. It was before the days of mass demos so the press were interested in us; after all, we were an unusual group – Jewish housewives from the NW London suburbs. And what is more there was a telephone box just near where we were standing. I stood in that box nearly all day and night and phoned every newspaper, TV and radio station that I could think of and said "Hello, we are a group of thirty-five girls, demonstrating outside the Soviet Embassy for the release of a Jewish woman imprisoned because she wants to go to Israel. She is 35 years of age and we are here for 35 hours". (This was not quite true, we were there for 24 hours, but it made a better story). I remember that after about 10 or 11 calls I phoned *The Daily Telegraph* and heard the man on the news-desk say "It's those 35s again". That was how the germ of the name came about. We had Nigel Wallis, Leon Harris and Cecil Oberman helping us and Nigel said "Let's call ourselves the 35s" as the Press wanted to know who we were. In a way the Press gave us the name and we took it from there.

> During the day we had been into the Soviet Embassy several times. Once we spoke to the First Secretary. He said to us "There is no Jewish problem. I don't know why you think there is, it's a purely Jewish

fabrication; there is no Jew who wants to leave Russia". That type of reaction was terribly important to us, it made us realise how sensitive the Russians were over the whole issue.

Barbara Oberman recalled:

on the day of the demo I spoke on the BBC's "World at One" programme as the leader of the 35s, the Women's Group for Soviet Jewry.

We were all so naïve; during our hunger strike the father of one of the group drove up in his Rolls Royce with food for the 'starving girls'. We had to ask him to disappear – fast...

Actually we weren't thirty-five, there were about 28 of us, but Raiza was 35 years old. I was thirty-five and a few others were as well. It was all so exciting. During the day Ijo Rager sent his secretary, in a very clandestine way, with a secret note saying that Raiza had already been moved from a KGB dungeon, to an ordinary prison in Odessa, so we knew that it was working.

On the 14th May 1971, *The Jewish Chronicle* printed the first of its many reports on the 35s... "the black-clad housewives in London have registered their first, albeit limited, victory".

For several weeks following the demonstration the 35s took a letter to the wife of the Soviet Ambassador every day, apart from the Sabbath, hoping to deliver it personally on a woman-to-woman basis.

Margaret Rigal remembers how much she disliked taking these letters:

I used to try and deliver the daily message; many times they refused to accept it. One day as I was walking towards the Embassy with the envelope in my hand, I heard footsteps close behind me and turned round to find that I was being followed by a very presentable-looking young man. He smiled charmingly at me as we neared the gate and I said "Perhaps you will be kind enough to deliver this for me". He asked who I was and when I told him I was representing the 35s his whole countenance changed. He was absolutely bursting with hatred and fury and he snarled at me – "You are a disgrace to womanhood. You should stay at home and look after your grandchildren instead of meddling in things that are no concern of yours".

As it became increasingly difficult to gain entry the deliveries became weekly and finally, due to rejection of the letters, they were sent by post. This continued for several years. Rita Bensusan recollects writing many of these letters: "It was a tedious task as it became very difficult to write something original each time. I tried to keep them as relevant as possible mentioning current events relating to Jews in the Soviet Union".

Barbara Oberman remembered: "The police were marvellous. They used to take us up to the Embassy gates in their car; they were never unpleasant. They would phone me and say, 'Mrs Oberman, can you make your demo for 12.30 – the boys go for lunch at one o'clock'."

In November 1975 at an Amnesty International press conference in London, Raiza Palatnik said that it was the public awareness of her suffering that led to improvement of her prison conditions and brought about her early release.

Chapter Four

Leadership

The names of four women have been synonymous with that of the 35s, the Women's Campaign for Soviet Jewry. In the beginning they were Barbara Oberman and Doreen Gainsford, and when they departed, Rita Eker Rita, Margaret Rigal, and for a short time Linda Isaacs took up the reins of leadership.[19]

Barbara Oberman's remark "there, but for the grace of God, go I" is a phrase which falls readily from the lips of most of the 35ers; it was and remains their *raison-d'être*.

Barbara had always been troubled by the realisation that more could have been done for the Jews of Germany prior to the 1939–1945 war. In 1970, after hearing a talk on Soviet Jewry by Dov Spurling, (an early refusenik and one of the first to renounce his Soviet citizenship), she knew that she had to act. Naomi Goldwater, a founder member, remembers that even before the birth of the 35s Barbara was recruiting friends to collect money and clothes for a needy family from Riga. In May 1971 when Barbara asked her "to sit on the pavement outside the Soviet Embassy all night" she rejected the idea out of hand. But, typical of the founder members, she then realised that, in all conscience, she could not refuse and she took part in the demonstration. Whilst they were there the news came through that Raiza had been moved, and she realised for the first time that by their actions they could make things happen.

Barbara had a private meeting with Chief Rabbi Jakobovits who told her to approach the Board of Deputies. She did this and was aghast to find that the Board was categorically against any form of public demonstration. In her opinion this was doubtless in deference

---

[19]   Barbara Oberman, Doreen Gainsford, and Linda Isaacs later emigrated to Israel.

to Israeli Government policy. She made further approaches to the heads of all the major organisations of the Anglo-Jewish establishment but without success.

> They were appalled. I think they thought "Who is this little upstart?" They had never been challenged in this way before. But when our campaign got under way some of them congratulated me!

> Then I heard Rager speak about Raiza Palatnik. I identified whole-wholeheartedly with her; we had so much in common it could have been me. I told Cecil (her late husband) "We must do something" and he encouraged me all the way. Rager was perhaps the final straw to push me into action after all the rejections of the official bodies that I had experienced during the preceding few months.

Shunned by the establishment, Barbara energetically canvassed amongst her friends and she spoke to over one hundred women on the telephone. By the time that Rager contacted her with a view to setting up a women's support group, she was ready for the first demonstration.

> Out of all the many to whom I had spoken, there were only a brave few who were prepared to stand outside the Soviet Embassy; people like Sylvia Wallis and Zelda Harris. I was severely criticised for using such tactics. Cecil and I were members of a respected North West London Jewish family and mixed in respectable Anglo-Jewish circles. Family members were not too happy about us; but I had to do it... We all worked so hard. I remember my husband and sons working all one night to make a massive banner reading KGB STOP TORTURING RAIZA PALATNIK which we used on the first demo. We also marched to *The Times* office with that banner. They were always quoting *TASS* as if it was gospel. We said they should formulate their own views and not just regurgitate *TASS*. William Rees Mogg the Editor came down to speak to this little army of women... and I must say that he reacted very

positively to our criticism and inferred that he wouldn't just quote *TASS* verbatim but would make other sources available to his readers.

The students came to work from our house when we had meetings there. PRAVDA once referred to our home in Golders Green as 'the centre of Zionist activity'.

Amongst those at the first demonstration was Doreen Gainsford who had been brought there by Gloria Brown, realising that as she worked in the field of public relations she would be a valuable asset to the group. It was after the following disturbing incident, a few months into the 35s campaign, that she assumed the role of leader.
Cyril Stein remembers:

> I went with Alan Freeman, Chairman of the Union of Jewish Students, and some students to the Soviet Consulate, ostensibly to ask for visas for Russia although we knew that one had to go to Intourist for visas.
>
> We really wanted to get some publicity for the Leningrad prisoners. We set it all up; we had alerted the television news who had a camera crew outside. When we got inside the Consulate we found anti-Semitic and anti-Zionist literature and took it to the window to show to the cameras. In the meantime the Soviets had sent to the nearby Soviet Embassy for the KGB, who came and threw us out. This really brought the struggle for Soviet Jewry on to the front pages.

Barbara Oberman became involved in the affair...

> My doorbell went at 3 a.m. and Rager was standing there to tell me that in the fracas Alan Freeman had lost his briefcase which contained my name, amongst others. He suggested that I lie low for a month. It was a bad incident and the Israeli Embassy had to apologise publicly to the Russians...
>
> Doreen Gainsford and Zena Clayton came to see me to try and persuade me to keep quiet for a while. As it

was never my intention to hurt the Israelis, and an international incident had blown up, I agreed to keep away from the 35s for a month. To his credit, my husband thought that this was not necessary, in fact stupid, but I listened to some Israeli friends of Cyril Stein and took their advice.

Very shortly after that I created the Committee for the Release of Soviet Jewish Prisoners, which continued until I went to live in Israel in 1978. There was a rivalry of sorts (with the 35s) to get news coverage which, in fact, didn't detract but rather added to the campaign.

Barbara Oberman's contribution to the work of the 35s may have been brief, but it was formative and effective. Together with Doreen Gainsford she is remembered to this day as a founder of the Women's Campaign for Soviet Jewry.

Speaking about Doreen Gainsford, Margaret Rigal said, "Doreen is capable of more concentrated drive than anyone I have ever met".

Doreen Gainsford had also been deeply moved by the plight of Soviet Jewry and after hearing about Raiza's incarceration in a KGB dungeon, her guilt feelings about the Holocaust, which had been dormant for years, rose to the surface. "If I were to be imprisoned tomorrow I hope that someone would do something for me".

She, too, was stung into action. With the departure of Barbara Oberman, and strongly supported by Joan Dale, a founder member, Doreen took on the leadership of the group. She described her feelings about the situation:

> The timing was just right. The Six Day War, the Leningrad trials, Raiza's imprisonment, and Rager's influence came at a time when Jewish women were learning to quit their roles as housewives and become people in their own right, enabling them, perhaps for the first time, to stand up to the Establishment.

This explosive mixture resulted in the creation of "the only exclusively female group in the Soviet Jewry movement".[20] [21]

> We were women, we were attractive, we had our 'gimmick' of dressing in black and demonstrating in silence. The other Human Rights groups wanted to climb on our bandwagon – the Balkans, the Ukrainians. But we said from the beginning that we were not anti-Soviet. We didn't want to confuse the issue; we were campaigning for the right of Jews to return to their National Home. We knew that we had to be single minded... we had a terrific task at the beginning. It wasn't like the 'Ban the Bomb' campaign. No one knew that Jews were being persecuted in Russia – and Russia seems a long way away to most people here... we used to sit outside the Soviet Embassy contemplating that formidable set of buildings and thinking 'How the hell are a group of ladies from north west London going to have any effect, not only on those officials in there but on the minds that rule the Kremlin?'[22]

From 1971 to 1978 Doreen Gainsford dedicated her life to Soviet Jewry through her work with the 35s in this country. Her expertise in public relations brought a professionalism to the group; perhaps her most abiding legacy. No opportunity was missed for a demonstration or campaign with an 'impact'. When an engineer lost his job and was forced to become a street cleaner, the 35s swept the streets of London. When a doctor was accused of poisoning a child, the 35s wheeled a hospital trolley down Regent Street, and when Colonel Davidovich died needlessly in refusal the 35s carried a symbolic coffin through Whitehall.

A 35er needed courage, particularly in the early years. Intimidation, insults, and criticism were commonplace and were frightening to these inexperienced women. Doreen Gainsford remembered when the leaders of the 35s were summoned to a meeting

[20] Michael Sherbourne and Sydney Gabrel were notable exceptions to this exclusivity.
[21] *Count us in – the Canadian role in the international struggle to free Soviet Jewry* by Wendy Eisen: Publ. Burgher Books, Toronto, Canada, 1995.
[22] As reported in the *London Evening News* of January 1978 prior to Doreen Gainsford's emigration to Israel.

of heads of Jewish organisations and told (after their second 1971 demonstration) "If you make too much noise about Soviet Jewry you will simply create anti-Semitism in this country. Do not think we are ignoring Soviet Jewry – we sent a cable from Geneva last year". And a letter to *The Jewish Chronicle* in July 1974 urged "a more restrained approach".

This was the attitude of much of Anglo-Jewry at that time and it is to the credit of these gutsy women that by their fortitude and imagination they raised the consciousness of the community *vis-à-vis* the plight of Soviet Jewry.

The work was not without risks. In August 1975 Doreen was arrested in Helsinki, and in June 1977 she was deported from Belgrade. Following the coffin incident in London she was arrested and charged with obstructing the highway. It also led to encounters way beyond the usual experience of housewives. Doreen visited the Foreign Office and she met, at times, with police officers of the Special Branch, with whom she developed an excellent relationship.

She recollected a nerve-wracking yet rewarding incident:

> Joe Gormley (President of the National Union of Mineworkers) told me about this man. He was the leader of one of the Trade Union branches and was going to visit Russia. I wanted him to speak with the Russian Trade Unions about some of the refuseniks. I rang him up – I remember it was late Friday afternoon and in the event I was on the phone for two hours and our Shabbat dinner was very late that evening! I said "Hello, I'm Doreen Gainsford. I understand that you are going to Russia..." He interrupted me "Young lady, I think I ought to tell you that I am one of those who believe that Hitler didn't do a good enough job on the Jews". Anyway, he agreed to take some details with him and I arranged to meet him at his hotel near Victoria Station. (Incidentally Joe Gormley had told me that the only way I would be able to influence him would be to seduce him!) I walked up the steps of this sleazy hotel wondering what I had let myself in for. I remember gazing up at the sky and praying, "Dear God, this is for the Jewish people". We talked for hours and it turned out to be very easy and he took our material

with him. I saw him when he came back. He said that
he had changed his opinion of Jews – "To tell you the
truth I had never met a Jew in my life". He
subsequently befriended a refusenik in Moscow.

The revival of the Israeli branch of the 35s in 1985, together with
the creation of the Mini-gift[23] enterprise are further examples of her
indomitable energy. The Israeli President's Award for Volunteers,
presented to her in 1992, was a fitting recognition of her services to
Soviet Jewry.

It would be difficult to find two more disparate people than
Margaret Rigal and Rita Eker. Nevertheless their efforts have always
complemented each other and the sum of their contributions over
almost twenty years is a remarkable achievement.

Margaret, deliberate and with a devotion to detail, Rita, volatile
and extrovert, have, since Doreen Gainsford's departure in 1978,
spearheaded the campaign with professionalism and a single-minded
dedication. As members of the organisation from its earliest days,
their motivation was similar to that of virtually all other 35ers.

> I was so disgusted when I found out how little our
> parents' generation did for the victims of the Holocaust.

> My parents always regretted not having done more for
> German Jews. They did what they were asked, but no
> more. I didn't want my children to turn round and say
> "Why didn't you help the Russian Jews?". I was asked
> by my Synagogue, St John's Wood Liberal, to ask my
> local librarian to sign a petition for Raiza Palatnik who
> was also a librarian. His response shocked me to the
> core. "I certainly would not do any such thing. If my
> Town Hall Masters change I might find myself
> disadvantaged as an anti-Communist!"

> At about the same time I had been asked to attend a
> demonstration for Syrian Jews and found myself outside
> the Syrian Airline offices. When I saw all these women
> standing in the gutter in Piccadilly, holding placards, I

---

[23] 'Mini-gifts'. This scheme is the brainchild of Doreen Gainsford in Israel, where
she employs Russian immigrants to design and manufacture attractive items of table
linen, religious articles, etc.

panicked, walked past and went into a shop. There I communed with my conscience as I remembered what my parents had said. I went back and joined in the demonstration, and I have to say, the earth didn't open at my feet.

Following the Syrian demonstration, Margaret Rigal was asked to work with the 35s, and this time there was no hesitation on her part. Margaret's main involvement has been with politicians and religious groups. The meticulously detailed files on all members of the British and European parliaments and of the House of Lords, together with the copious correspondence with the Foreign Office give testament not only to the 35s reputation for scrupulous accuracy but also to the very positive influence on Her Majesty's Government *vis-à-vis* Human Rights.

Margaret:

> We have a rule in the office; nothing is given out without confirmation. We have to be particularly careful because our information often comes from people who are not experts; therefore everything has to be checked. We were very concerned about saying things like 'prisoners are on the verge of death'. You can't go on year after year saying that people are dying if its not true, so we have to be very careful.

Rita's role is far less clearly defined than Margaret's. When asked how she would describe her work she replied "general dogsbody". "General", as being involved with most of the aspects of the work, would be a correct description. "Dogsbody", as being a drudge is also, on occasions, not far from the truth, but the phrase in no way sums up the flair and élan which epitomises Rita's approach.

Despite the generous funding of the office and its operation by Cyril Stein, large sums of money have been needed, particularly latterly, to support the medical campaign, the One-to-One work[24], and to aid travellers, etc. Small wonder then that her friends fear the sound of her voice on the telephone as she attempts to wheedle yet another donation from them. "No" is not a word in her vocabulary.

---

[24] One-to-One scheme, see Chapter Twelve.

When something has to be done, she first sets the wheels turning and then finds the ways and means to fulfil it. She has organised concerts, film shows, exhibitions, meetings, and speakers, to raise funds and to publicise the work of the group. Rita became Vice-Chairman of the National Council for Soviet Jewry in 1980, and visits Israel several times each year. Far from these trips being holidays, she invariably returns home exhausted after having monitored the absorption and aid work for the new immigrants with which the 35s campaign is concerned.

Her travels, on behalf of the 35s, have taken her to Paris, Madrid, Helsinki, Israel, and Washington. She has, over the years, also visited all the provincial groups. By contrast, her visits to the USSR have been sparse. Together with Margaret Rigal, Michael Sherbourne and others, her name was on a black list and she was refused a visa on many occasions, often just two or three days before an intended departure date.

Recognition of the value of the work of the 35s has been demonstrated by the receipt of a number of awards. Following the murder of Ross McWhirter by the IRA, a £1,000 peace prize was instigated in his name, to promote "the exercise of personal initiative and leadership". Rita Eker and Margaret Rigal were joint recipients of this award at the Haberdasher's Hall in March 1979.[25]

The All-Party Parliamentary Committee for the Release of Soviet Jewry once again showed their appreciation of the value of the work of the 35s by the presentation of their annual award for 1987 to Margaret Rigal and Rita Eker. The award for outstanding services, a Henry Moore lithograph donated and signed by the artist, bore the inscription "For Courage in defence of freedom". Other recipients of this award include Vladimir Slepak, Victor Brailovsky, Ida Nudel, Anatoly Sharansky, Iosif Begun, Alexander Lerner, and another 35s worker, Michael Sherbourne, in 1980.

In May 1991 Rita received the Israeli President's Award for Volunteers, on behalf of the group. A further acknowledgement of

---

[25] The McWhirter Peace Prize was also awarded to Arkady Polishchuk. He took part in a mass protest against the prevention of emigration. He was arrested in October 1976 and was eventually allowed to leave the Soviet Union. He said that he is convinced that he owes his release from prison to the work of the 35s.

its work was the receipt of an award from the French Committee of 15[26].

One of the proudest moments for Rita and Margaret was in February 1976 when Golda Meir, the Prime Minister of Israel, addressed the Brussels II Conference of American Soviet Jewry activists, British, French, and Israeli organisations working for Soviet Jewry. She drew attention to "the ladies in black" who were present in the hall, and referred to their sweeping the streets saying that she would be proud to sweep alongside the 35s.

Rita remembered:

> What a night that was. The atmosphere was electric – I get goose pimples now when I think about it. She stood on the stage, a lonely little woman, dressed in black. I cried, it was a most incredible moment, to be recognised like that. It was the first time that I appreciated that we were actually as much a spearhead of the movement as I had suspected we were.

> I never realised that we were pushing the movement along. That had been our real task, not to be deflected.

Margaret:

> We have kept ourselves focused. We've often helped other movements in the Human Rights world but only when we knew it would help Soviet Jewry.

When asked if they had any regrets about the campaign, they both expressed disappointment that they had not received more support from the Jewish community. They felt that if world Jewry had worked to the same extent as the 35s, all the refuseniks would have been out by now.

Doreen Gainsford, Barbara Oberman, Rita Eker, and Margaret Rigal are at pains to emphasise that without the frontliners (cf Appendix 1) the workers at Head Office, the London, provincial and international groups, very little would have been accomplished. These were women who, at the ring of the phone were willing to drop everything, often at the sacrifice of their family life, their leisure and

---

[26] The Committee of 15 is a French group of Jewish and non-Jewish members, which worked for 15 Jewish and non-Jewish families who had grave problems.

their health. It is impossible to give the same degree of recognition to all workers as to the "leaders" but in the course of the research for this book these four names crop up with great frequency and are spoken with justifiable pride and admiration.

Chapter Five

Growth

Having taken up cudgels on behalf of their oppressed fellow Jews, there was no going back. Within the space of a year the 35s had grown into an accountable and credible body. Whilst they could not claim a 'Land's End to John O'Groats' coverage, by the mid 1970s a network of 35s groups, affiliates, and supporters was in existence, extending from Edinburgh in the north to Bournemouth in the south, from Dublin in the west to Newcastle in the east and covering London and its environs. As it became established, Sylvia Becker, Zena Clayton, Zelda Harris, and Naomi Goldwater from the London office became responsible for visiting the groups to supply information and give encouragement. From 1972–1975 this was reinforced by a weekly analysis of all the latest information from Colin Shindler which was made on the suggestion of Ijo Rager. The groups worked closely with the London office but were autonomous. Each group devised its own campaigns and was instrumental in achieving extensive coverage both on the front pages of the local newspapers and on radio stations. As each enthusiastic band of recruits formed itself into a 35s group, natural leaders came to the fore and it was they, together with the "rank and file" who would create the distinctive character by which each group was to become known.

It now became necessary to develop into a group which was able to make contact with world powers, trade unions, parliamentarians, the news media and influential individuals. Amateurism was out; accuracy was to become their hallmark.

The trickle of names of refuseniks and their families, originally supplied by Michael Sherbourne from his telephone calls to the USSR, rapidly grew into an ever-widening stream. Names begot names, travellers returned with more names, and when the first immigrants came out they brought even more names. Detailed biographies of the refuseniks and prisoners were compiled. Many refuseniks had to wait up to fifteen years for an exit visa, and these biographies had to be revised regularly. Their detail and accuracy were admired by all the many organisations that made use of them.

The office generated a mass of documents: documents on legal cases, on emigration, refusals, permissions, appeals by prisoners and appeals by prisoners' families – all of which had to be translated by Michael Sherbourne. This documentation became the primary source of Soviet Jewry information in this country.

There was also a list of people about whom the organisation had only scanty details, insufficient for full-scale biographies. These names were kept on record with provision for details to be added as they became available. Perhaps a traveller would return with the name of someone they had met in a refusenik's apartment, or a traveller might be approached by a stranger in the street having been recognised as a fellow Jew.

Not every Jew wished to emigrate; age, health, family commitments, or fear of change were some of the factors which held people back. But they still desired contact with fellow Jews and with the outside world. News of the work of the 35s spread throughout the Jewish communities of the USSR and sometimes people would write asking for help. For every Sharansky, Shtern, Prusakov, or Zalmanson for whom a campaign was fought there were hundreds of "unknowns", many of whose stories were equally heartbreaking: of families separated, job dismissal, ill health, and the constant dread of KGB harassment. These hundreds ceased to be "unknowns" as a result of the work of the 35s.

The names developed personalities and became Mikhail Presman and Vladimir Bukovsky, Leonid Menes and Mark Nashpitz, Moshe Lats and Alexander Marysin, Boris Ryvkin, Helena Mai, Alexander Vilis, Elena Tendler, Joseph Essas, Irina Grivnina, Sender Levinson, Lazer Kagan, Igor Reichlin, Yehuda Tendler, Yefim Pargamanik, Katherina Chaimchev, Lev Gendin, Boris Katz, Lev Blitshtein, Leonid Volvovsky, Igor Kushnirenko, Edward Nizhnikov, Moishe Tonkonogy, Ida Taratuta, Natalie Rozenstein, Nina Soifer, Anatoly Starkman, Marina Vigdarov, Tonya Krivonos, Naum Falkovich, Yevgeny Tserlin, Rafael Adzashvili, Zina Abramzon, Alexander Podrabinek, Alexander Roitburd, Elena Khess, Irina Kuravsky, Isolda

Tufeld, Arkady Chepovetsky, Solomon Flaks, Yakov Ravlenko,
Emmanuil Likhterov, Alexander Gorshonsky, Leonid Lubman, Clara
Kazan, Svetlana Levina, Alexander Magidovich, Olga Kofman, Soibla
Khomak, Elena Friedland.

And the personalities rapidly became friends. Irina and Elena,
Katherina and Natalya, Nina and Clara and Moise, Mishe, Lazer,
Yakov and Yehuda were enveloped in the warmth of the 35s family.

Ask a 35er about 'her' adopted refusenik and her face lights up.
So often it is not the relevant details of the case which she remembers
– the number of years in refusal, the length of prison sentence, but the
minutiae of their lives.

Rita Eker, reminiscing about some of her friends:

> After Alex Lerner's wife died his beautiful setter dog
> called Red became his close companion. When I visited
> him he ordered Red "Say shalom" and the dog put his
> paw out to be shaken. Poor Alex, when Red
> disappeared something went out of his life – one more
> tragedy for him.

> Natasha Khassina worked for every Jew who needed
> help, and this was often detrimental to her own family.
> She saved so many Jews, helping them with documents,
> with food and medicines and money. She often put
> herself at risk. She told of an occasion when her young
> child was in Hebrew classes and a KGB man walked in
> and asked for Khassina Natasha's child. Those children
> had been so well disciplined that not one of them opened
> their mouths.

> Irina Brailowsky's husband was a prisoner – there was a
> big campaign for him throughout the worldwide
> scientific community and because of her connections she
> was followed by the KGB wherever she went. I visited
> her on one occasion and we decided to go for a walk.
> When we got outside she went over to this man standing
> near the door and said: "We're going for a walk, are
> you coming with us?" I said, "Who's that?" She
> looked at me with a grin and said "KGB". She had such
> courage.

Visitors to the office immediately sensed the atmosphere, vibrant with names and details of refuseniks and prisoners and their families. As historian Martin Gilbert recalled:

> This was the strength of the 35s, they were dealing not just with names but with real people, they turned statistics into people. Not only did they get names, they knew everything about each one of them and they became an extension of the 35ers' own families; they brought these people to the attention of the public. The 35s made brilliant use of the specific case and the specific name. This was, I believe, their main difference from all the other Human Rights organisations where names of individuals seldom emerged. The impact was enormous because an individual was clearly being persecuted... and they made these names, faces, needs, characters, desires, sufferings and hopes known not only in Britain but throughout the Free World. If it were not for those to whom the 35s introduced me, my book could not have been called *The Jews of Hope*. Nor would it have been the human story as opposed to the politico-sociological.

Hardly a week passed without someone from a 35s group or a 35s contact visiting refuseniks, the bulk of their luggage containing urgently needed medicines, clothes, books, tapes, as well as the little luxuries; the bar of soap, the bottle of scent and the pack of cigarettes.

But lists of names and files of biographies can in no way convey the saga of tragedy which they contained. One weekly newsletter, No. 7, November 1978, alone contained the following stories:

1. LERNER family. The Lerners first applied 7 years ago. They have seen many friends and colleagues leave the Soviet Union while they still remain. The situation has now become very dangerous for them. Prof. Lerner, who is 65, is a doctor of technical sciences and cybernetics; he was dismissed from his job when he originally applied but he holds private seminars every Monday. Their daughter, Sonia, left the USSR in 1973 with her husband and baby daughter. The wrench was even more poignant for the Lerners as their two oldest children were killed in the Second World War in the Ukraine. Sonia and her brother were

born after the war. Since emigrating, Sonia has had a second daughter who, of course, her parents have never seen. Vladimir, the Lerner's son, is still in the Soviet Union. Please send letters of support to show we have not forgotten them.

2. PRISONERS-OF-CONSCIENCE. Iosif MENDELEVICH and Hillel BUTMAN have been moved from Vladimir Prison to the same prison as Anatoly SHARANSKY. Please send letters of support to all three.

3. Iosif BEGUN. Alla DRUGOVA, wife of Iosif was visited by tourists who inform us that the temperature of Iosif's place of exile is 40°F below zero already. During her visit to Iosif, he was moved to a single room where the roof leaked and there was snow on the floor and bed. These dwellings are merely dilapidated wooden shacks. Alla complained to the Camp Commandant of the conditions under which Iosif is living. A reply came back saying that "conditions are suitable for someone of his character". Please send letters of support to Alla who is very depressed about Iosif's situation. Also send letters to Iosif sympathising with him in his plight.

4. Gregory GOLDSTEIN. When Isai returned from an earlier visit to Gregory he reported: "He is very pale and very thin but alive. He now has high blood pressure and vomits because of the dirt in the food. He spends eight hours a day as a metal worker, and has an abominable diet. The possible penalties for not attaining work targets are: no letters, no dinner, fifteen days solitary, beatings by other prisoners." Please send letters of support to Gregory. In your letters please tell him that you have written letters of protest on his behalf to the Camp Commandant (same address as Gregory) and also to General Roman Rudenko.

5. Dr Semyon GLUZMAN – Prisoner of Conscience. Semyon is very depressed and in desperate need of your support. Please write to him.

6. Alexsei MURZHENKO. Lubov Pavlovna, Aleksei's wife has had a letter from him saying that he does not receive any mail from her or the parcel to which he was entitled. The KGB have told her that her behaviour is 'slanderous' and she will be charged with leading a parasitic way of life. Papers have already been drawn

up. Their young son is being harassed at school and asked to denounce his father. Lubov Pavlovna is expecting their second child after a recent private visit. Prisoners in strict regime are allowed one private visit a year, lasting up to three days. Please send letters of support to Lubov. Also send letters of encouragement to Alexsei.

7. Anatoly MALKIN of Moscow. Anatoly Malkin the former Prisoner of Conscience is facing a fresh wave of harassment. His young wife is expecting their first child in the new year and they are now in very grave danger. Please send letters of protest to Deputy Minister of OVIR in Moscow and letters of support to Anatoly. (Malkin, a twenty-one-year-old student applied for permission to emigrate. He was refused and expelled from the Moscow Steel Institute and therefore became eligible for conscription. He renounced his Soviet citizenship to avoid military service as this would have meant at least seven years ineligibility to emigrate. He then met with harassment, arrest and imprisonment).

8. Lev ROITBURD. We are gravely concerned about the lack of news and information reaching us. We are worried because this silence could be ominous. Please send letters and cables of protest to Mr Zoitov, the Deputy Minister of OVIR in Moscow.

9. Kopel SPECTOR. "Nick's" aged parents in Israel are deeply concerned in case the free world have forgotten their son. He is completely alone in the Soviet Union. Please write letters of support to him. Please also write letters of protest to the OVIR office.

10. Dr Viktor BRAILOVSKY. In a telephone conversation he says that the family have received another refusal. He has also been told that he must not give any more private lessons. Viktor thinks that this is the first step in a parasitism charge and asks for more active support. Please write letters of protest to the Deputy Minister of OVIR in Moscow. Dr Brailovsky requests that Logunov (Director of Moscow University) be approached. PLEASE WRITE TO HIM.

The newsletter of November 1978 printed the following letter:

49

OPEN LETTER RECEIVED BY MICHAEL SHERBOURNE ON 4 NOVEMBER 1978.

TO: The Chairman of the Presidium of the Supreme Soviet of the
         USSR, L. I. Brezhnev
FROM: Sixteen Refusenik Pensioners

We are all pensioners who appeal to you in regard to the refusal to allow us to emigrate to Israel. Most of us have already been separated for many years from our children and grandchildren and are completely isolated from our people and from our national and religious culture.

Old age is the time when we feel the necessity to be able to express more deeply our religious feelings. We feel urgently the need to live in a Jewish milieu to be able to follow the age-old Jewish religious rituals and traditions, and to observe the Jewish religion, to be able to visit our Jewish holy places and in fact, to lead a full Jewish life in our Holy Land.

The refusal to grant us permission to emigrate to Israel is causing us indescribable anguish and suffering. Refusal to grant permission to people who, for many years, have not been working and are receiving old age or disability pensions can only cause astonishment to people of goodwill, whereas the granting of such permission by a humanitarian Soviet government can only result in approbation on the part of the outside world.

We therefore urgently beg you to grant us, the undersigned, and our families permission to emigrate to Israel as soon as possible.

> Naum KOGAN, age 70
> Faina KOGAN, age 63
> Alexander LERNER, age 65
> Judith PERELMAN, age 63
> Vladimir TUFELD, age 50 (invalid of the
>   3rd category)
> Arkady MAI, age 55 (war disablement
>   pension 3rd category)
> Yakov GRECHANIK, age 69
> Channa YELLINSON, age 61
> Saul GORELIK, age 65
> Salomon INDITSKY, age 66
> Channa ZASHCHINSKAYA, age 66
> Boris LIFSHITZ, age 69
> Clara LIFSHITZ, age 63
> Emmanuel LIKHTEROV, age 63
> Lydia LIKHTEROVA age 53

Another newsletter of March 1978 tells of the hunger strike of nearly 150 refuseniks from cities all over the USSR to mark the first anniversary of Sharansky's arrest.

The Soviet emigration figures showed a constant fluctuation which appeared to have a direct bearing on the prevailing relationship between the United States and USSR, but there was never any period during which the 35s could be complacent:

1973	34,000
1974	20,000
1975	13,000
1976	14,000
1977	16,000
1978	28,000
1979	51,000
1980	21,000
1981	9,500
1982	2,500

What a contrast with 185,000 emigrants in 1990.

Small wonder that the members were willing to sacrifice their personal lives. The refuseniks wrote that the Women's Campaign for Soviet Jewry gave them hope, but from the refuseniks the women received inspiration.

Alongside the specific Jewish issue of the refuseniks and their desire to live in Israel, there was the broader one of Human Rights. On a less emotive scale, but nonetheless pertinent, were matters not only involving Jews, but also other religious groups, particularly Baptists. It was virtually impossible to obtain prayer books of any sort as Soviet law prohibited the use of state-owned printing presses for the production of such literature, and all printing presses were owned by the state! The importation of prayer books or religious literature from other countries was also illegal. Religious education was banned as being seditious and obstacles were put in the way of religious worship other than in a very small number of strictly controlled token establishments.

Even those Jews who did not wish to emigrate or had no strong desire for religious expression were subjected to professional and educational discrimination. For example, the 1970 Census returns for Moscow showed that Jews comprised thirty-six percent of the population, but in the academic year of 1976–77 the percentage of

Jewish students at the Moscow Institute of Higher Education was only 1.8 percent, and no Jewish student had been accepted at the Moscow University in the previous years' intake.

In the spring of 1975, a group of women of different nationalities gathered in Geneva to lobby delegates of the participating countries at a session of the Conference on Security and Co-operation in Europe (CSCE). It was here that Doreen Gainsford, together with women from Canada, Denmark, France, West Germany, Eire, Sweden and the United States of America banded together as the International Women's Committee for Soviet Jewry (IWCSJ) and agreed to attend the Helsinki Accords meeting later that year.

In August 1975, President Brezhnev of the USSR and President Carter of the USA signed the historic Accords of the CSCE. This was the final act of recognition of the inviolability of the post world-war-two frontiers in Europe. It also pledged the 35 signatory nations to respect Human Rights and fundamental freedoms and to cooperate in economic, scientific and humanitarian activities.

Doreen Gainsford recalls:

> Helsinki was a gift from God; it was the catalyst. There were three baskets;- Trade, Human Rights and the Ratification of Borders, and we forced the Human Rights basket to become the most important. We were lucky because President Carter found Human Rights attractive to fight on. We opened Pandora's box and once the truth was available it had to be recognised. All the Human Rights organisations were there and we pressed all the heads of the delegations and once we presented them with the material they had to take action, and once they had taken action we wanted to know what was going to happen next.

In a letter to *The Daily Telegraph*, 12 August 1975, Professor Leonard Schapiro, an expert on Soviet affairs, observed that there were two reasons why the Russians were patently anxious for the conference. The first was their desire to put an end to all arguments about post-war frontiers of the Russian Empire, and the second was to try to use Helsinki in order to silence unwelcome criticism and interference in Soviet internal affairs.

The Jewish Telegraphic Agency (JTA) of 1st August 1975 reported a demonstration by the International Women's Campaign for Soviet Jewry in Helsinki outside the USA Embassy. Doreen Gainsford, together with some of her sister activists, were arrested by the Finnish police after they greeted President Brezhnev's arrival with banners bearing the message USSR HONOUR THE AGREEMENT – GIVE HUMAN RIGHTS TO SOVIET JEWS.

Doreen, (who confessed to possessing a very loud voice) shouted in Brezhnev's direction: "You are signing – and persecuting Soviet Jews. While you are signing, Anatoly Malkin is in prison. Free Malkin".

The women had reconnoitred the area the previous evening and knew exactly where to stand and in which car Brezhnev would be arriving. They were later released without charge.

With a typical feminine touch, before she left Helsinki, Doreen Gainsford sent a bouquet to President Kekkanon with a personally written apology for having caused his country any inconvenience. She also sent a single rose to Prime Minister Harold Wilson with the message: "I am proud of British democracy and the freedom we enjoy in this country".

The Soviet Jewry Action Committee of the Board of Deputies actively discouraged Doreen Gainsford and her group from demonstrating at Helsinki, but she felt that her actions had been justified. "I now know that our journey to Helsinki was really necessary because I heard the BBC report from Helsinki that 'the summit conference is the highlight of Brezhnev's career, only marred by a demonstration for Soviet Jewry rights'."

The women's delegation had written to the President of Finland as Chairman of the Conference on Security and Co-operation in Europe, explaining their motives for demonstrating, and in particular had singled out the imprisonment, on false charges, of Dr Mikhail Shtern from Vinnitsa, and Sender Levinson from Moldavia. They also noted that within the previous few weeks, three more Soviet Jews had been imprisoned; Lev Roitburd of Odessa, Anatoly Malkin of Moscow and Yaakov Vinarov of Kiev. They wrote: "...the actual crimes of these men is that they applied to emigrate to Israel. The above, and many others, contravene the spirit of the agreement (JTA).

"It was the USA might that mattered but it was the British delegates who pushed our Government and they, in turn, encouraged the US administration" recalled Margaret Rigal.

The Women's Campaign for Soviet Jewry began to expand with the setting up of groups throughout London, in the provinces and overseas, until by the late 1970s there were nineteen groups in Great Britain as well as groups in Europe, Canada Australia, New Zealand and Israel.

The Office allocated to each of these autonomous groups "their own" prisoner and refuseniks for adoption, and individual members within each group took it upon themselves to adopt a refusenik. Photographs were collected and filed at the office and copies were sent to the adopters; putting a face to a name humanised what was, all too often, a very one-sided correspondence.

At the time of writing this (1995), there are approximately 6,500 entries in the biography files. Many of these entries refer to families, not only parents and children, but often grandparents too. A rough estimate would suggest that since its inception the 35s campaign has helped about 20,000 people.

The 35s gathered and stored a very broad spectrum of information both for their own use and for distribution to other interested organisations or individuals.

A sample file-box from the mid 1980s contained the following data:

1. List of refuseniks in refusal for more than 10 years (1984–85).
2. Soviet emigration figures from 1968–1988.
3. British towns twinned with towns in the USSR.
4. Report on European Inter-parliamentary Conference on Soviet Jewry (1985).
5. List of Soviet officials.
6. List of searches, arrests and imprisonment of Hebrew teachers and Jewish activists (1985).
7. Soviet Jewish prisoners of Zion (1984).
8. Soviet Jewish ex-prisoners of Zion (1984).
9. Appeal to the Jewish people from the Jews of Kiev.
10. Jewish participation in the Soviet war effort in defence of the Soviet Motherland (1940-45).
11. List of matter forbidden to be taken into the Soviet Union.

12. "Keys to the Kremlin" 1977. List of all Ministers, addresses, Ministries, officials, telephone numbers, etc.
13. List of refuseniks adopted by British Trade Unions.
14. Petition to be signed by Trade Unionists at conferences in support of Ida Nudel and Vladimir Slepak.
15. Discrimination against Jews enrolling at Moscow University 1979.
16. Victims of Soviet persecution 1978/9.
17. List of Hebrew teachers in the Soviet Union (1981).

By 1977 the 35s had become a highly structured organisation with thirty-six frontliners and a back-up of over one hundred and fifty women who could be called upon to attend demonstrations at a moment's notice.

What started as a campaign for Prisoner Palatnik had developed into an international organisation the work of which was to encompass – "adoptions, information about anti-Semitism, Bar-Mitzvah twinning, campaigns, charity shop, clothes distribution, demonstrations, education, fund-raising, letter-writing, lobbying, medical aid, 'Mini-gifts', newsletters, 'One-to-One', poor relatives, prisoners, trade unions, travellers and trips". An impressive catalogue.

Despite the fact that, today, the organisation has no committee (or committee meetings), hierarchy, elections or agendas – it works. Its finances are precarious. From day one it had to rely on an amalgam of benefactors and begging to remain viable. From its inception its chief benefactor was Cyril Stein. Convinced by the urgency of the work and impressed by the 35s' proven ability to carry it out, he gave unstintingly for over twenty years. When his funding ceased, Rita Eker, with tiring regularity had to put her 'hands-on' work on one side, to cajole friends, acquaintances and strangers to contribute, in order to keep the 35s viable.

Nothing could be a better illustration of their chronic insecurity than its chequered history of office venues.

In the twenty-five years of their existence the 35s have moved offices six times. A pre-requisite of these diverse addresses appears to be a building which is under threat of demolition; hence the hasty moves, in the course of which many irreplaceable documents and photographs have been lost.

Initially the work was carried out in Doreen Gainsford's home. In the mid 1970s the 35s moved to Allandale, a dilapidated office block in NW11, where, housed in a leaking basement, they worked surrounded by buckets to catch the drips. Later the floor above became vacant and they moved upstairs into it, but by about 1978 they were flooded out and moved into a condemned laundry in Granville Road nearby, where they worked in the former machine room. The floor was damp, the bare plastered walls were cracked and draughty. Joanna[27] recalled:

> ...we had to be so careful as there was an enormous hole in the centre of the floor where a machine had been ripped out. We were frozen in the winter when we worked with our coats on. There were no lights in the room where we kept our records and we had to use torches to search through the filing cabinets.

Joyce[28]:

> when the laundry, which had moved to the other side of the road, was in operation, the whole room vibrated and our telephones would jump off the desk. We kept on getting notices to quit, but we had nowhere to go. First it was a 6 months notice, then 2 weeks, then 1 week, and then one day, and on that day, the day we moved, the demolition men were waiting outside, ready to bulldoze the building.

In the pouring rain everyone joined in; papers and files were crammed into boxes, trunks and cases which came to rest in the attics, garages and basements of various members. There they remained, often damp and deteriorating, until they were dug out by the author in 1992.

In true 35s style the next move, into the offices of the former Jewish Blind Society in West Heath Avenue, Golders Green, was made in typically adverse conditions. Margaret recalled:

> The day we moved the snow was thick on the ground. It looked so beautiful, like Sleeping Beauty's garden, undisturbed for years. But when we arrived the place had been empty for so long that we couldn't even get up the long front drive for the dense jungle of overgrown

27 Joanna Aron
28 Joyce Simson

rose bushes and shrubs. George (her husband) had to
fetch some secateurs and eventually cleared a way
through the thicket. We slipped and fell in the snow; it
came down our necks and into our boots and everything
got wet again.

Rita remembered:

On the ground floor the windows had been blocked up
for security and they were kept that way. It was
marvellous storage space but it was highly impractical,
searching for things in the dark and cold of a winter's
afternoon. It was a little better upstairs, but the roof
leaked so once again we had buckets all over the place.

In 1986 this building became due for demolition and, with nowhere
else to go, the office work was carried on in Rita's dining room,
spilling over into the playroom. Her husband, Moss, breathed a huge
sigh of relief when eventually the office was moved into two rooms
and a lavatory above a hairdressing salon in Finchley Road. The
all-invasive smell of curry from the adjoining Indian restaurant was
the least of their new problems, which included shattered windows,
broken floorboards and a chronic lack of space, necessitating working
in the lavatory which accommodated several filing cabinets. Evelyn
remembers an occasion when she even worked under a desk in a
desperate search for space.

Joyce recalls:

When Sharansky was released all of us in the office
were glued to the TV. On the pavement outside, queuing
up the stairs and crowding the landing were the ITN,
BBC, and NBC camera crews trying to record us
watching that famous newsreel scene of him walking
across the bridge – to freedom.

In 1988 they moved a few doors along Finchley Road to their
current offices on the top floor of Pannel House, and in 1992 they
extended into additional offices on the same floor, providing
much-needed space for the changed nature of the work.

To visit the office today, go round the back of the Lighting Shop, (ex car showroom) and up two steep flights of stairs into the office. Negotiate your way round the bulging black plastic bags waiting to be taken to the Charity Shop. Don't trip over the piled-up holdalls filled with much needed clothing awaiting transport to new immigrants in Israel.

Joanna in her office calmly copes with the constantly ringing telephone, with Peggy's[29] queries, with Rita's dictation, and with Daphne's[30] requests. Rita, invariably doing two things at once, is on the telephone, yet again wheedling a desperately needed donation from an acquaintance, whilst dictating a letter at the same time. Evelyn[31] briefs two travellers prior to their forthcoming trip to Moscow. Daphne wanders around looking for a clear desk on which to start filing the week's mail. Joyce, surrounded by newspapers, extracts items of interest for the forthcoming newsletter. Margaret attempts, for the third time this week, to get the photocopier to work. Peggy calmly continues typing biographies whilst Sue[32] checks the current list of refuseniks. Sylvia[33] and Joy[34] prepare the envelopes for the newsletter whilst Michael[35], on the red telephone conducts a conversation in Russian with a refusenik in Kiev who is still beset with problems.

Max[36] pops in and is immediately commandeered to manhandle yet another box of bric-a-brac to the shop and some black sacks to the tip (not all the clothes donated are usable).

Judith[37] and Rita debate the merits of helping Family A as against Family B through the One-to-One scheme whilst the other Rita[38] types the minutes of the Medical Committee meeting. A motorbike messenger delivers a package and is followed by an out-of-breath donor who had dragged a couple of cases of clothes up those stairs. Ten boxes of drugs arrive. Evelyn puts them aside for checking

---

[29] Peggy Fortuyn
[30] Daphne Gerlis
[31] Evelyn Nohr
[32] Sue Usiskin
[33] Sylvia Levine) *Both early 35ers who have willingly and cheerfully*
[34] Joy Lowy) *tackled every task demanded of them*
[35] Michael Sherbourne
[36] Max Nohr (Evelyn's husband)
[37] Judith Sheldon
[38] Rita Earl

against the medical files: A needs syringes for her diabetes; B needs blood pressure tablets; C needs heart drugs. Maybe her travellers can take them?

A typical day's work is underway in the office. In comparison with earlier days, the 35s are now housed in carpeted, centrally heated, palatial rooms. There is space for the ever-expanding shelves of files, the filing cabinets, the fax machine, the photocopiers, the computers and the typewriters, the "drugs department", the clothing store, and the overflow of black bags for the shop.

And the telephones. Margaret and Rita think that the telephones are no longer being 'bugged' by the Soviets, but they insist that they were not letting imagination run riot when they strongly suspected that there was a connection between the men who always seemed to be digging up the road outside their various offices and the mysterious clicks heard so often on the lines.

The site is due for development and again the hunt is on for new premises.

Chapter Six

Campaigns And Demonstrations

Demonstrate as much as you like as long as there is
no violence. The more you demonstrate the more
strength it gives your arm and gets the Russians to do
what we want.

Prime Minister Harold Wilson
to Greville Janner MP

"The 35s? Weren't they those women who used to dress in black
and who were always demonstrating at the ballet and outside the
Russian Embassy?"

Yes, they were, but the substance of their work was carried on in
the office year in and year out; quietly phoning, writing, pleading,
organising and lobbying for the thousands of little-known refuseniks
and their families. But were it not for the campaigns and
demonstrations little would have been achieved. It has been seen time
and time again that refuseniks, ex-prisoners, journalists and politicians
have testified to the efficacy of the glare of publicity which was
directed at the Soviet Embassy in London and on Soviet officials in the
USSR, who loathed the spotlight which revealed the callousness and
inconsistencies of their regime. They hated losing face and they
fought against the political pressures which were brought to bear as a
result of the campaigns. The ultimate humiliation was that all of this
was engendered by WOMEN – JEWISH WOMEN.

The very fact of the expulsion of (mostly) Jewish dissidents from
Moscow during the run-up to the Olympic Games held there in 1980,
reveals the sensitivity of the authorities to the publicity engendered
over their denial of Human Rights. In the summer of 1978 the 35s
launched a campaign against the holding of the 1980 Olympic Games

in Moscow. This campaign aroused a certain amount of dissension even among some Jewish activists. The Soviet Government was issuing more exit visas than in the previous year and it was believed, by some, that they were relaxing their emigration policy. But Michael Sherbourne was in regular contact with Moscow refuseniks (many of whom were being expelled from the city in the run-up to the Games) and he maintained that this was a pre-Olympic ploy and that the refuseniks themselves were in favour of the campaign.

Margaret Rigal thought that the campaign was certainly justified in that it brought the abuses and injustices to the notice of a wider audience, although some people became concerned and it did cause some hackles to rise. The issue was covered in most of the national newspapers. The *London Evening Standard*, *The Daily Telegraph*, *The Sunday Telegraph*, *The Times*, and *The Daily Mail* all carried leaders, articles or letters, most of which supported the position of the 35s and other protagonists.

From about ten months before the Games were due to commence, the front page of the newsletter featured an "Olympic Games tear-off countdown calendar", e.g. "38 weeks to the Games", which changed weekly. A typical newsletter of the time (No. 28, 15 May 1979) demonstrates the intensity of the activities:

1. Milk Race. 27 May–9 June. Details of the route have been sent today to the groups in the vicinity of the race. Please do your utmost to obtain publicity.

2. Soviet Exhibition, Earls Court, 23 May–10 June. DO YOU REALLY WANT TO HELP? The Soviets are mounting this propaganda exercise and it is imperative that every member participates in at least two or three demonstrations; also that everyone should be in regular contact with this office so that when they go to the exhibition they can ask the organisers relevant questions.

First demonstration, 23 May from 10.30 a.m. prompt to 1.30 p.m. No excuse for non attendance – think of Ida (Nudel), Vladimir (Slepak) and Anatoly Sharansky.

Georgian Dancers – Croydon and Wembley
The dancers and the Soviet Exhibition overlap so friends must be enlisted to join the demonstrations. Anyone who cannot travel to Earls Court should help the Wembley and Croydon groups.

There were also the following items:
(a) Reference to the BBC "World at One" programme which reported that the Russian authorities were showing signs of nervousness about

DON'T MISS

THE

GEORGIAN STATE
DANCE COMPANY

- From
  USSR

with **MARCELLO KOSYGIN**
RAQUEL BREZHNEV
LEE VAN PODGORNY
and the **KGB ENSEMBLE**

ANOTHER SMASH HIT!!

FROM THE PEOPLE WHO BROUGHT YOU...

THE SIBERIA STORY!!
THE PACT WITH HITLER!!
THE GREAT PURGES!!

AND NUMEROUS OTHER UNDEMOCRATIC SUCCESSES

THIS DECADE
*Soviet Productions unashamedly present
an Epic Campaign of Anti-Semitism*

ENTITLED

"KEEP THESE PEOPLE HERE"

Featuring: PRISONS, MENTAL ASYLUMS
AND CONCENTRATION CAMPS FOR JEWS
DARING TO APPLY FOR REPATRIATION TO
ISRAEL

*Leaflet produced for visit of Georgian State Dancers, London
Coliseum, 1973.*

anti-Soviet influence that may be brought in by some of the visiting Olympic teams, and that dissidents were being expelled from the capital to avoid embarrassing demonstrations. (b) Extracts from *The Guardian* (5 May 1979), *The International Herald Tribune* (10 May 1979) and *The New York Times* (14 May 1979), all of which discussed the decision to hold the Games in Moscow.

(c) An extract from *The Soviet Weekly* of 12 May 1979 extolling the forthcoming exhibition at Earls Court, with a reference to the Games.

In March 1980, Newsletter No. 25 reported that in the course of a debate on the subject in the House of Commons, MPs Jill Knight, Winston Churchill, and Ian Gilmour all spoke in favour of a boycott of the Games. During the debate the names of Sharansky, Nudel, and Sakharov were mentioned. Much of the information had been supplied to these MPs by the 35s.

35ers were urged to write to Lord Kilannin, the President of the International Olympics Committee, to the Moscow Committee for the Olympic Games, to Prince Philip (who was due to visit Moscow to advise on equestrian events), and to their own MPs in protest at the decision to hold the Games in Moscow.

Despite the huge effort expended, not only by the 35s but by many other groups and individuals, this campaign did not succeed in its purpose. Nevertheless, it aroused public consciousness of the situation of Jews in the Soviet Union and it helped to maintain the momentum of the overall campaign.

The campaigns and demonstrations, some of which extended over a period of many years, were extremely demanding on the women. But how could they do otherwise than continue to pursue their activities when they received letters such as the following?

"Brothers-in-arms, throughout many centuries of battle for our existence and of much suffering we appeal to you... Our history is a never-ending web of humiliation, oppression, pogroms... on the surface only a small part of the erupting volcano can be seen, all the rest is inside, hidden, concealed from view. What is being cooked-up down there in the depths is, as yet, unknown to us, but we shall no doubt very soon feel it and experience the full effect of the depths of the anti-Jewish prejudice being stirred up ready to vomit forth from the volcano... We shall continue with the fight for our freedom because we know that you are with us. We shall do everything in our power to restore and maintain the honour and dignity of our people. Am Yisroel Chai".[39]

This letter was written in 1977 and signed by 250 refuseniks. It was reprinted in Newsletter No. 42 of July 1980.

Such letters were often smuggled out, at great risk to their writers.

It was impossible to campaign for every refusenik listed in the files of the 35s; it was generally the activist refuseniks for whom campaigns would be launched. They were often the leaders of their community, or of a group of refuseniks, or they were sometimes teachers of Hebrew. They were the sort of people who were likely to be met by travellers to the USSR, and when these travellers returned home with the sadly familiar stories of tragedy and trauma, hardship and harassment, they would add yet another family to the campaign list. Sometimes an activist would inform a traveller of a particularly dire case which needed urgent action. One such example was that of 13-year-old Marina Temkin who had been kidnapped by the KGB in 1972 and placed in a militarised young communists' camp. In the Newsletter of 4 September 1979 it was reported:

> ...she is now 20. She has been subjected to forcible re-education; attempts have been made to change her personality by the mis-use of drugs. She is denied the right to visit her 82-year-old paternal grandmother. Nevertheless, she still wants to join her father, Professor Alexander Temkin, in Israel. She wrote that she wanted to establish contact with her father, that she remembers him as before and always remains his daughter... She suffers from the impossibility of being in touch with her father.

Adopters who worked for Marina were asked to publicise her case during the Year of the Child and the run-up to the Moscow Olympics and to send appeals to the chairman of the KGB, Yuri Andropov and to the director of OVIR, Konstantin Zoitov.

---

[39] "Am Yisroel Chai" (Hebrew) – "The People of Israel Live".

The 35s soon became front page news. Since the suffragettes, no other group of women had protested publicly with such perseverance and vigour. Unheard of for Jewish housewives to demonstrate (and in such a manner), they stood in silence on the streets, displaying their banners and placards aloft whilst the cameras clicked; the pictures of their demonstrations became a regular feature in many newspapers. The transition from stay-at-home housewife to demonstrating campaigner was gradual.

Delysia Jason:

> we were eased in slowly at first, starting off in a 'ladylike' way with quiet demonstrations and no gimmicks but steadily we became more adventurous. If Sylvia (Wallis) or Doreen (Gainsford) rang up, you just couldn't say 'no'. Without my 35s training I would never have done the work I did later with the Churches, or the 'Keren Klita'[40] work that I do now in Israel".

Sylvia Wallis was a founder member who originally was in charge of organising the demonstrations, and when she left to live in Israel this responsibility was taken over by Rochelle Duke, who recalled:

> ideas would fly around the whole time. The telephone would ring at the most ungodly hours – it would be Doreen or Rita with an idea. This would be finalised in the morning and we would be out on the street in the afternoon. I was the most shy person and I cringed at the thought of demonstrating on the streets. Half of me wanted to do it and half didn't – but I know that I HAD to do it. Our demonstrations were so creative, so inventive, and they made such an impact.

In time the novelty of genteel demonstrations began to pall and the women would vie with each other to devise ever more ingenious ideas. They dressed as prisoners weighed down with balls and chains, and when young mothers were separated from their babies they dressed in baby clothes, complete with nappies and dummies. When the KGB started to arrest refuseniks whilst they were still in bed, they

---

[40] "Keren Klita" (Hebrew) – Absorption Fund for new immigrants. Delysia Jason, the former leader of the Elstree 35s, founded Keren Klita and is at the forefront of its activities.

demonstrated in nightgowns and pyjamas, and when an engineer was imprisoned they hired a crane and drove it up and down Bayswater.

Before each Helsinki Accords meeting Linda Isaacs, dressed as Britannia in black garb, took a one hundred name sheaf of detailed refusenik biographies to each of 35 embassies of the signatories of the Helsinki Agreement. Newsletter No. 9, November 1980 reported that "...every country that signed the Final Act in Helsinki in 1975 has now received evidence of one hundred and thirty-two refuseniks or prisoners whose fate shows how little the Soviet authorities are honouring their obligations". The 35s produced an annually updated version of this list until the advent of "glasnost".

They developed a close relationship with the police, at times, perhaps, a little too close. Rochelle tells of being "propositioned" on more than one occasion by a high ranking police officer. She, Doreen, and Rita all had contacts within the Special Branch. Rita Eker recalled:

> we would swap information with the Special Branch; they would give us the venue and time of an appearance by a prominent Russian visitor and we would tell them our plans. During our demonstrations we would try to chat to a chauffeur or a policeman and in that way we would get to know their next "port of call".

Rochelle Duke: "we were on first-name terms with some of the 'top brass' which meant that on occasions we were able to stretch the boundaries a little".

By the end of 1971 the London group alone could count on thirty to forty members on immediate call and a supporting group of about three hundred and fifty women ready to attend demonstrations at twenty-four hours notice. This larger group was subdivided with a telephonist for each sub-group. A list dated April 1977 records that Rhoda Burns, Leila Cumber, Simone Goldfarb, Herta Graham, Mollie Greenby, Susan Herold, Myra Janner, Valli Kokotek, Zena Kut, Janet Millet, Enid Sherry, Ruth Urban, and Rosalind Witte were all standing by ready to call out "their" demonstrators.

Sometimes demonstrations were prevented or curtailed but, ironically, even such "failures" could become resounding successes as a result of the extra publicity obtained. An example of this occurred at the Henley Regatta in July 1974. Margaret Rigal and her son

David, Susan Rabin and her daughter, and a helpful minicab driver had hired a boat for the day, with the intention of confronting a competing Russian rowing crew at the end of their race, with their display of banners, written in Russian and English, "USSR STOP PERSECUTING JEWS AND RELEASE VICTOR POLSKY"[41]. However, the London Press Association News Agency had warned the regatta officials and a Thames Conservancy launch stopped the boat and towed it away. But the graphic photographs and detailed reports in *The Daily Telegraph*, *The Daily Express*, *The Guardian*, and the *Reading Evening Post* ensured that the demonstration gained even wider publicity than it might otherwise have done.

Plucky as these demonstrating women were, their daring pales into insignificance compared with the courage and heroism of the many refuseniks within the Soviet Union, who, on numerous occasions, attempted to express their frustrations and anger at their circumstances by demonstrating. During 1988 the newsletter reported fifty demonstrations in which twelve hundred Jews participated. There were seven hundred arrests, twenty-one cases of beating and one hundred and fifty were taken to court and fined. In Moscow alone there were five women's groups who met regularly and registered their views by meetings with Soviet officials, going on hunger strikes and holding placard protests. Unlike the demonstrators in this country, the Moscow women were confronted and attacked by hostile crowds, beaten up and dragged into vans by the police and were often held in custody without trial for weeks on end.

It was through the sheer "chutzpah"[42] of their demonstrations that the name and fame of the 35s spread. Photographs and articles in the press and broadcasts on radio and television brought their activities to the attention of both the Jewish and non-Jewish communities. Indeed, on 26 November 1987 The Times reported:

> the 35s Women's Campaign for Soviet Jewry clearly rattled the Russkies during the Leningrad Kirov Opera's tour of Britain this summer. Leningradskaya Pravda has just devoted a lengthy article to abusing the movement for its protests during the tour. Even more oddly the

---

[41] Viktor Polsky, a professor of mathematics, who was being held on a trumped up driving charge.

[42] "Chutzpah" (Hebrew) – cheek, effrontery.

paper has a bee in its bonnet about the campaign's '35' appellation, adopted because the first person for whose right to emigrate it campaigned for was a thirty-five year old woman. In an outburst at once ageist and sexist, the author notes 'the committee members have long ago passed the Balzacian age and at best are old enough to be the Odessa woman's auntie.

Such comments were grist to the 35ers' mill and they derived much satisfaction from having such a positive feedback from their campaigns and demonstrations.

SHARANSKY – THE ANATOMY OF A CAMPAIGN

> Nothing they can do can humiliate me. I alone can humiliate myself
>
> Natan Sharansky, *Fear No Evil*,
> page 8[43]

Two bulging box files contain the bare bones of the FREE ANATOLY SHARANSKY campaign. Fleshed out they reveal a relentless drive, commencing at the time of his arrest and ending only on his release from prison nine years later.

Ranged alongside the activities of the governments of Israel, the USA, Britain, and other European countries, USA Soviet Jewry activists, the Canadian Women's Soviet Jewry Campaigners, and numerous other Soviet Jewry groups here and abroad, the 35s campaign was but a small cog in a huge FREE SHARANSKY machine. But their contribution was out of all proportion to its size.

Anatoly Sharansky was a twenty-nine-year-old Moscow mathematician. He first became interested in the Human Rights movement through reading about Andrei Sakharov. This interest developed and led to the formation, with others of a group to monitor the Helsinki Final Act Accords. He made his first application to emigrate to Israel in 1973; this, together with his work for refuseniks,

---

[43] Weidenfeld & Nicolson , London 1988, p245. When he finally emigrated to Israel, Sharansky changed his Russian forename 'Anatoly' to the Hebrew 'Natan'.

led to his arrest, and in July 1973 he was sentenced to thirteen years imprisonment on charges of espionage and treason.

Launched by the Canadian 35s, a tremendous Sharansky campaign took off in this country following a visit to Canada by founder member Rochelle Duke in 1976. She returned home to England inspired by the Canadian "Broken Heart" campaign which featured a huge red heart, split down the middle, a poignant reminder of the heartbreak of Avital's and Anatoly's one-day marriage. In typical 35s fashion, Canadians Elaine Dubow, Wendy Eisen and Barbara Stern had promised Avital Sharansky, who they met in Israel in 1975, that: "Your problem is our problem". This pledge was reinforced by Rochelle Duke who, on her return demanded of Doreen Gainsford, with that oft-repeated phrase, "we must do something!" That "something" developed into a nine-year campaign unsurpassed in the history of the 35s. The European 35s were enlisted, and American Soviet Jewry groups were contacted and briefed. Daily the campaign gained momentum. FREE SHARANSKY went countrywide and worldwide.

One of the first tasks was to solicit the help of politicians and as a result one hundred and forty-three Members of Parliament, of all parties, signed the following letter to *The Times* of 7 May 1977:

> We, the undersigned, call upon the United Nations to note the arrest of Anatoly Sharansky, a leader of Soviet Jews who, since 1973, has been denied the right guaranteed to him by the United Nations Declaration on Human Rights, to leave the USSR and join his wife. We appeal to the General Assembly of the United Nations to take every possible action to ensure that the Soviet Union frees Anatoly Sharansky and ceases its anti-Semitic policies.

Rochelle Duke: "The campaign became Doreen's *cause célèbre*. She lived Sharansky day and night; it played a major part in her life during that period".

Such was the seriousness of Sharansky's pre-trial situation that in July 1977 the 35s contacted twelve thousand eminent people for their consent to the inclusion of their names in a full page advertisement to be placed in *The Times*, to coincide with the Helsinki Review Meeting on Human Rights in Belgrade. By August, fifteen hundred affirmative replies had been received and a daily notification of these signatures was made to the Soviet Embassy. Alongside this appeal was one for £6,000 to pay for the advertisement. Urgent letters were sent to Jewish philanthropists and charitable trusts, and their generous response resulted in the publication, in October 1977, of an advertisement bearing the signatures of nearly two thousand "prominent citizens". Members of the 35s recall working all hours to organise this.

Joanna Aron[44] recalls:

> it was all Doreen's doing. She was a slave-driver. The whole of the office staff and Doreen dedicated themselves to the two appeals. We worked non-stop. But at the same time it was exciting that we ordinary Jewish housewives could be involved in these demonstrations and do so much for the campaign.

Between July 1977 and January 1980 alone, the Sharansky files contain over ninety public handouts and press releases publicising demonstrations to mark his birthday, the anniversary of his arrest, public postcard signings, etc. In this way the gravity of his situation was brought to the attention of thousands of men and women in the street. Figure 1 illustrates a mischievous example of a leaflet handed out to passers-by outside the Aeroflot Office[45] in Piccadilly.

In his book *Fear No Evil*, Sharansky writes that he learnt that tens of thousands of people had written to him during his imprisonment, but the only letters he had received were from his family. Nor was he informed about their existence. Nevertheless he maintained that:

> it was extremely important that these letters were sent. To the regime they served as a constant reminder that

---

[44] At the time Doreen Gainsford's secretary, then Rita Eker's secretary and still a committed 35er.
[45] The official Soviet airline.

TASS (Travel Across Siberia Service)

invites you to a

"BREZHNEV PEACE MEDAL SPECIAL"

at: Aeroflot, 69 Piccadilly, W.1

TODAY : 19th September 1977

to commemorate the presentation

to LEONID BREZHNEV

of the UNITED NATIONS PEACE MEDAL

These tours are across Siberia for those who are looking for an adventurous endurance course. Also recommended for the conscientious weight watcher. You are guaranteed to lose from four to six stone during the time of your stay.

Below freezing temperatures ensure invigorating conditions. Although Yoga is not a feature of the course, it is accepted that those in charge will put themselves out to influence your mental approach on every-day issues.

Although these holidays are voluntary for the general public, they are compulsory for many Soviet Jews.

Ask inside for details about trips to
LEFORTOVO (Moscow)
where Anatoly Sharansky has been held since May 1977
or apply to: T.A.S.S c/o The 35's tel: 01·458 7147

see overleaf for further details/

TASS leaflet produced on occasion of Brezhnev being awarded a Peace Medal. These were handed out to passers-by outside the Aeroflot Office, Piccadilly, London.

people all over the world knew about me and cared about my fate... so the many letters which themselves did not survive, nonetheless helped to save my life.

The files contain copies of heart-rending pleas from Sharansky's mother, Ida Milgrom, to prominent mathematicians in the West, to the Chairman of the Praesidium of the USSR, N. Podgorny, to the editorial board of the *Literaturnaya Gazeta* and to the Procurator General, R. Rudenko. These, together with copies of lengthy reports on the proceedings of each day of the trial sent by Anatoly's brother Leonid, demonstrate the countless hours devoted by Michael Sherbourne to the translation of these documents. Sherbourne recalled that "I would come home from school and then start translating, often through the night to get these transcripts out ready for distribution next day". During the whole of the campaign there is scarcely a newsletter which did not carry Sharansky's name. With a circulation of approximately 1,500, this fortnightly publication enabled the readers to be kept informed of the state of his health, where and in what conditions he was being held, and of what actions were being taken or were planned by the 35s. Many prominent people were enrolled to give endorsement to the campaign and were exploited in a variety of ingenious ways. "Showbiz personalities" were always a draw and valuable publicity was afforded by names such as Peggy Ashcroft, Nigel Davenport, Edward Fox, Doris Hare, and Yvonne Mitchell. Janet Suzman and Henry Cooper were the guests of honour at a 'prisoners' luncheon' at the House of Commons, and Ken Dodd visited the blood donor session organised by the Liverpool 35s.

Amongst the host of photographs printed in all sections of the press throughout the campaign, there is a series featuring the Sharansky shop. This was opened in November 1982 in the Bayswater Road, opposite the Soviet Consulate, and displayed a large neon sign SAVE OUR SHARANSKY, which was switched on by actress Pamela Stevenson in a blaze of publicity. It served to keep the plight of Sharansky, and refuseniks in general, in the public eye. "We were a thorn in the flesh of the Russians. Every time they looked out of the Consulate window they saw our Save Our Sharansky shop," recalled Margaret Rigal.

There were the few lighter moments in the campaign. Seeing the police and the media in attendance, one raincoat-clad gentleman crept into the SOS shop and asked if they had any interesting videos for sale. His disappointment was obvious when he learnt that it was not a Soho-style video shop.

In his book *Fear No Evil*, Sharansky wrote of a visit paid to him in Vladimir Prison by his mother and his brother, Leonid: "As the meeting was drawing to a close, Leonid stood up and said 'Tolya, your name is written on your outfit, right? Look, I also have something written on mine'. Pulling open his shirt he revealed a T-shirt with his brother's face and name, with the words written in English – FREE ANATOLY SHARANSKY." Anatoly recalls that he laughed in delight (p.242).

The T-shirts were another of the 35s inspired creations, which had reached across the thousands of miles from London to Vladimir.

On file there is a report of a meeting held in December 1977 at the Foreign Office with the Foreign Secretary, Dr David Owen. Sir David Renton, the Rt Hon. Jeremy Thorpe and John Gorst were present together with Doreen Gainsford and Margaret Rigal. The Foreign Secretary admitted that concern over the Sharansky arrest had cast a shadow over the Belgrade Helsinki Accord meeting and that he would find it difficult to sign any document in connection with this if his arrest continued.

A moving inclusion in the file is a specially composed prayer for Sharansky and other prisoners which was read in churches throughout Great Britain on Mothering Sunday, 20 March 1977, less than a week after his arrest.

There are reports of meetings of the International Committee for the Release of Anatoly Sharansky, whose joint chairmen were MPs John Gorst (Conservative), Helene Hayman (Labour) and Russell Johnstone (Liberal). They were supported by a group of about fifty other MPs; Doreen Gainsford was the secretary. They organised a 'Mock Enquiry' on behalf of Sharansky at the time of his trial. Amongst the participants were The Rt Hon. Sir David Renton, Jeffrey Thomas, The Rt Hon. Jeremy Thorpe, Lord Foot, Donald Farquarson, David Freeman, and Judge Anthony Tibber. Members of this committee wrote letters to *The Times* to support Sharansky's case. Bernard Levin's article in *The Times* of 5 April 1978 summed up the dangers of his situation at that period. Levin's support for a widespread campaign of public protest added to the growing current of concern in the days leading up to the trial.

There was much correspondence during March and April 1977 regarding the contentious issue of the direction of the campaign. The files contain a telegram purporting to have been sent by Avital Sharansky from Israel to Shmuel Hatzor at the Israeli Embassy in London, protesting that non-Jewish Russian Human Rights activists should not be involved in the campaign. Michael Sherbourne states that when he questioned Avital about this, she denied having sent the telegram. Sharansky had worked with non-Jewish Human Rights groups and was one of the founder members of a Helsinki Watchdog monitoring group. Many of its members had been imprisoned or exiled. Sharansky had therefore become particularly vulnerable as he was both a Jewish Refusenik and a Helsinki monitor. Doreen Gainsford explained that because of this the Israeli Government was nervous to be seen to be involved with him. They wanted the Jewish struggle to be totally separate.

The Israeli Government was not alone in failing to support Sharansky. Michael Sherbourne suspected that the Israeli Government had brought pressure to bear on the Anglo-Jewish establishment, as they were opposed to the manner in which the 35s and other activists were conducting the campaign; they were all too active.

The Israeli Government's claim that they were holding 'behind-the-scene' negotiations may or may not have been true, but most of the former dissidents and refuseniks believe that their eventual freedom was due to the open and aggressive campaigns conducted by the activists all over the world, in France and Holland, in Canada and the USA, in Australia and in Switzerland.

Sharansky's mother, Ida Milgrom, told Jane Moonman and Zelda Harris[46], in reply to their question of what would happen to the dissidents if there was no support from abroad: "none of us would be here. After our first move we would be put in prison".

She expressed her deep gratitude to all the women who had supported her son, and felt sure that their help would result in his freedom in the end.

Whilst in prison, with another seven years to serve, Sharansky was vainly optimistic about the forthcoming SALT[47] talks. He remarked to a fellow prisoner that he knew that their supporters wouldn't stop

---

[46] *The Jewish Observer and Middle East Review*, June 1977, following a visit to Moscow by Jane Moonman (now Biran) and Zelda Harris.
[47] SALT – Strategic Arms Limitation Talks

their struggle for a moment[48]. And after his release he said "it is an important lesson that no quiet diplomacy, even at the highest level, can help if it isn't accompanied by a strong publicity campaign to convince the Soviet Union to let my people go".[49]

This view would seem to justify the 35s determination to pursue their style of campaigning.

"Avital's spirit is on every page of this book even when her name does not appear. She was like the air I breathed; from the moment we met she was with me always".[50]

Towering above all other Sharansky campaigners was Avital, his wife of one day.[51] Rita Eker recalled:

> Avital is a very special person; in all those long years
> she never lost hope. She's exquisite to look at, gentle
> but tough, with such charisma – well, they both have
> that. And Natan's mother as well; another remarkable
> human being; and his brother Leonid; he never missed a
> day in court during the trial and he produced a daily
> report of the proceedings. He could have gone to Israel,
> but he stayed for his brother.

In an interview in *The Daily Mail* (24 April 1981), Avital said that when she heard of the charges against her husband, "I screamed; I knew what was about to happen. I knew I would have to go on screaming if his life was to be saved".

She screamed to Presidents and Prime Ministers, to the media and to the public. She demonstrated, she went on hunger strikes. Throughout the 1970s and 1980s she paid repeated visits to England to participate in a campaign orchestrated by the 35s, travelling countrywide from Newcastle in the north to Bournemouth in the south. Under the wing of Lord Bethell, she had meetings with prominent people and met Margaret Thatcher on two occasions.

In her tours of this country and throughout Europe and the USA she was supported by Cyril Stein, who once again furthered the cause

---

[48] *Fear No Evil*, p.258.
[49] *Jerusalem Post*, August 1986.
[50] *Fear No Evil*, preface p.xviii.
[51] Married 4 July 1974 – separated 5 July 1974.

of Soviet Jewry in his customary practical manner. Wherever there was a summit meeting Avital would be there. The constant travelling, combined with the hunger strikes badly undermined her health and at one period she required hospitalisation. In 1981 she was in Paris and Washington, and in 1982 she was pleading her husband's case at the United Nations. Journeys to Paris, Madrid, London, Rome and New York in 1983 and again to Rome, Paris and Oslo in 1984 represented just a fraction of her exhausting itinerary.

The 35s devoted themselves to organising her travels during those enervating years, years when she dedicated her life totally towards Anatoly's release. Rita Eker recalled:

> I went to Israel to see Natan arrive. You just cannot put into words the emotions at Ben Gurion airport, but even more emotional was walking into a room and seeing Avital and Natan together – what we had worked for all those years.

"FROM RUSSIA WITH LOVE"
(Daily Express front page banner headline)

Exhausted as they were by this protracted and often disheartening campaign, it was with renewed energy that, eight months after his release, the 35s organised a triumphant "Anglo Jewry Welcomes Sharansky" rally. Pulling out all the stops, they booked the Albert Hall, hired audio-visual equipment, liaised with the police on security, had tickets, posters, handouts and leaflets printed, booked hotel accommodation, organised a press conference, and issued invitations to VIPs representing the clergy, the arts and sciences and the entertainment world (and remembered to write thank-you letters afterwards). With characteristic 35s thoroughness they used the occasion to pursue their ongoing campaigns by placing a leaflet on every seat, urging the recipient to adopt another refusenik, and they produced a video recording of the proceedings. Rochelle Duke remembers:

> When we were organising the rally, I remember standing on the stage of the Albert Hall with Rita (Eker) and Cyril Stein (who financed the rally), and gazing out at that vast auditorium. It was the most daunting

prospect I've ever experienced. Cyril said we've got to put bottoms on seats; we filled that place, we could have sold the seats four times over.

Rita Eker reflects:

The planning was incredible, we all worked so hard. Joyce (Simson) did the press side of it. She really excelled herself; she was brilliant. Cyril was wonderful. He said no one should make a penny piece out of it. We could have made thousands of pounds and sold those seats over and over again, but Cyril said that this was for 'the little people', the housewives, the students, all the unknowns who had worked for Natan. When Natan walked on the stage I think it was the most emotional experience of my life. He received such a standing ovation. It went on and on. In the end we had to ask everyone to sit down.

"It was so moving," Joanna Aron. "All those years of work and there was our reward – on the stage."

Following the rally, the Chief Rabbi, Sir Immanuel Jakobovits wrote to Rita Eker and Margaret Rigal on 8 October 1986:

"...the community will owe you an enduring debt for your initiative and enterprise which will long be hailed as a unique experience"

And author and columnist, Chaim Bermant, known to be sparing with praise, paid tribute to the organisers of the event who all rose to the occasion. Nonetheless they could not rest on their laurels. Marian Bernshtein, Dmitri Shteinberg, Yakov Grinberg, Ida Nudel, Anna Ostroverkh, Arkady Abramson, Irena Kaploon, Alexander Fridson, Boris Lobobikov, Galya Gennis, Natasha Magazinik, Vladimir Zukerman and many, many others still needed their support. Their task was not yet over.

SOME MEMORABLE DEMONSTRATIONS

A number of early 35ers were asked to name their most memorable demonstration. Of the hundreds which had been organised the following examples were mentioned time and time again.

Manchester, May 1973

When the Mayor of Leningrad paid a civic visit to Manchester, about fifty London members travelled north to support their provincial colleagues. In their sombre black outfits they were the cynosure of all eyes as they filed into a motorway café at five a.m.

"Going to a funeral, love?" asked a sympathetic lorry driver. This was a common reaction to their mournful attire and they generally found it easiest to say 'yes'. Throughout the journey they were busily sewing slogans on to black umbrellas.

On arriving in Manchester they boarded their hired, open-top, double-decker bus, planning to drive around Albert Square, the heart of the city centre and the location of the Town Hall. As if by design the bus broke down and became the focus of a huge traffic jam. The police were furious and the Lord Mayor showed his displeasure; they could not believe that the incident had not been deliberately planned. Much to the delight of the 35s the bus would not start and they took advantage of the hold-up to unfurl their umbrellas and display their slogans: "LET MY PEOPLE GO" and "FREE SHARANSKY NOW".

Art Exhibition, London 1973.

In 1973 there was an exhibition of Russian art at the Cavendish Hotel in Jermyn Street. Rochelle Duke and Rita Eker went along beforehand to 'spy out the land'. They had decided that when the exhibition opened Rita would chain herself to a display stand. "We needed to measure the distance between the stands but I had forgotten to bring my tape measure, so bold as brass I went up to the receptionist and told her that I had just seen a painting that I was thinking of buying and could she please lend me a tape measure. When we returned the following day I padlocked myself to one of the display stands and Rochelle, who had the key, stayed outside. When the receptionist saw me she almost had hysterics and kept repeating 'but she... she... she... borrowed my tape measure yesterday'. The police arrived, armed with the most enormous pair of chain cutters, chopped off the chain and marched us out".

London, May 1974

Many are the tales told about the various (and sometimes controversial) demonstrations connected with the visits of Russian artistes, particularly the ballet companies with their relevance to the situation of the Panovs. Rita Bensusan described the manoeuvres which led to the successful outcome of one such demonstration.

"I am sure you know all about the extended demonstrations which took place nightly at the Coliseum Theatre when the Bolshoi Ballet was performing there. You may not, however, have heard the tale of how it began...

"We knew approximately on which flight they were arriving but the police had strictly forbidden any demonstration at the airport. So my son, Stuart, and his girlfriend went off to the airport to try and let us know when to expect their arrival at their hotel, where a demonstration was to be set up. The girls all sat in cars or waited round the corner from the hotel with their banners well hidden. Stuart had a very loud horn on his car which made a noise like a roaring bull. He waited until the Bolshoi coaches left the airport, drove ahead of them, and as soon as he approached the hotel he sounded his horn. The girls knew that this was the signal to move, so that when the dancers arrived at the hotel they were greeted by the 35s, and many others, carrying huge banners telling them that as long as Jews were persecuted in Russia, they were not welcome in England".

Rita Eker recalls – "We had three minicab drivers who used to take us around on our demonstrations. When the Bolshoi Ballet came and we were demonstrating outside the Coliseum Theatre on behalf of the Panovs, we dressed one of them – John – as a ballerina. He was such a sport. He stood night after night outside the theatre in a tutu and plimsolls (his feet were too large for ballet shoes). These boys were terrific; they helped us with so many things. They even helped us to make that coffin which caused us so much trouble".

The Baby Demonstration, London, October 1974.

This was held in support of Dr Mikhail Shtern who had been charged with poisoning babies. He was being used as a scapegoat to deter others from applying for exit visas. Rita Bensusan remembered the occasion – "the idea was for some of us to be photographed dressed up as babies. I went with my daughter to pick up Margaret Rigal and together we drove to the destination for the demonstration, a side street in Kensington. It was about 8.30 in the morning and when we arrived the street was deserted except for one man, David Fifer, a member of the Brighton and Hove Soviet Jewry Group, who was joining us. Margaret looked out of the window and said 'hello' and he got into the back of the car. He was wearing a bowler hat and a raincoat and carried an umbrella. These he discarded and then proceeded to remove his trousers, under which he wore a pair of tights. With great difficulty Margaret and I then helped to pin a napkin on him and he also put on a baby's bonnet. He, Margaret and my daughter, Tina, then left the car and met up with Valerie Green, Barbara Lyons and Doreen Gainsford, who were also dressed in baby clothes. The photographs were taken and the demonstration ended.

"They got back into the car and the man removed his nappy, put on his trousers, his raincoat and his hat, got out of the car, hung his umbrella over his arm, raised his hat, said 'good morning' and went on his way. From that day to this we never met again".

Portsmouth, May 1976

Rita Eker remembers that when the Russian destroyer *Obraztsovy* came into port to receive the Freedom of the City, it was decided that the 35s would also give them a very warm welcome. An advance party went down to Portsmouth and paced out the cliff tops so that they knew the length of banners that would be needed. They then went into some public houses and chatted to people to get as much information as possible about the visit, following which they had a mysterious phone call offering them the complete itinerary of the Russians in exchange for £25, so they got to know the entire route they would be taking. They recruited their husbands and the husbands of friends and anyone who had a little boat.

Everything was in their favour on the big day. Firstly, the Russians had forgotten to change their clocks to British Summer Time, with the result that they missed the tide. This enabled the 35s to sail round and round the destroyer in their own flotilla of little ships. The Russian crew was lined up on the deck, standing to attention; none of them gave the slightest hint of noticing them or their placards which were written in both English and Russian. This went on for nearly an hour.

A bus had been hired to follow the Russian contingent and, to crown it all, the bus became stuck under an arch in the city centre so once again their banners were displayed to a captive audience. The Russians were convinced that the police had planned it deliberately. (After all, that's the way things are done in Russia). When they came out of the Guildhall they found the 35s waiting for them again. Some of them were dressed as prisoners, each with the name of a Soviet prisoner on her chest, and some of them were lined up on each side of the Guildhall during the reception by the Lord Mayor.

Chess – Game and Match, London 1982

Effective publicity which was launched during the international chess finals at County Hall, London, engendered much press coverage. The deadly rival of Karpov, the Russian star player, was Igor Korchnoi (whose father, a Grandmaster, had defected to the West). Igor was refused permission to leave Russia so the 35s brought his father over from America and booked him into the same hotel as the Russian team. Outside the County Hall a daily demonstration was mounted, with banners proclaiming "KGB PLEASE FREE MY SON".

Joyce Simson: "We were with Korchnoi in the foyer of the hotel one day when he came face to face with Karpov. They eyed each other and immediately faced up like a pair of fighting cocks. Rita and I had to hold Korchnoi back whilst his KGB minders did the same for Karpov. I felt that this really symbolised the conflict between the East and the West – Rita and I on one side and the KGB on the other.

"When the musical *Chess* was playing, we managed to get five chess Grandmasters to demonstrate outside the theatre with us. We were campaigning on behalf of another Grandmaster, Boris Gulko and his wife, who had been refused permission to play abroad".

Fishy Business, London 1984.

During Gorbachev's first trip to London in 1984, Joyce Simson recalls how they demonstrated outside the Café Royal where he was lunching and then followed him to the Ministry of Agriculture and Fisheries where he was making an official visit.

"The previous day I had gone to Stollers, the fishmonger in Finchley Road and bought half a stone of fish heads. The trouble was that they were too fresh for our purpose so Margaret put them in her boiler room overnight. It was literally a stinking journey as we made our way as near to Whitehall as possible. We then set out the fishheads on paper plates on the pavement and displayed our banners inscribed "ALL JEWISH PRISONERS GET TO EAT IN THE GULAG IS STINKING FISH". (We reckoned that the Whitehall cats had a real feast that night).

"We had another stinking car load on the occasion of a visit by the Mayor of Moscow at the invitation of the Greater London Council. We found out that he was going to inspect the Beckton Sewerage Works on the Isle of Dogs. It was very difficult to find the entrance there, and by the time that we eventually arrived we were becoming overwhelmed by the stench from the load of horse manure which we had picked up from a riding school. When we found the entrance gates we deposited the manure outside them and unfurled our banner which read 'HUMAN RIGHTS IN THE SOVIET UNION IS A LOAD OF HORSE SHIT'.

"The aide of Ken Livingstone (one time leader of the former Greater London Council) called us Nazi thugs because of this demonstration, but the remark was withdrawn when we protested.

"Mysteriously, the visiting mayor had to curtail his tour and return to Moscow. A little while later we learnt that he was sent to Siberia on corruption charges".

The visit of a Soviet statesman was seen as the opportunity for innovative exploits. During the visit of Gorbachev, when he was Minister of Agriculture, the 35s mounted a four-day vigil. From the moment that he arrived in England until the day of his departure he was constantly confronted by the 35s and their banners. When he visited the British Museum in order to see a letter written by Lenin, they stood on the entrance steps holding a banner which stretched the whole width of the steps, bearing the slogan in Russian, "LET SOVIET JEWS GO FROM THE COMMUNIST PARADISE TO THE CAPITALIST HELL". Joyce Simson remembers that it took her eleven days to make that banner.

The 35s went to Highgate Cemetery where Gorbachev was to have made a pilgrimage to the tomb of Karl Marx. On this occasion, however, they were thwarted as he had been warned in advance and had cancelled the visit.

Joyce Simson: "It was a pity as we had a large urn with 'ASHES OF HELSINKI' written on it. But still we got the publicity because when I turned the radio on in the car on my way home, I heard an item about it on LBC. When he visited the Ministry of Agriculture in Whitehall, we stood on an island in Parliament Square with a loud-hailer and put it to good use until the police confiscated it. When the Gorbachev entourage passed by we saw them taking photographs of us".

Talk of the Town, London.

Simone Goldfarb: "We heard that a party of Russian generals were to be entertained by their British counterparts at 'The Talk of the Town' (a well-known London nightclub). Rochelle Duke, Leila Cumber and I reserved a table there and went in with our banners, but when we tried to unfurl them we were asked to leave. We went out on to the pavement and unfurled them there and confronted the generals as they came out. The British generals were convulsed with laughter as, in the confusion, we were displaying the banners upside down. After the Russians had been put in a taxi, rather the worse for wear, the officers asked us about our demonstration and we all ended up in a nearby pub for the rest of the evening. They were utterly charming and we had a marvellous time".

A Spirited Demonstration.

Highgate Cemetery was also the venue for another demonstration, which was rather more successful than the previous one there. On learning that a party of Russian historians was visiting this country, the 35s phoned the curator of the cemetery with the suggestion that they (the Russians) should be invited to visit the tomb of Karl Marx. It worked. On the day of the visit they made sure that the press was there. They had draped themselves in white sheets, with just their eyes showing and at the right moment, they "floated out" from behind the tombstones with placards which read "WHERE IS THE SPIRIT OF HELSINKI?"

Coats for Goats, Geneva 1985

On the occasion of the meeting between Reagan and Gorbachev in Geneva, hundreds of Jewish students from all over Europe, including a strong contingent from England, held a magnificent demonstration in the Place Neuve, in front of the Grand Theatre where the conference was being held. Goats were released in the city wearing specially made coats bearing the slogan "MR. GORBACHEV, FREE JEWISH SCAPE GOATS!"

Who but the 35s would have known where to hire a herd of goats? It so happened that a member of the office staff, Jacob Gabay, had a friend who knew a Swiss goat farmer. Who but the 35s would have sat up night after night sewing goats' coats from the cloth which they used for their demonstration banners (complete with laces for fastening under the goats' bellies)? The animals were herded to the Conference Centre where, with untypical Swiss regard for their surroundings, they deposited their dung in front of the buildings. But with typical Swiss efficiency, a policeman, armed with brush and shovel, soon restored the square to its former pristine condition. All traces of the goats' presence soon disappeared but recollections of the episode still remain.

The Demonstration within a Demonstration

Rachele Kalman remembers "we were on our way to a demonstration – a 'prisoner meal' in Westminster, on behalf of Vladimir Bukowsky, when we heard on the car radio that the French Government had just released an Arab terrorist. We were all absolutely furious to think that this vicious man was being set free, and quite spontaneously we decided to go to the French Embassy. There were six of us and we stood in the freezing cold, in the snow, eyeball to eyeball with the police. We made our protest and then continued on to Westminster".

A Lullaby of our times

Go to sleep, my baby, close your pretty eyes
Your Mummy's demonstrating, she's joined the 35s
The night is cold and wintry, but Mummy had to go,
So snuggle up, my little one, deep sleep will help you grow.

Daddy came home early to see you off to bed,
You've had your bath, and nappy changed and also you've been fed.
Grandma's downstairs knitting, the cat's sitting on her lap
She's looking at the telly whilst pussy has a nap.
But Mummy's demonstrating, it's the first time that she's been
Outside the Soviet Embassy, Kensington Palace Green.

The women's group assembled there are known as 35s
With banners held they do their stint 'til other girls arrive.
Moses said, in days of old, "Let My People Go",
The same words are repeated still, by persons high and low.
So, Mummy's demonstrating as all who care can see
For our people far away to be as we are – free.

So hush-a-bye, my darling, be happy every day,
You learn so much, so swiftly, it's a joy to watch you play.
Babies grow up quickly, dear, and soon you'll be a man,
What is no concern of yours just yet, one day the flames could fan
For Prisoners of Conscience that Human Rights sustain
So freedom and justice might evermore remain.
Now go to sleep, my baby, it's good to know you thrive
Whilst Mummy's demonstrating with the other 35s.

(Written by Lena Alford, mother of 35er Helen Boyan)

Chapter Seven
Internal Development

During the growth years the image of the Women's Campaign for Soviet Jewry was seen as helping refuseniks and prisoners in the USSR primarily by holding demonstrations, but not many people were aware of the multitude of tasks which the group undertook in order to achieve the professionalism for which they became renowned. During the 1970s the office staff grew until there were about seven part-time workers as well as dozens of regular volunteers. Together they ran the following sections:

- Telephoning
- Letter writing
- Travellers and trips
- Adoptions and twinnings
- Youth and education
- Fund-raising
- Anti-Semitism Watch
- The newsletter

A most important element of the early days of the 35s was the telephone chain, a resourceful method of circulating the latest news of the refuseniks throughout the British Isles and the United States of America. The strongest link in this chain was Michael Sherbourne. Sylvia Becker explained that when Sherbourne received messages from the USSR he would translate them and pass the transcripts to her and she would telephone them through to Enid and Stuart Wurtman in Philadelphia. If they were not available she would call Rae Sharfman in Michigan and Glenn Richter in New York. Within twenty-four hours this information would be published nation-wide through the vigilance of these members of the Union of Councils for Soviet Jewry. This American umbrella organisation developed excellent relations with Capitol Hill and the information was passed very quickly to the State Department. Enid Wurtman recalls:

> I warmly remember Michael's calls with urgent news to be disseminated through the Union of Councils and Student Struggle and locally in Philadelphia so that we could be responsive quickly to the fate of the refuseniks and the prisoners – to whom Michael was a remarkable lifeline and link. Michael was the clarion caller from London with news about Soviet Jewry. His crisp, vivid and lucid translations of appeals, news, missives, reports from the refuseniks and prisoners, etc. were outstanding. Michael has a remarkable memory, he is a cherished friend.[52]

In London the transcripts were forwarded to the Israeli Embassy, to Colin Shindler, editor of *Jews in the USSR*, and later to Nan Griefer who succeeded him and who also regularly telephoned reports from Russia.

Michael Sherbourne maintains that the Israeli Government tried to impede the work of the activists. He remembers an occasion when Vladimir Slepak tried to telephone him to give him some important information, but being unable to contact him, he passed the information directly to Nehemiah Levanon's office in the Israeli Soviet Jewish Department, with the request that it should be passed on to Sherbourne. This was not done and Sherbourne cites this as one of a number of similar incidents.

The telephone conversations between the 35ers from all over the British Isles and the refuseniks in the USSR were a lifeline, sustaining hope in the darkest days. The Soviet authorities recognised this and clamped down on these contacts. Michael Sherbourne remembers speaking to a Moscow refusenik who interrupted the conversation, saying "I have to go now, the KGB are coming up the stairs". Lines were 'bugged' and connections were obstructed. The author recalls attempting to speak to Fanya Roisman of Mogilev Podolsk, in the Ukraine. She heard the Russian operator tell the intermediary Paris operator that there was no such place as Mogilev Podolsk! On trying

---

[52] The Americans named in the telephone chain were committed workers in the American Soviet Jewry movement. Enid Wurtman's recollection was sent to the author via Martin Gilbert.

again the following evening she heard the Russian operator say that there was no such number in Mogilev Podolsk. On the third attempt she was told that there was no reply from that number. The fourth attempt was successful.

When Margaret and George Rigal were in Moscow in 1978 visiting Viktor Yelistratov, a very active refusenik, he told them that it had been many months since he was able to speak to Michael Sherbourne. They took the risk of taking him back to their hotel and he spoke to Michael for over an hour on their bedroom telephone. Although the rooms were undoubtedly 'bugged' it was well past midnight and they took a chance that no one was listening in at that late hour. But when the Rigals left Moscow the next day it became obvious that someone had listened to a tape recording in the meantime because, as Margaret put it "they isolated us; they put barriers around us – they took us apart".

Despite the difficulties and frustrations the 35ers persisted and many thousands of telephone calls have been made over the years.

From its inception the 35s have conducted a letter-writing campaign of unparalleled and unremitting intensity. They initiated letter and postcard campaigns in Jewish and non-Jewish schools, churches, synagogues, youth groups, etc.; letters to prisoners and refuseniks, letters to Soviet officials and letters to British and American politicians. They have written birthday cards, anniversary of arrest, trial and imprisonment cards, New Year and Chanukah cards[53], as both individual and co-operative efforts.

In one five week period during 1980 the newsletter printed exhortations to write to the following people:

- A list of ten birthdays to addresses in Russia, Latvia and Byelorussia, for August.
- A list of seven birthdays in Moscow, the Ukraine and Leningrad, for September.
- A list of ten birthdays in Moscow, Leningrad, Kiev and Kharkov, for October.
- Dr Arkady Dumanis – sentenced to two and a half years in a labour camp on a charge of giving a ten rouble bribe. Please write to him assuring him of your support. We are looking for adopters who will write to him on a regular basis.

---

[53] The New Year and Chanukah are Jewish religious festivals.

- Semyon Gluzman, and send him birthday cards for September.
- Lev Roitburd whose situation in Odessa is deteriorating. He is having to work double shifts to support his family. He is being watched and followed by the KGB. Please write also to Senator Kennedy as Lev's name is on his list.
- The Dolganov family in Leningrad. They are separated from their family and have written a tragic letter to their adopter, who is hoping to involve his local MP, Sir Keith Joseph, in the case.
- Victor and Irina Brailovsky, long term, very courageous refuseniks.
- Elena Vinkovetsky, who has recently had a stillborn baby and suffers from a heart condition. She has been refused permission to emigrate to Israel with her husband because her parents, who have had no contact with her for five years, refuse to give her permission to leave.
- Vladimir Kislik, who has been charged with "hooliganism". (This is to keep him from meeting foreigners during the Moscow Olympic Games). He was being held in a police cell and complained of severe chest pains (he has a heart condition), and has been sent to the psychiatric ward of the hospital.
- Alexander Magidovich is charged with "anti-Soviet agitation". He has been transferred to the notorious Serbskiy mental hospital. We are very worried about the situation.
- Igor Guberman on the first anniversary of his arrest (five years in a strict labour camp). Please write letters of support to his wife and children.
- Grigory Geishis, he is due to be tried. Any Russian speaker please phone his father; also write.

This is a tiny sample of the tens of thousands of communications sent to the USSR in the course of the campaign. Most of these were never received by those for whom they were intended. But they were seen by the KGB and other officials there, serving to remind them of the West's unflagging support of the refuseniks.

A constant theme running through the 25-year campaign is the testimony of the refuseniks referring to the succour afforded to them by visits from travellers[54].

Prior briefing was a necessity, initially undertaken by Rita Eker and for the last sixteen years by Evelyn Nohr. In the grim dark days, people placed themselves at considerable risk in visiting refuseniks and taking them goods. Many were followed and some were arrested by the KGB and their hotel telephones (as well as those of the refuseniks) were "bugged". The author remembers visiting refuseniks in a Moscow apartment and watching with amazement as they placed cushions over the telephone – to her it was bizarre, to them it was a matter of course.

Travellers were eager to visit the well-known refuseniks, but in order to prevent "A" receiving fifty visitors and "B" none, the 35s preferred that all UK travellers, whatever their affiliation, were briefed by them. Travellers had to be told, in very clear terms, how to avoid getting into trouble in the USSR. They were given detailed information and advice on any known eventualities which might arise. Maps and details of transport services, a guide to the Cyrillic alphabet and suggestions as to which gifts were most acceptable were also supplied.

Evelyn Nohr keeps detailed lists of all known Jewish communities in the Former Soviet Union, stretching from Kaliningrad, an isolated community of about two hundred Jews near the border with Poland, to Petropavlovsk, Kamchatskiy, on a far-off Siberian peninsula jutting into the Pacific ocean, with a population of one thousand to two thousand Jews. As new information filters through, her list is regularly revised. A traveller who wishes to visit Kaunus, in Lithuania, for example, can learn the approximate size of the community, names, addresses and telephone numbers of any officials and useful contacts, the address of the synagogue, details of Hebrew education, communal organisations, etc. Gradually, a very substantial travellers' dossier has been built up. Evelyn has learnt to speak and read Russian, enabling her to translate map instructions and, certainly on paper, knows her way around the centres of the major Russian cities. She has been a Human Rights activist for most of her adult life. Before joining the 35s in 1979 she was a member of Amnesty

---

[54] Travellers – the term used by the 35s for those who visited the USSR in order to visit refuseniks.

International and worked with anti-apartheid groups when she lived in South Africa. Seeing the segregation of the black people there reminded her all too vividly of her girlhood in France during World War 2 and witnessing the segregation of Jews prior to deportation. She cites Human Rights as her main motive in working with the 35s.

The travellers are also requested to send a report to her on their return, as it is vital that her information is kept up-to-date. Does "C" still need medication? Why can't we get through to "D" on the telephone anymore? Do they still need Hebrew language books in "E"? What is the address of the synagogue in "F"?

One such report by Carole Spiers[55] after her 1979 trip included the following details: she visited nine families in Leningrad and twelve families in Moscow. She gave a concise but detailed survey of each of the refuseniks including their financial, health and emotional conditions. She gave a list of things taken in and a list of their requests, e.g. cassette recorders, radios, art books, calculators, cameras and films, clothes and food. She described in detail her experience of going through the Soviet customs and of being followed, etc. She reported that she took a minimum of her own clothes as all spare case-room was for goods for the refuseniks. On her return from her 1984 visit she sent a detailed report to Malcolm Rifkind, Minister of State at the Foreign Office and to Rhodes Boyson, Member of Parliament for Brent, on the situation of Soviet Jewry. She also compiled the following checklist of dos and don'ts for travellers:

1. Make sure that your baggage is not overweight.
2. Make sure that the (gift) garments that you take are of your own size.
3. Book yourself on at least two tours.
4. Join in the tour activities as much as possible.
5. If questioned by the KGB admit only to being a tourist; if they are persistent insist on seeing the British or US Consul.
6. Regard yourself as a tourist first, traveller second, even at the expense of seeing fewer people.
7. Expect to be searched going in and going out.

---

[55] Chairperson of the Brent group since the mid 1970s.

The Adoption and Twinning programmes which developed out of the Board of Deputies "link-up" scheme have proved to be popular in their combination of a strong emotional relationship with a practical application, such as the sharing of a Bar-Mitzvah or Bat Chayil, and the sending of material help. Sue Usiskin, who became the scheme's organiser explained:

> The scheme encouraged more people to become involved in the campaign. We sent lists of names to all the groups and they in turn asked each of their members to write to a family. It was channelled through the office as we didn't want too many people writing to the same ('well-known') family. The names of the adopters would be entered into the refuseniks' biographies and we asked the adopters to send us copies of any letters they might receive in return so that we could keep our information up-to-date. We didn't ask them to do any more than to write and help to give the family moral support, but if they wished to do more and send them material goods or to involve their Member of Parliament, then that was all to the good. From this we developed the Bar-Mitzvah and Bat Chayil schemes in which the ceremony and celebration of the reaching of religious majority of a British child would be linked by proxy with a Jewish child of the same age in the USSR, who was unable personally to enjoy religious freedom. These were immensely popular and worked very well, and, of course, we were involving children, both here and in the USSR, which was a good thing. The youngsters were thrilled to feel that they were sharing their special day with a Russian youngster who had been so completely cut off from his or her Jewish roots. We organised individual ceremonies and group ceremonies through the Jewish schools.

One such proxy Bar-Mitzvah was a symbolic ceremony outside the Soviet Embassy in London in March 1976, for Sasha Roitburd the son of Lev Roitburd, a Prisoner of Conscience. The ceremony involved twenty boys and was conducted by Rabbi Unterman. Similar ceremonies for Sasha were held by 35s groups in other parts of Britain and Ireland.

Many paired families became warm friends and have continued their friendship to the present day, visiting each other here and in Israel.

Sylvia Wallis, a founder member, who campaigned for Sylva Zalmanson, explained her involvement with Sylva and the 35s by contrasting their lives. They shared a similar Russian-Jewish background. Sylva Zalmanson's grandfather was relatively wealthy and stayed on in Russia; Sylvia Wallis's grandfather was poor and left Russia in the hope of finding a better life for his family. When Sylvia Wallis wanted to emigrate to Israel there were no problems whereas, for Sylva, there were nothing but problems. Yet again the phrase "There, but for the grace of God, go I", was quoted to explain Sylvia's motivation.

A time consuming but necessary activity was that of giving talks on the work of the 35s and of the prevailing Soviet Jewish situation. In locations ranging from Synagogues and Churches to youth groups and schools, both Jewish and non-Jewish, to radio and television, 35ers from every group gave up even more of their free time to spread the message. Talks are still being given albeit that the emphasis has changed somewhat.

In the 1970s, Rachele Kalman, an early 35er, was responsible for the liaison between the 35s and the students and young people. In 1979 she was asked by Zelda Harris, an early 35er, to help in a National Council for Soviet Jewry scheme to educate Soviet Jews about Judaism, a subject about which most of them were sadly ignorant. She spent one day a week at the Council's office helping to sort out the many hundreds of books on Jewish topics, which were then sent to the USSR. She recollects speaking at a meeting of Amnesty International in Conway Hall after they had asked for a representative from the 35s to be present:

> Our discussions were not always sympathetic but at least they learnt of things of which they were not aware. It seemed to me that they had a total blind spot regarding Israel. I saw some vicious anti-Israel leaflets in the lobby which perhaps coloured our discussions.

The newsletters carried regular reports of similar activities in the provinces, for example:

Birmingham 1979 – Talk on "Semyon Gluzman and psychiatric abuse in the USSR".
Newcastle 1979 – Talks to the Round Table and to the Jewish Youth Council.
Glasgow 1985 – Talk on "The plight of Soviet Jewry" on BBC radio.

These are instances of the way in which the message was carried to the public at large.

Single minded as the women would like to be, from time to time their energies have to be diverted to the mundane task of fund-raising. As the nature of the work has changed, money is increasingly needed for providing material help for refuseniks and new immigrants into Israel, through schemes such as One-to-One and Keren Klita. Despite the continuing generosity of many benefactors there is a perennial shortage of cash. To this end fund-raising events are held regularly, often in conjunction with other Jewish charities. This also serves to raise awareness of the campaign.

In addition to major events organised by the office, each group organises its own fund-raising, in order to pay their expenses and also to help support their adoptees. Apart from the run-of-the-mill concerts and film shows, etc. they often devise novel ideas ranging from a sponsored parachute jump by the Brent 35s, to a sponsored London marathon run by Sydney Levine for the Leeds 35s, to "Walking in the footsteps of Moses", a sponsored Israel Trek arranged by the "Head Office" in 1994. They sell pens and badges, Chanukah and New Year cards, and they hold "sponsored silences" and supper quizzes.

A typical newsletter item reading – "Brent 35s are organising a supper quiz. Please come along and support it" is but a bald statement of the work involved which includes:

- The printing of tickets
- The selling of tickets
- Ordering the food
- Organising the sound equipment
- Organising the raffle and the prizes

- Hire of table linen
- Manhandling tables and chairs
- Booking a hall
- Organising "Adopt a Family" leaflets
- Arranging the quiz itself
- Dealing with things that went wrong
- Writing "thank-you" letters

Leeds 35s have produced a calendar annually for many years. Each monthly page is sponsored by local firms or individuals and gives details of a refusenik or a prisoner or carries an apposite quotation. The front page of the 1993 calendar bears the following quotation from Professor Norman Stone, professor of Modern History at Oxford University, writing in *The Sunday Times* on 1 September 1991:

> There were some characters or privately funded institutions who got it right and endured much flak while doing so. Those who campaigned for Soviet Jewry, including their champion, Bernard Levin, never faltered in their uncompromising critique of the Soviet Union.

As well as raising money for their campaign the calendar was an effective way of spreading the message.

In a wan comment beneath the photograph on the cover of their 1983 issue, they report "forty-eight refuseniks were featured in the calendar last year. Guly Yevgeny Barras has been allowed to leave the USSR. His place has been taken by Peter Gennis, aged 15. All the rest are still waiting".

Another activity of the 35s is the monitoring of manifestations of anti-Semitism, not only in the Former Soviet Union but worldwide. A phalanx of files testifies to the prevalence of this age-old evil and the newsletter contains regular reports of its resurgence.

Officially anti-Semitism did not exist in the Soviet Union, but in fact, it was endemic there and remains so. During the Second World War many Ukrainians and Lithuanians were happy to collaborate with the Nazis in their extermination of more than two million Jews[56]. One

---

[56] *The Jews of Russia* by Martin Gilbert, published by the National Council for Soviet Jewry 1976.

of the main reasons, therefore, for the desire of Jews to leave the land of their birth and with which they have strong emotional ties, is the discrimination, oppression and harassment which lurks beneath the surface of their lives. Ironically since "glasnost" and "perestroika", with the subsequent easing of totalitarian rule, anti-Semitism has become more blatant with organisations such as Pamyat openly flourishing[57].

Faina Shemeleve of St Petersburg, wrote to the 35s in June 1992:

> ...all through our lives we have lived in fear of pogroms, we have been humiliated, we have been discriminated against, we have been prevented from getting jobs, we have found it difficult to study, but now things are so bad that we just have no strength. In the centre of the town they gather for "the meeting" and they curse the Jews. They say we are responsible for all the sorrows of the Russian people, that we should be wiped out, thrown out, etc. We live poorly, old people becoming as poor as beggars, poverty stricken. There is nothing to wear and the food situation is bad. We live in hope of better times, but when...? And how are we expected to live now? People are so spiteful...

Despite the easing of restrictions on emigration, Faina chose to stay in St Petersburg. As well as caring for her elderly mother she stays to give assistance to the thousands of elderly, needy Jews there. In August 1991, she wrote to a 35er, "I see it as a mission in life".

In March 1993 two Jews were murdered in Donetsk. In July 1993 the Moscow synagogue was vandalised for the fourth time in a month, and in St Petersburg the Jewish cemetery was desecrated. The scurrilous pamphlet *The Protocols of the Learned Elders of Zion* is once again being printed in Russia.

The years of work demonstrated in the meticulously documented evidence of anti-Semitism contained in these files can hardly be described as a labour of love.

From its earliest years the 35s have produced a newsletter, otherwise known as the circular. At its maximum circulation over one

---

[57] PAMYAT – an ultra xenophobic Russian political party.

thousand one hundred copies of each issue were sent, but financial constraints have reduced this to six hundred. This fortnightly publication, originally edited by Sylvia Becker, and for the last twelve years by Joyce Simson, is despatched not only to 35ers and other Soviet Jewry groups but also to government offices, libraries, the news media, centres of higher education and research departments both at home and abroad. Throughout this book the numerous references to the newsletter show the wide scope of its contents. It is probably the only reliable source of information on the Former Soviet Union and in addition to news concerning Soviet Jewry, its contents now include information regarding the general political, social and economic conditions in that area of Europe.

Chapter Eight
External Development

As the demands and urgency of the campaign became more apparent, the 35s realised that their own resources were not sufficient to enrol the Western world into the dual fight for Soviet Jews and Human Rights. Influential outside help was needed and contacts were made and established with news media, politicians, trade union officials, Church leaders, etc.; disparate bedfellows indeed, but all working for a common cause, albeit sometimes for their own ends.

First rate press, television and radio coverage has been the backbone of the 35s campaign. Journalists from these media, always hungry for unusual stories, found them in the entertaining, novel and (mostly) good humoured demonstrations organised by the Women's Campaign.

News of the women's exploits reached into the furthermost corners of the world, but many of the broadcasts of the BBC's World Service could not be received in the main Russian cities because they were jammed by the Soviet authorities. Joyce Simson recalls that when Vladimir Slepak was in exile, in a far-away Siberian outpost, he was able to listen to an unjammed BBC. He telephoned Moscow to tell them that he had heard about the 35s' demonstration and the Moscow refuseniks telephoned the office in London to thank them for their support.

In her early years as Press Officer, Joyce Simson received valuable help from Kevin Keighley of *The Guardian* foreign desk. "Look," he told her, criticising her 'copy', "let me show you how to write a press release." This basic lesson became the foundation of what many experts in the field agree to be a most effective media campaign.

To this day it is the 35s to whom the press, television and radio refer when they want up-to-date information on the situation of Jews in Russia or in what was the Soviet Union.

Joyce Simson's involvement with the press began when she visited Moscow in 1979. Outside the main synagogue in Arkhipova Street, she met Masha Slepak, whose husband had been exiled to Siberia. In tears, Masha explained that Vladimir was very ill. Joyce promised to pursue her case on her return. Back in London she telephoned John Miller, then Diplomatic Correspondent of *The Daily Telegraph* and told him "this has to go on the front page", and on 9 May 1979 a report in the foreign news section stated that the 35s were attempting to send a doctor to visit Slepak in Siberia. Her initial involvement in the 35s had been due, in part, to the anger she felt at the arrest of Sharansky. But this was as nothing compared with the rage she felt during her second visit to Russia, together with her husband. They were arrested, ostensibly "for selling Western goods" but in reality for meeting activist Elena Oleynik. Elena, who was three months pregnant was also arrested, but whereas the Simsons were released after being harshly interrogated for several hours in a militia post, Elena was imprisoned for fifteen days and suffered a miscarriage, probably as a result of this.

Before the Madrid Conference in 1985[58], Rita Eker and Joyce Simson attended a briefing at the Israeli Foreign Office in Tel Aviv. They were categorically told not to attend the conference. They pointed out that whereas Israel was not a signatory to the Helsinki Agreement, Britain was. It was a very distressing situation but Rita insisted that they intended to go.

Said Joyce:

> one can understand the Israeli stance. At this time they were pursuing the establishment of diplomatic relations with the USSR. This was a well known fact; the Israelis and the Russians were often seen together in the coffee shops of Vienna. The Middle East situation was so precarious; both the Russians and the Americans had invested so much weaponry in that region. The Israelis were very nervous of tipping the balance. Whilst we

---

[58] To review the Helsinki Agreement

understood their motives, we had our own motives, and, of course, we did go.

Madrid was the venue for the 35s press conference that nearly wasn't! After the conference was announced, at which Avital Sharansky was to be the 'star turn', it was surreptitiously cancelled. On their arrival in Madrid, Rita and Joyce noticed that they were being accompanied everywhere by a representative of the Israeli Foreign Office. Word came to them from journalists that it was he who had cancelled their press conference. However, they were able to re-convene it at the 11th hour, and Avital, who had spent the morning at a beauty parlour, took the normally hard-boiled Press Corps by storm with her glamorous image. "She had to be so strong in the face of the Israeli Government opposition, but she was a triumph," Joyce remembered.

The 1986 Reagan/Gorbachev summit meeting in Iceland presented many difficulties for the press. The two Heads of State were deliberating, holed up in an isolated house, and journalists were desperate for stories. Liz Phillips and Joyce Simson, accompanied by former refuseniks Mikhail Sherman and Iosif Mendelevich, found this to be an ideal opportunity to present the tragic case of Sherman, who was dying of leukaemia. His only hope was to receive the compatible bone-marrow transplant from his twin sister who, if she left Moscow, would not be allowed to return home to her family.

Due to a shortage of hotels in Reykjavik, the press contingent was scattered throughout the town. The Russians, very cleverly, had booked the only available hotel for each day's press conferences. Joyce Simson and Liz Phillips (cf. Medical committee) had press passes (from *The Hendon Times*) and sat in the front row next to the BBC correspondent. When called upon for a question, Joyce Simson stood up and, in a loud voice introduced herself as being from "*The Times*" and in a quiet undertone added "of Hendon". She asked: "Now that Sharansky has been released, isn't it time for the Soviet Government to release the four hundred thousand Jews who want to join their families in the West?"

In the ensuing uproar she drove home the point by bringing up the case of Sherman's twin sister[59]. "We made a story with the Human

---

[59] Mikhail's sister was eventually allowed to leave, but the permission came too late; her brother died.

Rights issue. There were so few stories coming out of Reykjavik. We really hit the headlines on BBC Radio, the Canadian Broadcasting System, Agence Presse France, *The Times*, etc."

Soviet Jewry and Human Rights issues were inextricably linked. A double page advertisement appeared in *The Times* in November 1974 in the form of an appeal to the USSR for the release of Soviet Jewish Prisoners of Conscience and bore over three hundred signatures of well-known people. Although published under the auspices of the Board of Deputies, much of the groundwork was done by the 35s, as was also the case with the above mentioned full page advertisement appealing on behalf of Sharansky which was printed in *The Times* (6 October 1977) and signed by nearly two thousand prominent citizens.

Andrew McEwan, the Diplomatic Editor of *The Times*, was very supportive in the fight for George Samoilovich who was seriously ill with lymphoma and unable to receive the appropriate treatment in Russia. He wrote a sympathetic article in *The Daily Telegraph* on 27 January 1989, and on 8 March this newspaper carried a banner headline – "GEORGE SAMOILOVICH – SOVIET VISA BAN ON CANCER VICTIM".

The previous Vienna Agreement had stipulated that if medical treatment could not be forthcoming within six weeks, permission to leave had to be granted to receive treatment in another member country.

George Samoilovich became a diplomatic case and a test of Gorbachev's promises on Human Rights. It took a six-month campaign to procure his release. George still recalls his amazement at receiving a bouquet of flowers from the Foreign Office on his arrival at the Royal Marsden Hospital. He remains ever grateful, not only for the help he received from the 35s but also for the support and encouragement of Margaret Thatcher and Geoffrey Howe.

Perhaps the most rewarding press conference in the history of the 35s was that at the Albert Hall in September 1986 following the great public gathering there on the occasion of Sharansky's visit to London following his release. The world's press was there but the 35s ensured that neither TASS nor Pravda were admitted.

Joyce Simson said:

We were extremely useful to the media during the Sharansky campaign. Whenever Avital came over she made news. After all, it was obvious that the Human Rights issue was one of the three key elements in the whole of East/West relations; the others were economics and defence.

Sharansky also appeared on the *Wogan* and *Frost* television programmes. His schedule was so packed that Simon Jenkins, then a feature writer on *The Times* newspaper, found that the only way he could interview Sharansky was to accompany him in his taxi from venue to venue throughout the day.

The 35s utilised as many media outlets as possible. In centres such as Brighton, Leeds, Liverpool, Manchester, and Newcastle, the women took advantage of their local radio stations to publicise Soviet Jewish issues. In November 1979 Newcastle Radio featured the 35s, detailing the harsh situation of Anatoly Sharansky in Chistopol Prison. In November 1986 the BBC "Today" programme broadcast a taped message from Inna Begun pleading for her husband Iosif, who was incarcerated in the same notorious prison because of his insistence on studying and teaching Hebrew. This message was followed by Joyce Simson enlarging on the Begun case and those of other refuseniks.

Ever hungry for something different, radio stations were happy to seize upon some of the more novel demonstrations. In June 1979, Rita Eker was interviewed both on BBC Radio 4 and on Capital Radio following a traffic stopping motorcade on "Ida Nudel Day" when a fleet of cars, festooned with banners and posters and crammed with 35ers, made its way tortuously from the office at Golders Green to the Soviet Embassy. They were caught up in numerous traffic jams en route, which enabled them to use their loud-hailers to good effect.

Publicity in the news media is by its nature ephemeral, but lasting recognition of a 35s campaign was achieved by an entry in the *Encyclopaedia Britannica* following a demonstration in February 1977.

During International Women's Year, 1975, the signatures of over one hundred thousand British women had been collected, with the intention of presenting a petition, entitled "Haven't all human beings the right to freedom?" to President Brezhnev on behalf, of all persecuted Jewish women in the Soviet Union, during his planned visit to this country. But the visit never materialised, so it was decided to hand over the petition to the Cultural Attaché at the Soviet Embassy.

The petition was loaded into a supermarket trolley, labelled BASKET NO. 3[60] and a delegation of five prominent women: Margaret Drabble, Doris Hare, Helene Hayman, Cleo Laine, and Caroline Rhys-Williams pushed it up the Embassy drive. However, as Mr Parastaev, the Cultural Attaché refused to accept it, remarking that there was no persecution of anyone in Russia, they dumped it on the Embassy steps and rejoined the crowd of over one hundred 35ers and their supporters who had come from different parts of the country.

The demonstration was widely reported in all the media, but a more permanent record appeared in a subsequent edition of the *Encyclopaedia Britannica* in the section devoted to Human Rights. A picture of Doris Hare and Cleo Laine pushing the trolley with 35ers holding their placards in the background is a fitting reminder of their battle for Human Rights.

As well as the national dailies, local London and provincial newspapers also gave the campaigns and demonstrations invaluable coverage. *The Croydon Advertiser*, *The Hendon Times*, *The Ilford Recorder*, *The Enfield Times*, and local papers in all the towns and cities where the 35s were active, were among the publications recording their work. The activities of the group were also noted in newspapers overseas.

Joyce Simson recalls a *New York Herald Tribune* extract taken from a *Washington Post* article which in turn had been taken from a 35s newsletter citing their analysis of East/West relations.

Even in far distant Iceland the 35s were news and were featured on the front pages of the Reykjavik newspapers during the Reagen/Gorbachev summit meeting of 1986.

Joyce Simson:

> We had constant attention from the media when we had our 'Save our Sharansky' shop which was right opposite the Soviet Consulate in Bayswater Road. We were reported by the BBC, The Voice of America, and Radio Free Europe, amongst others. We had a very good relationship with the BBC, particularly with the Russian unit of its World Service. I spoke pretty regularly to

---

[60] Basket No. 3 at the Helsinki Accords Agreement dealt with Human Rights.

Weeping Willow tree planted in Valentine's park by Ilford 35s in 1973 for Sylva Lalmanson.

© *Leon Gabrel 1996.*

Newcastle 35ers demonstrate for Sharansky and Begun during visit of President Jimmy Carter, May 1977.

Against a background of his paintings, ex-refusenik Boris Penson lights the Chanucah candles at a reception given by the Brighton and Hove Soviet Committee, December 1979.

Liverpool 35ers demonstrate for Sharansky at Liverpool Pier Head, 1975.

Birmingham 35ers with Father O'Mahoney and ex-refusenik Boris Levitas campaigning for Alexander Feldman and his daughter Marina. Background from left to right: René Johnson, Ruth Direktor, Lorna Goodkin.

South London 35ers, June Kenton and Barbara Benjamin, dressed as the Wombles of Wimbledon, present petition to Russian tennis star T. I. Kakulia on behalf of imprisoned Soviet Jews, June 1974.

London 35ers outside Soviet Embassy demonstrating for Raiza Palatnik, 1971.

*South London 35ers demonstrating for Smeliansky family over
proposed visit of Shelepin, March 1975.*

London 35ers demonstrating for prisoners.

London 35ers storming the stage at Earls Court during Russian gymnastic display, May 1973.

See Campaigns and Demonstrations appendix, July 1972.

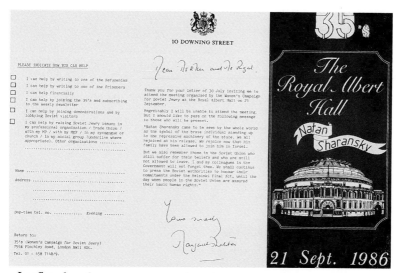

Leaflet placed on every seat at the Albert Hall Rally to welcome Anatoly Sharansky. The reverse side gave details of refuseniks still imprisoned in the USSR, September 1986.

Seven 35ers on hunger strike for seven hours for seven scientist prisoners outside the Soviet Embassy, June 1973.

South London 35er June Kenton slips on the ice at Streatham ice rink in front of Russian skaters as she goes to present them with a Sylva Zalmanson medallion, October 1973.

35ers demonstrate outside London's Royal Festival Hall during a series of Russian musical concerts, November 1972.

John Simpson of their Foreign Desk (now the Foreign Affairs Editor). Well, as regularly as possible as he is a very difficult man to get hold of. Sometimes I used to cheat. They would say "Who is speaking please?" and I would say "Mrs Sim(p)son" – I always got through.

For all our professionalism the 'Jewish Mother Syndrome' would keep breaking through. We always felt so sorry for Ian Glover-James, the ITN Correspondent in Moscow; he always looked so gaunt. We used to send him Mars Bars and chicken-soup cubes.

The dogged determination of some journalists to reveal the sham of the public face of communism was of enormous value. One such journalist was David Floyd, Communist Affairs Editor of *The Daily Telegraph* in the early 70s, who wrote a number of articles in that paper. On 12 November 1978 his report of persistent anti-Jewish campaigns in Russia inspired an editorial on the subject. So reliable was the information put out by the 35s that it was frequently used by Stuart Parrot, the Bureau chief of Radio Free Europe and by his colleague, Roland Egleston, an experienced commentator on Russian affairs. Whenever Joyce Simson and Liz Phillips met Egleston at meetings and conferences they would put him in the picture regarding the latest information and he would relay it directly into the Soviet Union.

The 35s appeared in and helped the BBC "Panorama" and ITV "World in Action" programmes. Such was the impact of the Sharansky case that "World in Action" featured it in three programmes. Much of the film material used had to be smuggled out of Russia. One of these programmes was "used in evidence" against him during Sharansky's trial. Prosecutor Solonim claimed that Michael Sherbourne had given the commentary but this was not so. Sherbourne had been interviewed in a second "World in Action" programme, after Sharansky's arrest, when extracts from the original programme were shown again.

Since its inception, the Women's Campaign for Soviet Jewry has kept a watching brief on the media, for two reasons. Firstly, in order to correct any misinformation (generally by writing letters to the press) and secondly, in order to include newsworthy items in the organisation's newsletter. Instructions in the 'Frontliners List' of

1977 states "the following will read the press early and pass (items of interest) for attention immediately". There followed a list of the names of twelve women, together with the names of the newspapers to be read, but the system soon broke down. A Press-cuttings Bureau was utilised for a while, but this was found to be too expensive. Muriel Sherbourne then undertook the task, and for many years, despite prolonged bouts of ill health, she monitored the newspapers as well as supporting her husband, Michael, in his ongoing campaigns. This scrutiny resulted in many letters being published refuting instances of blatant propaganda, misinformation, prejudice and anti-Semitism, thus informing and educating the public. The value of this work cannot be overestimated. The scope of the outgoing letters covers a wide variety of subjects; from a contrast of American democratic government with the Russian "regime imposed by a minority elite", (Margaret Rigal, *International Herald Tribune*, 14 May 1984), to the enforced separation of parents and children as illustrated by the case of Igor Gutz and his baby son, Daniel (Leeds 35s, *The Daily Mail*, 1 February 1979), to the protest that by the Southern Electricity Board's purchase of £80,000 worth of Russian Trekmaster vans, the British taxpayer was contributing to the slave labour which was producing and assembling the engine parts in prison camps (Margaret Rigal, *Daily Telegraph*, 17 August 1979).

During the run-up to the 1980 Olympic Games, there was a constant flow of letters to the newspapers protesting against the Moscow venue. On 28th January 1980, a letter from Rita Eker in *Newsweek* highlighted the lack of freedom for those Moscow citizens who were being exiled to Siberia to prevent them from meeting the foreigners who would soon be arriving there for the Games. And on 19 July 1980, *The Daily Telegraph* printed a letter from Margaret Rigal reminding readers that even as the Olympic flame was being lit there were two thousand refusenik families in Kiev alone who were unable to obtain exit visas. Amongst other published letters on the same subject during this period, from individuals, Trade Union officials, etc., there were many which had been prompted by the 35s.

As well as letters sent to the press, matters of significance in the areas of Human Rights, anti-Semitism, Soviet Jewry, etc. were reproduced in newsletters, thereby over the years building up an important database. The results of this work were adequate compensation for the labour involved. Nevertheless there were

'Looks as if they're expecting another demo...'

Cartoon that appeared in the Daily Mail, 18 May 1984.
By kind permission of The Daily Mail

moments of pride when recognition came from time to time. In January 1983 *The Daily Telegraph* referred to the 35s as "those indefatigable women of the Campaign for Soviet Jewry".

Writing of Joyce Simson in *The Times* of 4 March 1991, Bernard Levin referred to her as: "one of those extraordinary Jewish ladies who spend their days and nights giving comfort – and more important – practical help to the Soviet refuseniks".

But to feature in a *Daily Mail* cartoon (18 May 1984) was surely the ultimate accolade for the 35s.

An account of the 35s and the news media would not be complete without reference to Bernard Levin, whose many articles in *The Times*, on Human Rights and the plight of Soviet Jews in particular, had direct links with the 35s. "Those splendid and indefatigable ladies – the Women's Campaign for Soviet Jewry" (*The Times*, 21 April 1989).

In Bernard Levin, the 35s found a staunch protagonist. From as early as 1972 he was championing the cause of Soviet Jewry through his articles in *The Times*. Not for him the demonstrations in the High Street or the postcard signings in Trafalgar Square, but, with his incisive pen, on numerous occasions, he laid bare the sham of the Soviet Union's lip-service to Human Rights. Indeed, in a brilliant article on 16 July 1993, entitled "How was the cruel lie perpetrated?" he asked how so many people – scientists, writers, artists, politicians – came to swallow the evil lie of Communism – "without the slightest endeavour to discover the truth about the Soviet Union", an aberration from which Levin certainly did not suffer.

His articles in *The Times* were a small but significant effort to inform these same people of the facts of life under Communism in the Former Soviet Union and of the present regime in the CIS[61]. He was forthright in his condemnation of the violations of Human Rights by the USSR, steadfast in his support of refuseniks and unstinting in his praise of the 35s and their work.

Levin wrote his first article on the Prusakovs on 4 July 1972 after a meeting with Michael Sherbourne and ever since then he has been writing about the evils of Communism, and the lawless and erratic regime which succeeded it. In more than fifty articles he has been trenchant in his fight for Human Rights, but a mere list can in no way

[61] Confederation of Independent States

convey the brilliance of his elegant and sardonic presentation of his views. He fought not only for Jews but also for many non-Jews who were also victims of the Soviet oppression (e.g. Sakharov, Solzhenitsyn and Father Gleb Yakunin).

In an article in *The Jewish Observer and Middle East Review* of September 1977, Michael Sherbourne said, in reference to Bernard Levin: "it is beyond doubt that his help in giving publicity to their cases has been a factor in obtaining freedom for, amongst others Valentin Prusakov, the Panovs and Dr Mikhail Shtern..."

Most of Levin's information on the subject came from the 35s. On 4 June 1993, in an article on anti-Semitism, he wrote: "never mind Mary Tudor. When I am dead and opened you will find the number 35 graven on my heart. The 35s are a group of Jewish ladies... who dedicate their lives to the succour of the Jews of the Soviet Union".

Levin's article "Was it really all in vain?" (29 March 1994) was a masterly précis of his thirty-year fight "to record and denounce the evils of totalitarian rule, the centre of which was the Soviet empire" against the background of its changing face. He grieved for the madness of today's situation, a situation in which thugs murder in order to obtain an apartment, in which "wicked baboons like Zhirinovsky are elected and... an era which is at least as anti-Semitic as the worst since Stalin, so that another exodus may yet be needed".

The impact of an article published in *The Times* cannot be overestimated. It has been shown time and time again that the Russian Government responded to publicity in the West (cf Sharansky, Azbel and others). When Levin met the Prusakovs in Vienna, after their release, they told him that "the continuous public pressure on the Soviet authorities from outside the Soviet Empire is the biggest single hope of those who wish to get out". (*The Times*, 2 November 1972).

He went on to say: "Valentin startled me a little by telling me that he had read my columns on the subject – it seems that British newspapers brought in by tourists often find their way into the right hands and are passed eagerly about".

Indeed, the author's own experience bears this out. On her trip to Russia, whilst being searched for printed matter at Leningrad airport, she saw papers being confiscated from a non-Jewish fellow passenger. He told her later that they were a series of Bernard Levin's articles in *The Times*.

In recognition of his resolute support of the campaign, Levin was presented with the All-Party Parliamentary Committee for the Release of Soviet Jewry Award for services to Soviet Jewry by Roy Hattersley, Deputy leader of the Labour Party in December 1988.

One of the most fruitful branches of the work of the 35s in this country has been their association with the politicians. In the early years, Doreen Gainsford initiated these contacts and from 1974 until the present day, Margaret Rigal has been responsible for lobbying, briefing and liaising with the Foreign Office and with members of both Houses of Parliament. She wrote to each new Prime Minister and to all new Members of Parliament apprising them of the situation of Soviet Jewry *vis-à-vis* the abuse of Human Rights. More often than not she received positive replies, the writers deploring such abuses. During the vigorous campaigning years of the 70s and 80s, this initial approach would be followed by requests to participate in the campaign, perhaps by signing an Early Day Motion, or a petition, or by asking a question in the House.

Margaret Rigal remembers: "when I sent a letter out to all the MPs I had an answer from at least a third of them, which is a good response".

Margaret is always ready to supply whatever help may be needed by the All-Party Parliamentary Wives Group for the Release of Soviet Jewry, and to the All-Party Parliamentary Committee for the Release of Soviet Jewry. Over the years more than three hundred members of the two Houses have given practical help. From a signature in a *Times* advertisement[62] to visiting refuseniks in the USSR, their various efforts made a considerable contribution to the work of the 35s. Many Members 'adopted' refuseniks and every Soviet Prisoner of Conscience was 'adopted' by one or more Members.

From her early years in Parliament, Margaret Thatcher demonstrated an active sympathy, not only for the broader issue of Human Rights, but also for the individuals trapped in a barbaric system. From February 1975, when she wrote to the Foreign Office

---

[62] *The Times* of 6 October 1977 – a full page letter signed by nearly two thousand prominent citizens, called upon the Secretary General of the United Nations, the British Foreign Secretary and the President of the USSR, on the occasion of the meeting of thirty-five nations in Belgrade, to review the progress in the defence of Human Rights as laid down in Helsinki 1975. It was headed "A day to think about Human Rights and Anatoly Sharansky". This was organised by the 35s.

about the plight of thirty Prisoners of Conscience, and on numerous subsequent occasions throughout the 1970s and 1980s, she espoused the cause with a genuine concern. Sharansky, Panitsky, Nudel, the Beguns, Sosner, Ovsisher, the Yussefoviches, Tufeld, Schvartstein, Zelichenok and Samoilovitch are just a few of victims of injustice on whose behalf she made personal appeals to the Soviet authorities.

In the summer of 1983, Avital Sharansky was in England campaigning for her husband and she had a personal meeting with the Prime Minister. Later, during a meeting with his mother and his brother in Perm 35 prison camp, seven years into his sentence, Sharansky learnt of Avital's meeting with Mrs Thatcher; on his release in 1986, she was one of the first people that he and Avital met on their celebratory tour of the country.

Despite the undoubted pressures on her time by her many commitments during the annual party conferences, the Prime Minister always managed to fit in a meeting with representatives of the local 35s group. Cecily Woolf, secretary of the Brighton and Hove Soviet Jewry Group which is affiliated to the 35s, writes: "Each of my three meetings with Margaret Thatcher grew progressively warmer... In October 1988 I had a private interview with her in her heavily guarded suite. As instructed by the 35s in London, my mission was to ask her not to sign the Helsinki Accord unless the Russians recognised the Human Rights treaty. She was very well informed about the refuseniks' situation and seemed to be genuinely concerned about their plight. She followed up our meeting with a long letter in support of Human Rights, personally signed... Whatever one may think of her politics, Soviet Jews lost a good friend when she left office".

In November 1988 the 35s enlisted the help of Mrs Thatcher as part of their campaign to prevent the Conference on Human Rights from being held in Moscow. At the same time Rita Eker and Margaret Rigal also asked for her assistance as yet again they had been refused visas to visit the USSR to accompany members of the All-Party Parliamentary Wives group

During her meetings with President Gorbachev in Moscow in March 1987, she placed the issue of Human Rights high on her agenda. Equally important to her were the individuals for whom the 35s were campaigning. In October 1989 she found time to write personally to George Samoilovitch in reply to his letter of gratitude for all that she had done to enable him to receive medical treatment for malignant lymphoma at the Royal Marsden Hospital, London. She wrote: "...you and others like you won your freedom by your own faith and courage. I am so glad we were able to help...".

In May 1990, as guest of honour at the annual luncheon of the Women's International Zionist Organisation she said:

> ...but Israel does have cause to rejoice, as do we all, over the freedom to emigrate now being given to Soviet Jews. I remember when I spoke in Israel during my visit there nearly four years ago. I said that I believed that persistence in their just cause would be rewarded. Well, we did persist, and we are now seeing the reward... Many people played a part in that, and none more so than the Women's Campaign for Soviet Jewry in this country and we congratulate them on their efforts.

Prior to her visit to Kiev in June 1990, Mrs Thatcher was briefed by the 35s on a number of cases in need of urgent medical treatment, especially following the Chernobyl disaster. She was able to raise these matters and was also able to meet some refuseniks and bring their plight to the notice of Soviet officials.

Whilst in Kiev, in a generous and imaginative gesture, she laid a wreath at the Babi Yar memorial, which commemorates the mass murder of Soviet Jews in 1941.

In a letter to the 35s regarding the Helsinki Agreement, Margaret Thatcher wrote: "I have nothing but the greatest admiration for the way in which you have pursued your objectives with such conviction and persistence".

Margaret Rigal's appraisal of Margaret Thatcher summarises her invaluable contribution to the fight for Soviet Jewry: "She had a genuine personal regard for Soviet Jews. She knew more about them than most of those who went to see her; she knew of all the prisoners; she really cared".

From the Prime Minister to the humblest back-bencher, support for Soviet Jewry has always been forthcoming. Most of the information supplied to the Foreign Office and to Members of Parliament regarding Soviet Jewry came from the 35s. The politicians could be confident that the information provided to them was backed by rock-hard research; they knew that they were working for an overwhelmingly just cause, in a superbly conducted campaign.

Another Parliamentarian who helped was Dr Rhodes Boyson the Conservative Member of Parliament for Brent:

> Together with my wife, we worked for Soviet Jewry for twenty years. As soon as I came to Brent I was approached by the 35s and I identified with the cause from the start. It was a specific cause and I could see that something was being done. It was a complicated yet simple issue: how do we get them out? The 35s are a formidable body of women; they show such courage and determination; they are an example to all of us – they just get on with it. They are un-put-offable. I have come to know them very well and now see them as close friends.

The first Foreign Secretary to receive and support the 35s was David Owen[63]. In December 1977 he was briefed by Doreen Gainsford and Margaret Rigal on the situation of Sharansky who was then in prison awaiting trial "...thereby putting the issue of Human Rights firmly on the Foreign Office agenda. From that time on the 35s have always had the backing of the current Foreign Secretary" said Margaret Rigal.

Later, when Sharansky was suffering an excessively harsh regime in the punishment cells of Perm labour camp, the Foreign Secretary, Francis Pym[64], summoned the Soviet Ambassador to the Foreign Office. *The Jewish Chronicle* commented that this was the first occasion, on British soil, that a foreign diplomat had been called upon to account for one of his own citizens!

Prior to his departure to take up his appointment as British Ambassador to the USSR, Sir Rodric Braithwaite received Rita Eker and Margaret Rigal at the Foreign Office (August 1988).

The visit of a Soviet official was always an opportunity for person-to-person representations. In March 1989, William Waldegrave, then Minister of State at the Foreign Office wrote to Janet Fookes, MP: "Obviously Soviet Human Rights will be very high

---

[63] Later Lord Owen, a Minister in the Labour Government at that time. He later became a founder member of the Liberal Democratic Party.

[64] A Conservative government was then in office.

up on the agenda when Mr Gorbachev comes to London in April and you can be sure that the Prime Minister will be highlighting the continuing refusenik problem".

In January 1990, the Foreign Minister, Douglas Hurd, informed Margaret Rigal that he had raised the issue of Human Rights with the Soviet Foreign Minister, Edward Shevardnadze:

> I also raised a number of individual cases of refuseniks and 'Prisoners of Conscience'. Mr Shevardnadze undertook to look into these cases, and we are following this up during official high level talks on Human Rights in Moscow.

On a more personal level, Frazer Wheeler of the Russian desk at the Foreign Office, wrote to George Samoilovich in October 1989: "...the campaign on behalf of you and your family succeeded, of course, because it was a team effort. (How could we have coped, for example, without the incomparable badgering of Rita (Eker) and Liz (Phillips) to keep everyone in line)..."

Most of the London and provincial groups received support from their local MPs, who covered the full spectrum of political parties in the House of Commons. A random selection of MPs and Peers shows the diverse range of both help and affiliations.

David Alton (Liberal)[65] accompanied a petition to the Soviet Embassy on behalf of Sharansky in January 1980. He campaigned for Ivor Gutz (separated from his pregnant wife) and in 1990 he visited refuseniks in Moscow.

Donald Anderson (Labour) also showed great sympathy. He, too, was a signatory of *The Times* petition, the "Sharansky letter", and the Sharansky appeal of 1985. In addition he took an interest in a number of individual refuseniks.

Peter Archer (Labour), a former Chairman of the All-Party Parliamentary Committee for the Release of Soviet Jewry, signed *The Times* petition (1972) and the "Sharansky letter" to *The Times* and *The Daily Telegraph* in January 1983[66]. He showed enormous sympathy and helped in a variety of ways.

---

[65] Now Liberal Democrat.
[66] In January 1983, a letter signed by sixty-three MPs appeared in *The Times* appealing to newly-elected President Andropov concerning Sharansky.

Kenneth Baker (Conservative) was the first British Minister to ask the British Embassy in Moscow to arrange a breakfast meeting with refuseniks (October 1988). Thereafter, the Embassy facilitated meetings between visiting British Ministers and refuseniks on a regular basis. Whilst in Moscow he brought up the cases of nine refusenik families, "about whom the British Government is concerned". His representations regarding Professor and Mrs Nadgorny, who had first applied to leave in 1981, appeared to bear fruit as they received permission to leave Russia just a few days after his return to this country. *The Birmingham Post* (October 1988) reported that Mrs Nadgorny believed that her meeting with Mr Baker gave the Soviet authorities the final push.

Dennis Canavan (Labour) was another intrepid worker for the Sharansky campaign. He signed an Early Day Motion and wrote to the American Ambassador on Sharansky's behalf and also worked for other refuseniks including Dr Iosif As.

Lynda Chalker (Conservative)[67] was hostess to Sylva Zalmanson when Sylva visited Britain after her release. She signed the Brussels Greeting[68], Early Day Motions, *The Times* advertisement for Sharansky, and was Chairman of the Ida Nudel Committee for many years until Ida's emigration to Israel.

Patrick Cormack (Conservative), the first Chairman of the All-Party Parliamentary Committee for the Release of Soviet Jewry, asked a question in the House on Human Rights in May 1977. He also signed the Sharansky Appeal, "adopted" Anatoly Malkin, and met refuseniks during a visit to Moscow.

Janet Fookes (Conservative) wrote to the US Ambassador in December 1981 on behalf of the "Free Sharansky" campaign. She also signed a petition to Geoffrey Howe, the Secretary of State for Foreign Affairs, on the Human Rights issue, was a member of the Ida Nudel Committee, and was one of the many hundreds of signatories of the Sharansky Appeal letter to *The Times*.

Michael Foot (Labour), when he was Leader of the Opposition, in reply to their letter requesting his help, informed the 35s that he would take every opportunity to exercise some influence, either directly or indirectly, on the Government of the USSR.

---

[67] Later Baroness Chalker.
[68] From British MPs to the Brussels Conference.

John Gorst (Conservative) was joint Chairman with Helene Hayman (Labour) of the Parliamentary Committee for the Release of Sharansky, from its inception. Vivian Bendall (Conservative) later took over until Sharansky was released.

John Marshall (Conservative) was unstinting in his help in numerous ways over a long period of time. He was one of the first MPs to be called upon when the 35s were in need of assistance, and was instrumental in helping to secure the release of many refuseniks including Ida Nudel and Anatoly Sharansky.

Prior to his visit to Moscow in November 1988, Geoffrey Howe, the Secretary of State for Foreign and Commonwealth Affairs, was asked a number of parliamentary questions by the following Members: Donald Anderson, Peter Archer, David Atkinson, Vivian Bendall, John Blackburn, Andrew Bowden, Alistair Burt, Hugh Dykes, Ivan Lawrence, Anthony Steen, David Sumberg and John Wheeler.

The questions concerned Human Rights in general and also made specific mention of the cases of Alexander Cherniak, Vladimir Kislik, Yuli Kosharovsky, Evgeny Lein, Yuri Orlov, George Samoilovich, Igor Uspensky and Raoul Zelichenok.

Alan Beith (Liberal Democrat), Betty Boothroyd (Labour), David Know (Conservative), Tim Sainsbury (Conservative), Andrew Welch (Scottish Nationalist), David Wigley (Plaid Cymru), and Alec Woodall (Labour) are but a few of the other MPs in the very long list who have given tangible support.

Members of the House of Lords also cooperated with the 35s. A random selection shows a few of the more active supporters.

Baroness Birk (Labour) was a member of the International Committee to Free Sharansky, and also worked for the release of Mikhail Shtern and other refuseniks.

The Earl of Caithness (Labour) spoke in the Upper House on Human Rights and the situation of the refuseniks.

The Duke of Devonshire gave much support to the 35s' campaign against the holding of the 1980 Olympic Games in Moscow and also helped in many other issues.

Baroness Seear (Liberal) was a member of the International Free Sharansky committee. She "adopted" Prisoner of Conscience Alexander Kholmiansky and assisted in getting a question asked in the House of Lords.

The cause of Human Rights was also raised in the European Parliament by Baroness Ellis (Conservative) and Lord Bethell (Conservative). Lord Bethell tabled a resolution on behalf of George Samoilovich who had been refused an exit visa despite his urgent need of medical treatment for malignant lymphoma. He also accompanied Avital Sharansky during her many visits to Britain. Winifred Ewing (Scottish Nationalist Party) was a constant champion for Ida Nudel and tabled a Motion concerning her in the European Parliament in November 1982.

It must be stressed that the politicians who have been mentioned represent only a few of the many hundreds who added their weight to the fight for Human Rights in the Soviet Union.

From July 1970, when he was first elected to Parliament, Greville Janner has been an unswerving supporter of Human Rights and Jewish causes. In 1979, he was one of the twenty-five leaders of international organisations who had an audience with the Pope, when he asked for his help in stemming persecution of Soviet Jews. Over the years he has asked many questions in the House on Human Rights, on visa refusals and on the plight of refuseniks. He pursued many individual cases including those of Sharansky, Semyon Livshits, Mikhail Penkov and Professor Lerner.

Janner took a particular interest in Vladimir Slepak and had a very close, albeit long distance, relationship with the Slepak family which was conducted mainly by telephone. The Barmitzvah[69] of Vladimir's younger son, Leonid, was celebrated in May 1972, by proxy, by a number of thirteen-year-old Jewish boys in this country, including boys at Carmel College, Britain's only Jewish Public school. The All-Party Parliamentary Committee for the Release of Soviet Jewry made a recording entitled "A Bar Mitzvah Gift for Leonid Slepak", on which were included messages from Patrick Cormack (the Chairman of the committee) and Greville Janner (The Honorary Secretary). Janner recalled, with emotion, speaking to Leonid on the eve of his Bar Mitzvah and listening to him recite the Bar Mitzvah blessings in Hebrew. The Committee had obtained a standard Hebrew prayer

---

[69] Bar Mitzvah. The attainment of the age of religious majority by a Jewish boy at the age of thirteen years. This is usually marked by a religious ceremony and in normal circumstances is an occasion of rejoicing by the extended family.

book which was then signed by the Prime Minister, members of the Cabinet, and over two hundred Members of Parliament. They attempted to send it to Leonid, but the authorities refused to allow it into the Soviet Union, as the import of religious books was forbidden. "So much for religious freedom" the recording comments. This undelivered prayer book became a symbol and its influence was felt by many Soviet officials, including President Brezhnev, as the Committee tried, on a number of occasions, to have it delivered to Leonid.

The All-Party Parliamentary Committee for the Release of Soviet Jewry, formed in February 1972 and the brainchild of Greville Janner, was a small but very active and influential group which worked closely with the 35s to mutual advantage. Greville Janner recalled:

> when the 35s had demonstrations, we would bring the
> MPs along – we always brought the troops out for them.
> I feel that our greatest success was to project Soviet
> Jewry as a Human Rights issue not as a Jewish one.
> The All-Party group was led all the time by non-Jews
> from whom much of the enthusiasm and leadership
> emanated.

As early as November 1971, a group of wives of both Jewish and non-Jewish MPs staged a one-hour vigil outside the Soviet Embassy to protest against the treatment of Sylva Zalmanson, who had been sentenced to ten years imprisonment in a labour camp. Later their efforts were coordinated and they became the All-Party Parliamentary Wives Group for the Release of Soviet Jewry. They made regular contacts with the leaders of the parliamentary parties and enlisted their help in support for Soviet Jewry.

In June 1979, the Parliamentary wives, as they became known, met Margaret Thatcher to ask her to press for the release of Ida Nudel. Their delegates, Susan Sainsbury, Valerie Cocks, Margaret Morris and Pat Tuckman, visited Moscow in 1988. This practical help and encouragement was greatly valued by the refuseniks and gave impetus to their struggle. From Moscow the Parliamentary wives went on to Vienna to participate in the Conference on Security and Co-operation in Europe (CSCE – the Helsinki Agreement) where they lobbied on behalf of the refuseniks. They requested a meeting with

Mrs Gorbachev during her forthcoming visit to the UK with her husband later that year.

Nineteen eighty-nine found them engaged in a continuous campaign to try to prevent the adoption of Moscow as the venue for the CSCE Conference on Human Rights.

The contacts which they made enabled Margaret Rigal and her colleagues to take up the cases of many refuseniks such as Natasha Khassina, Fima Fromenblit, Solomon Flaks, Vladimir Tufeld, Ida Nudel, George Samoilovitch and Anatoly Sharansky amongst others. They were always listened to with sympathy and action was taken where possible.

In his memoir *Fear No Evil*, Sharansky wrote, in reference to the tens of thousands of letters sent to him from all over the world:

> ...but although I never received them, it was extremely important that these letters were sent. To the regime, they served as a constant reminder that people all over the world knew about me and cared about my fate. That was why the authorities sometimes retreated, and it probably explains why they kept me alive during my prolonged hunger strike in 1982. The moment the KGB feels that interest in a prisoner is declining it immediately increases the pressure.

Since 'glasnost'"[70], contacts between the 35s and the politicians have lessened, but there are still refuseniks and prisoners needing help. In November 1992 when President Yeltsin visited London, lists of some of the outstanding refuseniks' and prisoners' cases were supplied to Mr Major (at the request of the Foreign Office) for him to pass on to the Russian leader. The 35s were represented by Joyce Simson at President Yeltsin's press conference. In December 1992, Rita Eker and Margaret Rigal accompanied a delegation to the Russian Embassy where they handed to the Ambassador, Mr Boris Pankin, a letter signed by nearly five hundred parliamentary candidates, asking Pankin to use his influence with all the governments of the CIS[71] in order to obtain exit visas for the Jewish refuseniks without delay. Pankin agreed that "refusal" was out of date and should go. The

---

[70] "Glasnost" (Russian – literally 'openness'). The USSR policy introduced by Gorbachev in 1990.

[71] Confederation of Independent States which replaced the USSR.

meeting took place in a very cordial atmosphere and it was agreed that the 35s should provide some medical supplies for Pankin to distribute to those most in need in Russia.

As described elsewhere, the 35s received much co-operation and help from the police during their demonstrations. Why was there such co-operation? Whilst it is probably true that the police enjoyed working with the women who seldom caused problems and invariably lent a light hearted touch to their otherwise mundane duties, could it be that they received instructions not to impede these women? Both Greville Janner and Margaret Rigal feel that, in view of the traditional anti-Israel stance of the Foreign Office, the British Government found it advantageous to take up the Human Rights issue as it enabled them to demonstrate that they were not anti-Semitic.

Margaret Rigal considered that: "sometimes we gained from many peoples' desire not to be overtly anti-Semitic, and they balanced their anti-Israel attitude by their support of our group".

It can be argued that were it not for the 35s and similar organisations, the Human Rights issue may well not have been pursued with such vigour by the Western governments. Doubtless it is true that this issue was an opportune "stick" with which to "beat" the Russians. However, it must have been equally fortuitous for the Russians to have such a valuable bargaining counter – human lives in exchange for diplomatic concessions!

In July 1973 Sir Alec Douglas Home, Foreign Secretary, stated:

> It follows that the item on our agenda which deals with co-operation on the Human Rights field is, in my judgement, the most important item of our business. If our conference is essentially about people and about trust, then it is necessary that we do something to remove the barriers which inhibit the movement of people and the exchange of information and ideas... That is why the United Kingdom will continue to press for a practical approach.[72]

There are conflicting opinions about the role of the Israeli Government in the overall Soviet Jewry campaign. Depending on their standpoint and relations with the Israeli Establishment, the views

---

[72] At the Conference on Security and Co-operation in Europe meeting in Helsinki.

of the activists differed widely ranging from Cyril Stein's frustrated outburst, "they did nothing, absolutely nothing" to Doreen Gainsford's, "they did, and still do a good job". Doubtless the true picture lies somewhere between these two extremes.

The existence of a Soviet Jewish department within the Israeli Foreign Office demonstrates that government's desire to assist in the plight of Soviet Jews, both in their lives in the USSR and in their desire to emigrate to Israel. This department was created after a visit to the USSR by an Israeli official, Nehemiah Levanon, who, on his return, said to the Prime Minister Golda Meir, "we must do something for them". He became the head of this department but as he had direct responsibility to the Prime Minister rather than to the Foreign Office, the normal channels of communication became fragmented. Because of this, great hostility arose between Levanon and various activists both in Britain and in the United States of America.

Prior to the Six Day War, after which diplomatic relations were severed, Israeli representatives in the Soviet Union supported Soviet Jewry in a number of ways by giving them encouragement and supplying them with religious material. Ijo Rager agreed that the Israelis were not inactive and maintained that they were helpful to the Jewish student activists in this country. In December 1995 he wrote to the author:

> I was sent by the Israeli Government to London and my MAJOR assignment was to do everything possible for Soviet Jewry. I sent weekly reports to the Israeli Government about my activities and got full backing.

The meticulously documented information on refuseniks and prisoners culled, often with great difficulty by the 35s and other activists, was initially sent to the Israeli Soviet Jewry Department. Eventually, after confrontation, Michael Sherbourne discovered that Levanon had suppressed this information instead of using it to help the would-be immigrants, saying that he deplored the publication of such lists. Sherbourne also declared that Levanon's office had spread lies about him (and other activists) by warning Moscow dissidents "not to give him any information as he doesn't pass it on".

Doreen Gainsford recalls the lack of co-operation from the Israelis during the Sharansky campaign. True to their ultra-cautious approach they were nervous of being seen to be behind Sharansky.

She explains:

> They said that he was too dangerous and that he was involved with others, the Human Rights people. I really fought with the Israeli Foreign Office over this. I said that he was a Jew who wants to go to Israel and we want you to recognise him as a refusenik. I felt that on this they were too frightened of their own shadows... It was only when I went to Russia that I began to understand Israel. The 'founding fathers' in the early days were mostly of Russian origin and they had the same bureaucratic inertia. The Government might change but the civil servants remained the same. They didn't want to rock the diplomatic boat. Levanon was one of these people. Remember, the Soviet Jewry Department was working for citizens inside a country with which Israel did not have diplomatic relations. The Establishment just can't understand a non-Establishment approach.

Michael Sherbourne suggests that after their initial support for the campaign they saw the way that it was developing, and they needed to control it as it was slipping from their grasp. This point of view is reinforced by Colin Shindler: "The Soviet Jewry Office in Israel tried to run a tight ship and frowned on uncontrolled individualism".

In a long interview with Avraham Shifrin[73], who disclosed a number of Israeli sabotaging incidents, Michael Sherbourne asked him about the activities of the Soviet Jewry Office in Israel. Shifrin suggested that the ruling Israeli Socialist Government were nervous of a large Soviet immigration:

> They realised that the Jews of the USSR were so fed up with socialism that they hated to see here any Socialists or red flags, and therefore they, the ruling Socialist party, afraid of opposition, did not want this immigration.

---

[73] Avraham Shifrin – Director of the Research Centre for Prisoners and Concentration Camps in the USSR. Israel December 1978.

However, Doreen Gainsford, who said that the Israelis were helpful to her, considers that the Israeli Government was working behind the scenes: "they were working at getting people to work".

Rita Eker agreed with this analysis: "they instigated a lot of the activities; at times we were their puppets. We used to have meetings with them, sometimes at the Israeli Embassy and sometimes in the 35s office".

In an article in *The Jerusalem Report* (22 February 1996) Natan Sharansky helps to clarify the enigmatic role of the Israeli Government. He explains that the Liaison Bureau (Lishkat Hakesher), the agency responsible for Jews behind the Iron Curtain, was a secret organisation reporting directly to the Prime Minister. It supported the Aliyah movement in a number of clandestine ways and it quietly organised protests in the West. But in insisting on making Soviet Jewry an Israeli strategic issue, it attempted to control the activities of the refuseniks (including threats against refuseniks who refused to submit). Sharansky goes on to say, "but the moment we reached Israel we could also see that the Bureau was irreplaceable". He underlines the need for the continuing work of the Liaison Bureau (Israel). Despite opposition from officials such as Jewish Agency Chief Avraham Burg, he views the current situation in the former Soviet Union with foreboding. Politically, nationalist and pro-Communist forces are in the rise which could easily lead to a deterioration in policy not only to emigration but to the Jews in general.

A picture emerges of a government in an extremely sensitive situation. Whilst there is no doubt that help from the Israelis was forthcoming, time and time again it is the activist groups and individuals whom the refuseniks thank for their eventual freedom, and whom they remember with affection as the people who came to see them, who wrote, who telephoned, and who were at the airport to meet them when they finally came out.

The issue of Israel's role remains contentious.

An intensive campaign over a period of about eighteen years led to a rewarding liaison with the Trade Unions. Ros Gemal was responsible for organising this aspect of the work during this period. She recalls her initiation into the 35s group:

I used to ask my father about the Holocaust – what were people doing for the Jews of Europe? When I read about the 35s' first demonstration I knew I had to do something, so I telephoned to offer my help. I was thrown in at the deep end. Doreen (Gainsford) said to me 'You'll be our Trade Union Officer'. I said that I knew absolutely nothing about it. 'You'll learn,' she said, and I did – the hard way. I had no qualifications and no training. I didn't have a clue on how to go about it; I was so ignorant. I sat thinking about it for hours. I wondered how I was going to get them interested. Then I had an idea. I went through the refuseniks' biographies until I found one of an artisan who was on trial for "parasitism". He was a metal worker called Sender Levinson. In 1975 he was sent to prison and in the meantime his wife and children had obtained permission to leave. Then I found out when the next Trade Union Conference was to be held and we decided to leaflet them with his story. Ken Gill was the secretary and he was an ardent communist. I thought 'how can I catch their imagination, they are all so pro-Russian'. So I got up a petition and we went to the pier at Eastbourne where the conference was being held. We got permission to stand outside and I thought that we would get them as they came out for lunch; but we didn't stand a chance. They came out in a mad rush, anxious to get down their lunch-time pint before they convened again. We were so disappointed but we were determined. As they returned, I got all the girls lined up outside and they had to run our gauntlet and we handed out the petition forms for them to take back to their branches – and that's how our Trade Union campaign got off the ground. They were a smashing lot of chaps in that Union. They really worked for Sender Levinson.

The campaign for Levinson widened to involve other refuseniks. Support came from the EETPU[74] which became one of the 35s'

---

[74] EETPU – Electrical, Electronic, Telecommunication and Plumbing Union.

affiliates (together with NALGO)[75] and from the AEU[76]. Many representations to Russian trades unions were made on behalf of Levinson; amongst those was one made in June 1975 by the Secretary of the Federation of Shipbuilding and Engineering Union, who wrote to his Russian counterpart pleading for the imprisoned metalworker. Terry Duffy, a member of AUEW[77] executive, wrote an article on Soviet Jewry in *The Way* (the eight hundred thousand circulation journal of the Union), exposing the cases of Iosif Begun and Sender Levinson.

Not all the Unions cooperated; many of their members were communists and took a pro-Russian stance. Some of them were also anti-Semitic and subsequently, when the Arab/PLO influence became strong, their attitude was even less sympathetic. They perceived the 35s as being anti-Communist and added anti-Zionism to their anti-Semitism.

Rachele Kalman remembers:

> at the Brighton TUC Conference in 1978, we were standing outside with our banners and handing out leaflets. Never in my life have I come across such blatant and vicious anti-Semitism. It was directed straight at us, face to face. I just couldn't believe what I was hearing; I found it absolutely nauseating. This came from the rank and file; the executive gave us their support. I came away shocked and shattered.

It is indeed ironic that, at a TUC Conference which then represented many millions of British workers, there would be a sizeable proportion who applauded a repressive regime embodying the kind of tyranny from which they had fought long and bitterly to escape.

---

[75] NALGO – National Association of Local Government Officers (now National and Local Government Officers Association).
[76] AEU – Amalgamated Engineering Union.
[77] AUEW – Amalgamated Union of Engineering Workers.

1978 TUC Conference
Brighton

HUMAN RIGHTS

This Congress reaffirms its policy on human rights adopted in 1973. Congress believes that acts of repression against workers and trade unionists by totalitarian regimes have continued and indeed become Worse since that time.

Congress calls on the General Council actively to support a charter for basic human rights in all countries for:-

(1) release of all non-violent political prisoners;

(2) right of all workers to organise free trade unions;

(3) right to free and democratic election by ballot;

(4) freedom of speech;

(5) freedom of assembly;

(6) freedom of religious worship;

(7) free press; and

(8) freedom to demonstrate and protest in a lawful fashion.

Electrical, Electronic, Telecommunication & Plumbing Union
PASSED UNANIMOUSLY

IF YOU ARE JEWISH IN THE

U.S.S.R.

and apply for an Exit Visa under the terms of the

HELSINKI AGREEMENT

YOU CAN

LEGALLY

BE PUNISHED WITH JOB LOSS

BE CHARGED WITH 'PARASITISM'

BE SENT INTO EXILE

BE SENT TO PRISON

TRANSPORT TO EXILE OR PRISON

"Barred prison compartments on the train built for 4 are crammed with 25 people . . .
Food for each 4 days was a chunk of bread and one salt fish . . . thirst was unbearable.
. . . the journey was full of violent incidents . . . occasionally there were deaths . . . Sanitary conditions were non-existent . . . FOR ANYONE WITH EVEN THE SLIGHTEST SENSIBILITY THE JOURNEY IS A BRUTALISING NIGHTMARE."

Leaflet handed out to delegates at Brighton TUC conference, 1978.

At the 1978 TUC Conference at Brighton, the 35s distributed their leaflets which listed the freedoms denied to Russian Jewish workers who wished to emigrate: "Freedom of assembly; Freedom from want; Freedom from fear; Freedom of religious worship; Freedom of education; freedom of choice; freedom to demonstrate and protest in a lawful manner and freedom for Human Rights... Behind the facts and figures are broken homes, broken marriages, children with irreparable psychological damage as families go on for years in isolation and terrible depression. People beyond the pale".

Attendance at the annual conferences of the various unions was, perhaps, the most productive aspect of the work and much of it was done by the provincial groups of the 35s. Blackpool and Brighton were favourite venues and year after year the groups from Liverpool, Manchester, St Anne's, etc. in the north and those from Brighton and Hove, Bournemouth, etc. in the south would be on duty lobbying, leafleting, picketing and parading. The women tried to think of a fresh "gimmick" for each conference.

Ros Gemal recalled:

> At one TUC conference in Blackpool we had huge pencils made with 'Remember Slepak' and 'Remember Levinson' printed on them. Leila Cumber and I brought a whole load of them. We found out where the big dinner was being held and we got into the dining room and put one at each place. They all thought it was a lovely gift until they saw the inscription.
>
> A Russian 'observer' was at the conference and Sylvia Sheff, one of the Manchester group, chatted-up a chambermaid and found out his room number. We knocked at his door and when he opened it we handed him a model of the Blackpool Tower and then tried to give him a petition which he wouldn't accept. So Sylvia said 'well let me read it to you' and there and then, in the middle of the hotel corridor and in a very carrying voice, she read it out.

Cicely Woolf:

> For over two weeks, in September 1976, we organised an exhibition on 'Prisoners of Conscience in the USSR'

at the Brighton Library, featuring Jewish and gentile prisoners, to coincide with the Brighton TUC Conference. Former refusenik Viktor Fainberg came with us to the Metropole Hotel where the Russian 'observer' (well known as KGB agent Boris Averyanov) was enjoying his capitalist steak dinner. How he choked over it when Viktor invited him to our exhibition.

In marked contrast to some of the other Unions, APEX[78] and their President, Dennis Howell MP, showed their sympathy for the cause in many practical ways. In November 1979, the 35s appealed to Dennis Howell[79] on behalf of Ivan Oleynik (a physical education instructor) and his wife Elena, who were being harassed and threatened by the KGB. They had become victims of a carefully planned programme of persecution, calculated to make them scapegoats as a warning to all the other Jews in Kiev who might have been thinking of applying to emigrate. Howell was due to meet V. Propokov and Y. Agladze, members of the Moscow Olympics Committee. He had demonstrated his sympathy on previous occasions and it was hoped that he would speak to his guests on behalf of the Oleyniks. The *APEX Journal* of October/November 1978 carried an article protesting against the Russian denial of violations of Human Rights following the Helsinki Agreement, and at their annual conference in March of the following year they passed a resolution condemning the victimisation of Soviet workers who had applied for exit visas.

The APEX union also wrote a letter to the Soviet Engineering and Instrument Making Union, maintaining that Human Rights violations were taking place in the USSR. They raised the issue that restrictions were being placed on Jews wishing to emigrate to Israel. The Soviet Trade Union denied these allegations and the *APEX Journal* subsequently printed the exchange of letters on this topic. This was a tiny, but incalculably effective means of informing an otherwise unknowing readership about the situation. Dennis Howell spread the message to a much wider public in January 1980, at a worldwide conference for white collar workers in Venezuela, when he stated that APEX had taken every opportunity to protect against abuses and injustices in the Soviet Union. He called for the implementation of the

---

[78] APEX – Association of Professional Executive, Clerical and Computer Staff.
[79] In his capacity as Opposition Spokesman on Sport.

Helsinki Accords and condemned the Soviet practice of job-dismissal as a means of dealing with dissenters.

In September 1975 the 35s were instrumental in getting Tom Jackson, General Secretary of the Union of Post Office Workers, to sign a petition against the arbitrary dismissal of Jewish trades unionists.

The Leeds 35s sent telegrams to the Transport and General Workers Union conference at Scarborough in July 1979, protesting against the Russian trades unions' lack of interest in the case of Sharansky, and the Liverpool 35s held demonstrations at the Trades Union Congress (TUC) conference in Blackpool in September of that year. At the TUC conference in Brighton the following year, the local group of the 35s held a demonstration and circulated a petition in support of the striking farmers of Ilyinka, a small collective farm, consisting of Jewish members, mostly related to each other, who wished to emigrate to Israel. Over eight hundred signatures were recorded.

During the period 1978-80, the 35s attended nine of these annual conferences. These three years are a typical sample of the eighteen or so years of intense lobbying of the Trade Unions. The Women's Labour groups were particular targets as the Women's Campaign for Soviet Jewry hoped to gain sympathy and practical support from their sisters. For years they campaigned on behalf of Ida Nudel. They sought support at their conference in Folkestone in 1979 and at the Women's Labour Conference in Felixstowe in June 1979. The Birmingham 35s enlisted the support of the Women's Labour Conference at Malvern in May 1980, as a result of which the conference agreed to submit a resolution for Ida at the forthcoming International Women's Conference at Copenhagen.

Lobbying and demonstrating at a four-day conference demanded very precise and detailed organisation and involved the members in a sophisticated balancing act between the clamorous claims of families, homes and jobs on one hand, and the campaigning activities on the other. In addition, the annual Trade Union (and political party) conferences often coincided with the dates of the Jewish New Year, presenting an almost insoluble logistical problem. But they were always there.

The conference work, with all its excitement and stimulus, was only a small facet of the involvement with the Unions. An examination of the files of the 35s reveals correspondence with every Trade Union over a period of fourteen years, attesting to the painstaking work of Ros Gemal. She and her co-workers never missed an opportunity to pair an appropriate Trade Union with a refusenik. Ros recalls:

> One of our most important achievements was to have articles printed in the Unions' journals. The rank and file members knew virtually nothing about what was happening in Russia and they found it very hard to believe what we told them. I said to those who wouldn't, 'believe me, you find out about it. You don't have to take my word for it'. We were absolutely scrupulous; we checked and double checked all our facts and screened out anything we were doubtful about. We were giving out hundreds of biographies (of refuseniks) and some of the Trade Union members were just looking for inaccuracies. We had to work on them all the time. It was one thing for a resolution to be passed at a conference; it was another for it to be acted upon".

In July 1986, Alan Sapper, General Secretary of the ACTT[80] was asked to enlist his Union's help for Alexei Magarik, a young musician who had never been permitted to practise his profession. Sapper agreed to institute an appeal on his behalf. Was it just a coincidence that Magarik's sentence was halved and his treatment improved, following Sapper's visit to the USSR in November of that year where he met Russian Trade Union officials in his capacity as President of the International Federation of Audio and Visual Workers?

In August 1987, APEX, AUEW, TGWU[81], NALGO and EETPU were all asked to adopt refusenik families. Among those that responded was NALGO; they adopted the Yelistratov family who had been "in refusal" for sixteen years. As was the norm at that time, they received no replies to their many letters. Eventually they were able to send in a letter by hand and were thrilled when Viktor

---

[80] ACTT – Association of Cinematograph and Television Technicians.
[81] TGWU – Transport and General Workers Union.

Yelistratov managed to communicate with the Union by phoning them from a public callbox[82].

The women were up to their ingenious tricks again in June 1979, as shown in the following report published in *The Jewish Chronicle*:

> RED FACES AT EXHIBITION. Some Soviet officials at the USSR National Exhibition at Earls Court are in trouble this week – for instead of giving out the official exhibition leaflet they spent two days giving out nearly identical ones prepared by the Women's Campaign for Soviet Jewry, the 35s.
>
> Members of the 35s obtained the official leaflet, whose cover proclaims 'The USSR National Exhibition' and carefully doctored it to read 'The real truth not on show at the USSR National Exhibition'.
>
> The 35s leaflet, which they had specially printed, is a typographical copy of the real thing, with the text altered to refer to Soviet Jews. It was placed next to the official leaflets and subsequently given out to visitors to the exhibition by the Soviet officials themselves.
>
> Two days later, when they realised what they were distributing, the embarrassed and furious officials blocked a youth demonstration and confiscated leaflets being brought into Earls Court.

Ros Gemal remembers the occasion:

> We had contact with a Trade Union official and he gave us an advance copy of the leaflet... When they discovered the 'exchange', they threw them in the waste-bin in disgust, but a member of the security staff rescued them and gave them back to the girls who carried on distributing them outside.

There have always been close links between the 35s and the Church groups, resulting in an appreciable non-Jewish effort on behalf

---

[82] Use of a private phone could be too dangerous as the phones of many refuseniks were 'bugged'.

of the refuseniks. As early as 1974 Christian clergymen of different denominations joined the South London 35s "prisoners' lunch" in Croydon.

Manifestations of solidarity were shown in a variety of ways ranging from an exhibition in front of St Giles Cathedral during the 1980 Edinburgh Festival, to a variety of supportive activities from Liverpool clergy of different denominations. When Sylvia Lukeman and Debby Lazarus had their book of poems *With a View to Freedom*[83] printed, great interest was shown by the local Catholic newspapers, which resulted in radio interviews with Canon Gordon Gates and Father Graeme Kidd. Sylvia and Debby were also invited to give talks to Catholic church and school groups. Both the Archbishop of Liverpool and Bishop David Sheppard gave constant support to the campaign.

Sylvia Lukeman:

> Bishop David Sheppard phoned me on the eve of the Day of Atonement (the most important and solemn occasion in the Jewish religious calendar). He asked if he could demonstrate outside the Liverpool Philharmonic Hall where there was to be a troupe of dancers from Odessa. He knew that we would be at the Synagogue service that evening and were, therefore, unable to demonstrate ourselves.

In Brighton, in the early 1970s, a friendly "showbiz" vicar presented dramatised case-histories of Sharansky, Leonid Kerbel, Ida Nudel and Sylva Zalmanson, at St John's Church, Hove, in collaboration with Dame Flora Robson and Alan Melville. The evening also included a few minutes of silent prayer.

The 35s also instituted campaigns for non-Jewish Soviet dissidents, as Cecily Woolf explained:

> We tried to help non-Jews in the USSR wherever appropriate and included campaigns for such figures as Pastor Vins (imprisoned for his Baptist beliefs),

---

[83] Published by Sylvia Lukeman and Debby Lazarus; c/o Harold House, Dunbabin Road, Liverpool 15. Sylvia Lukeman has had many poems published, some of which feature the plight of Soviet Jewry. She has donated the proceeds to the 35s and to other charities.

Dr Anatoly Koryugin[84], and Veronica Rostropovich (sister of the famous cellist), for whom we staged a demonstration outside the hall where a concert was being given by the Moscow Philharmonic Orchestra in May 1981. We presented the conductor, Dmitri Kataenko, with flowers on her behalf and on behalf of Sharansky as well.

In January 1981, the 35s held a thirty-six-minute evening vigil outside the Soviet Embassy in London for Raoul Wallenberg, the Swedish diplomat who had been missing for thirty-six years after trying to help Jews to escape from Hungary.

The list of demonstrations (see Appendix 2) shows that virtually every provincial and London group reported co-operation from their Christian friends. Liaison with the Churches was started early in the history of the 35s by Delysia Jason, and was continued from the mid 1970s by Margaret Rigal who, in 1975, wrote to twenty-one bishops canvassing their support for the 35s campaign. Responses ranged from the very sympathetic to the very indifferent, but by far the greater number replied positively, as exemplified by the Bishop of Crediton's response in the Anatoly Sharansky campaign of March 1979. He wrote to the Soviet Minister of Justice asking that Sharansky's family be allowed to organise his appeal. The Sharansky campaign was also supported in June 1981 by Cardinal Hume who urged his dioceses to give it their support. In June 1982 he wrote to the director of Chistopol Prison expressing his concern about Sharansky's condition and asked "that compassion be shown to him in his present condition of health". During the visit of Avital Sharansky to London in May 1983, the Cardinal received her, together with Margaret Rigal and Rita Eker.

Margaret Rigal remembers the valuable work done by Elsie Lucas whom she described as "an incredible women; one of the best of the good Christians I've ever met". Elsie is a supporter of Keston College Edinburgh, which, amongst other things, conducts research into the victimisation of Christians on account of their faith. She worked closely with the 35s for many years, helping to right religious persecution in the Soviet Union. Annually she took an exhibition

---

[84] The campaign for Dr Koryugin was in collaboration with The Campaign Against Psychiatric Abuse.

around the country, featuring prisoners and prison camps in the Soviet Union, and she always made a point of distributing postcards for visitors to send to the prisoners.

A heart-warming response was reported when the 35s appealed to the Churches to remember the Prisoners of Zion in their 1986 Christmas services.

Joyce Simson recalled:

> When the Patriarch of Moscow visited England we were telephoned by the Canon of Liverpool Cathedral, the Reverend Paul Oestreicher, who pleaded with us not to demonstrate. He wanted to show 'our' unity with the Russian Church. We just couldn't agree to this, and in fact when we demonstrated outside St Paul's Cathedral we were joined by a number of Christian groups whose members (e.g. Baptists) were also suffering under the Soviet rule.

An Interfaith committee was reactivated in 1987. Although this came under the umbrella of the National Council for Soviet Jewry, Margaret Rigal, who was the convenor, utilised the information, expertise and services of the 35s, making it, to all intents and purposes another affiliate of the 35s. The Bishop of Oxford, the Right Reverend Richard Harries was the Chairman, and after months of discussion, it was agreed to call the group "The Interfaith Committee for the Rights of Jews, Christians and Muslims in the USSR". The aims of the committee were to show[85]:

1. That much could be achieved through support and solidarity by and for each community,
2. The whole area of Human Rights in the USSR was neglected,
3. The value of the committee by demonstrating that different groups of names within British society were involved and interested in the fate of Soviet Jewry,
4. The importance of developing professional education programmes on issues of religious rights in the USSR and interfaith discussions,
5. The committee recognised that the right to emigrate was one issue in the attempt to lead what people in this country would call a normal religious life.

---

[85] From the Minutes of the Interfaith Committee, 3 December 1987.

The committee promoted a weekend of prayer for religious believers in the Soviet Union at the end of May 1988.

A Prayer for Religious Freedom in the Soviet Union, composed by Rabbi Zalman Kossowsky, was recited in many churches, mosques and synagogues.

On United Nations Day, 24 October 1988, the committee organised a 'Unique Event'. "For the first time ever leaders of the three faiths will work together on behalf of their afflicted members". The meeting included an up-to-date appraisal of the present situation for adherents of the three faiths by experts on the subject: the Rev. Michael Bordeaux, Dr John Anderson, and Michael Sherbourne[86].

At this meeting concern was expressed about the one hundred and sixty-eight known "religious" prisoners still in Soviet incarceration.

Rose Ellis, who worked together with Margaret Rigal, observed that:

> ...the main response of many of the churches seemed to be 'we shall pray for you'. Some did include the subject in their sermons which meant that many more people became aware of the problem. It was very moving because we began to receive donations from these people, often people who were not very well off. I particularly remember a postman who sent us money on a regular basis. Some of the churches 'adopted' refuseniks. It did show a caring attitude and an awareness – the dawn of an understanding of what was happening there. Some of them went on demonstrations with us and we had groups like the David House Fellowship in Wales, who sent us van-loads of clothes for distribution. All in all, it was a very mixed response. I have to say that with the exception of some nuns, the Catholic Church was less forthcoming than the Church of England.

> When missionary work started after the inception of 'glasnost' we were very wary of giving out lists of names of people who were in need of help. To be

---

[86] From a Press Release, October 1988.

honest we were suspicious of the motives of some of the groups.

Throughout the years, many non-Jews have worked alongside and within the 35s. Manchester and Ilford are two of the many groups which numbered non-Jews amongst their members. In March 1979, a non-Jewish member of the Manchester 35s approached the Lord Mayor, Councillor Trevor Thomas, to ask him to plead on behalf of Boris Kalandarev during his forthcoming visit to Leningrad. She said that she felt obliged to do this as "she couldn't live with the memory of the Holocaust".

Two stalwart workers, Trish Hosking and Dorothy Baker of the Millmead Baptist Church, have, up to June 1995, made twelve trips to Russia where they visit their co-religionists and distribute medicines, clothes and Bibles to their Christian and Jewish friends. After having previously driven a four-and-a-half-tonne truck to Romania, manhandling the dozen or so suitcases which they always take is child's play to them.

In Gwent, Meg Thomas worked tirelessly to help the Shlyater family through the One-to-One scheme. Vadim Shlyater, who was suffering from cancer, yearned to join his wife and son in Israel. He was finally given permission to leave. The whole family felt that Meg's help and encouragement gave them strength to carry on in the face of continued adversity.

A number of Christian groups work through the 35s, giving aid to refuseniks. One such group, the International Christian Embassy of Jerusalem, organised coaches to transport Jews from Kiev to Warsaw, to enable them to reach Israel more quickly. In one of their newsletters it was stated that: "the flow of Jews coming out of the Soviet Union needs to be accelerated. At its present rate it will take six years before all the remaining two million Jews are free".

Many of the Christian groups are driven by missionary zeal and they pray and work for the ingathering of "the Children of Israel", which to them anticipates the return of the Messiah. Their publications contain many quotations from the Bible and the New Testament, to substantiate their work. It cannot be denied that some of the groups have helped in a positive manner by donating money, visiting refuseniks and 'adopting' families. But when one reads of the activities of groups such as 'Jews for Jesus' who are operating in Israel amongst newly-arrived Soviet immigrants, it is apparent that not all of their help is entirely altruistic. In an article in the *Jerusalem Post* of 6 September 1991, A. R. Nellhams wrote that "...this organisation is very active in Israel amongst Soviet immigrants. The message tailored to Jews is that a Jew who accepts Jesus does not have to become a Christian – he becomes a 'completed Jew'.

This contention is contrary to Jewish doctrine and is of concern to the 35s inasmuch as they are regularly approached for lists of refuseniks who need help. Most Soviet Jews are very vulnerable to such approaches as, after seventy years of religious suppression, they are ignorant about the tenets of their faith. To them, the fact that Jesus was a Jew is particularly confusing.

However, loyal friends such as Lord Soper and members of the General Assembly of the United Reformed Church help to counteract the negative influences of the missionary groups. In May 1979 this Assembly passed several resolutions sympathetic to Soviet Jewry and the work of the 35s.

The following incident probably reflects the more typical attitude of concerned Christians. During a demonstration in support of Sharansky in March 1979, attended by Newcastle clergy, including the Provost of St Nicholas Cathedral and local Rabbis, passers-by despatched two hundred postcards. One of these cards carried the following message:

> Dear Anatoly, it is difficult to find words that could be of comfort to you. All I can say is that today I was stopped in the street by an organisation that does care for people like you and is working for your release. More importantly God is with you and caring, whatever happens. I am praying for you. I hope it helps.

This expression of feeling conveys the attitude of most of the non-Jews who have worked for, and continue to work for, Soviet Jews.

The revival of the Medical Committee for Soviet Jewry, which operates under the umbrella of the 35s, was a result of the concern felt by Rita Eker and Valli Kokotek following their visit to Moscow in 1982. They discovered that the six refuseniks – Benjamin Bogomolny, Lev Goldfarb, Igor Uspensky, Vladimir Kiplis and the Katchachurions, father and son, who were briefing them on the current situation, were all suffering from stomach ulcers and that medicines were difficult to obtain.

The 35s called and still call upon the expertise of general practitioners, consultants in every field of medicine, and pharmacists from all parts of the country. Previously the Scientists for the Release of Soviet Jewry committee had dealt with medical problems, but it is only since the time of the 'glasnost' and 'perestroika' policies of the early 1990s that the appalling deterioration of the health of the citizens of the Former Soviet Union and the inadequacy of medical technology, facilities and supplies have been revealed.

The help given covers a wide spectrum, from consultants freely offering expert advice, to doctors travelling to give on-the-spot assistance; from the sending of desperately needed drugs right through to the financing of surgical operations in this country, as these do not come under the provision of the National Health Service and are performed privately at the cost of many thousands of pounds. One of Rita Eker's 'dogsbody' functions is to beg/cajole/plead in the hopes of raising sufficient money for yet another life saving operation. On occasions the patient is already undergoing treatment in this country before sufficient funds have been raised. If the patient's condition warrants it Rita ensures that they receive the necessary treatment as speedily as possible; somehow the money is obtained. In this exercise she has been generously helped by Jarvis Astaire, past President of the Variety Club International, and the members of this committee and by the equally generous support of many surgeons and their colleagues who have donated their services. The expertise of Michael Sherbourne is again called upon for the translation of case notes as, with the aid of a Russian/English medical dictionary, he struggles with a technical terminology not normally within the range of his vocabulary. Pharmacists, too, have very generously supplied medical and allied commodities enabling the 35s to send, for example, one hundred kilos of medical supplies to Moscow in December 1992. In February 1993 a further three hundred kilos of medical supplies was sent to Armenia with the co-operation of Baroness Cox. They also worked together with Christian aid groups to send a consignment of medical supplies to Russia.

The committee deals not only with the many seriously ill patients who are seeking help. It also fought for their Soviet colleagues on Human Rights issues. As a result of their representations, in 1983 the

World Psychiatric Association threatened to expel the USSR All-Union Society of Neuropathologists; this was pre-empted by their resignation 'en-bloc'.

In March 1986 the Committee sent a petition to the Foreign Secretary, Sir Geoffrey Howe, prior to the Conference on Security and Co-operation in Europe, to be held in Berne the following month, pointing out that contrary to Basket 3, Section 2 of the Helsinki Final Act

> ...the USSR has failed consistently to permit members of the medical profession... to attend conferences and to travel abroad...

It also condemned:
1. The refusal of permission to emigrate
2. Postal interference
3. Denial of work
4. Denial of permission to attend conferences.

Letters of appeal from Dr Iosif Irlin were included, giving evidence of the difficulties which he experienced in continuing his work and his desire to emigrate.

This petition was signed by fifty-three eminent members of the medical profession in this country, of whom there were six Nobel Laureates, five Presidents of Royal Colleges, and twenty-two Professors.

The Medical Committee prompted a report in *The Lancet* of 18 March 1989[87] which gave details of the persecution and victimisation of Dr David Blatnoi, George Samoilovich and Mikhail Kogan. The newsletter of 24 March 1989 drew attention to this and commented:

"Let us hope that the Soviet Minister of Health will take heed of the plight of these victims when he learns of the publicity".

For many years Liz Phillips[88], an early 35er, acted as the intermediary between the cases in the Former Soviet Union and the Medical Committee. As well as obtaining medicines to send to the Former Soviet Union, finding families to care for patients whilst

---

[87] "USSR. Abuses of Legal and Medical Systems". Diana Brahams, *The Lancet*, 18 March 1989, p608.

[88] In 1992 Liz Phillips emigrated to Israel where she continues to work for the 35s and where she acts as Rita Eker's right hand.

undergoing treatment here, and liaising with the hospitals and doctors involved in the cases, she attended to the innumerable details which could spell the difference between life and death for these ailing people. This work is now continued by Evelyn Nohr, in addition to her other 35s commitments. Liz Phillips recalls:

> At first we used to do whatever we could to help sick people over there, sending advice, medicines, etc. Then gradually we began to 'take on' cases, sending doctors over and financing the patients for consultations and operations over here. I remember every person who came over. Each one was memorable but I have to say that George Samoilovich was exceptional. He is a very special person.

During the six months of his treatment for lymphoma at the Royal Marsden Hospital George lived with Liz and her family. She nursed him through the debilitating effects of his chemotherapy, through his weeks of nausea, despondency, lethargy and, at times, despair – encouraging him and nurturing him.

A number of the 35ers have given unstinted hospitality to the families of patients whilst they were here for operations or treatments. This often extended over a period of months. Not every case was fraught with problems or crisis. In 1990, three year old Kyril Sherman arrived at the home of his hosts as a typical "hole-in-the-heart" sufferer; blue lips and finger nails, unable to run, listless, breathless and lacking the sparkle of normal childhood. Four days after his operation he was walking around the ward – four days later he was out of hospital and four days after that he and his mother were on the plane returning to Moscow. The Russian doctors were perfectly capable of performing what is today a standard operation but they lacked the intensive care and nursing facilities which Kyril was able to enjoy at Harefield Hospital where his operation was performed by the renowned Professor Sir Magdi Yacoub.

Letters arrive at the office from all parts of the Former Soviet Union pleading for help. These are passed on to the Medical Committee for assessment. Sadly, it is not always possible to help because of financial restraints or a poor medical prognosis. On occasions patients have arrived in London against 'doctor's orders'. Such is the parlous state of their medical services that some people are understandably hypochondriacs and not all their complaints have a physiological origin. There have also been those who came over for surgery and then attempted to remain in this country and thus outstayed their welcome. It is hard to say 'no' to these cries for aid; it is harder still to face failure. There have been two deaths among patients for whom the 35s and others have worked, and a third patient, after initial improvement, now no longer responds to treatment.

The 35s and the Medical Committee were part of a worldwide race to find a compatible bone marrow donor for Katya Macharet, who died from leukaemia before one could be found. However, a positive aspect of this was that a great many names were added to the bone marrow register of the Anthony Nolan Research Centre.

Closer to the heart of the 35s, because they had so much personal contact with him, was fourteen month old Grisha Dudinov who died after his second open-heart operation at the Great Ormond Street Hospital for Sick Children.

Little Grisha lies buried in a London Jewish cemetery[89].

The following are some examples of the work of the Medical Committee (in association with the 35s) since its revival:

1983   Visit to Leningrad by Dr Stanley and Mrs Eileen Freedman to ascertain assistance needed by refusenik doctors. Visited Dr Arkady Chepovetsky who requested a stethoscope and a book on pharmacology. Dr Freedman attempted to bring out an abstract of Dr Chepovetsky's thesis in order to help him, but this was confiscated at the Customs on departure.

Visited Dr Anatoly Kodner who, after applying for an exit visa, had been dismissed from a senior research post.

1987   Visit by American physicians who liaised with the Medical Committee in London. Medicines were delivered to twenty-three refuseniks in four cities. They detailed medicines requested for future visits. An eye specialist evaluated the condition of twenty-seven people with eye problems, and asked the London Committee to find out about

---

[89] His gravestone was paid for by Barry and Barbara Harris.

the medical condition of other refuseniks whom they had been unable to visit.

1988   Up-to-date report obtained by a visitor of the state of health of Vladimir Kislik who is suffering from cirrhosis of the liver. Kislik feels sure that this was caused by nuclear contamination when he worked in the Urals as a geologist and was subject to large doses of radiation.

1988   Ongoing campaign on behalf of Semyon Gluzman

1990   Advice sent regarding a forty-eight-year-old woman who needed a liver transplant, but they were unable to help her.

1991   Help requested from a father whose daughter, in her twenties, was suffering from multiple sclerosis.

1991   Ongoing campaign to raise money for heart-patient Grisha Dudinov. (Two operations were necessary but he did not survive the second one).

1991   Campaign to raise funds for surgery on another patient with heart disease.

1991–3 Together with Belmont Soviet Jewry Campaign helped to raise funds for a series of orthopaedic operations on a young man.

1992   Advice sought and given about a rare condition, Waldenstrom's Disease, but the patient died before sufficient funds could be raised for treatment.

1992   Plea for advice and medication by the father of a fourteen-year-old girl suffering from alopecia (baldness).

1993   Money raised for a heart operation on a two-year-old child. This was successful but a second operation will be required in a few years time.

For many years the 35s collaborated with the Lawyers Committee which had been formed to support defendants in the USSR who were being subjected to fabricated charges and perverted trials. The lawyers' approach was of a more precise nature than the general giving of sympathy and support; they needed to obtain concrete evidence and information in order to establish the legal grounds on which they could act on behalf of the refuseniks. The 35s were instrumental in helping them to obtain this evidence, especially in the cases of the prisoners. This enabled the Committee to approach appropriate members of the judiciary on behalf of the falsely accused. The 35s arranged for tourists and visitors to the USSR to meet refuseniks and to transmit messages, food and material comforts to the prisoners. This was of inestimable help to the lawyers, especially during the 1970s and 1980s, when the persecution was particularly active.

Jonathan Arkush, the secretary of the Lawyers Committee commented: "When we needed that sort of help, Rita Eker was my first port of call. The chain of travellers organised by the 35s was magnificent. I cannot speak too highly of the complete tirelessness and dedication of these women".

142

Chapter Nine
The 35s Network

Jewish communal work in the provinces is more demanding than in London as the same willing heads have to wear a variety of (communal) hats. A number of communities are isolated from mainstream Jewry and lack the stimulus flowing from London's constant stream of visitors and of access to "people in high places". Without the regular input of new faces, ideas and contacts, the dedication shown by the provincial groups is all the more to be admired.

In cities with a large Jewish population the 35s group will comprise a core of dedicated women, tackling the job in a highly professional manner on a virtually full-time basis, backed up by a large number of other volunteers who will support a campaign by turning out for demonstrations or by writing many hundreds of postcards.

Contrast this with the West Sussex 35s group as described in a newsletter of July 1979:

- "A small isolated group who achieve results out of all proportion to their size".
- "One of the members visited Moscow and met refuseniks including their 'adopted' Lev Roitburd from Odessa".
- "A letter of protest and a bouquet of flowers was handed to the Soviet Music Ensemble in Crawley".
- "A few members participated in London and Brighton demonstrations".
- "Two members have given talks to women's clubs and Church groups".

- "The group concentrates on writing to Alexsei Murzhenko, Lev Roitburd and Vaisman, and from time to time letters are also written to Begun, Shneerman, Slepak, Gluzman and Nudel".

Somewhere between sparsely resourced West Sussex and the abundant reserves of cities such as London and Manchester lie a host of 35s groups and other organisations, affiliates – and the magnificent men. Men who babysat and cooked, carried and chauffeured, men who supported demonstrations and painted banners, men who held the fort at home and who supported their partners up to the hilt. The 35s are unanimous in their testimony that without the support of their menfolk their task would have been infinitely more difficult.

In addition to Michael Sherbourne, a number of men have worked in the office from time to time. And it is the men who have provided the considerable financial support which has been the mainstay of the Women's Campaign for Soviet Jewry.

The previously referred to contributions of journalists, doctors, trades unionists, churchmen, etc. have all added considerably to the strength of the 35s campaign.

A special role has been played by the historian (now Sir) Martin Gilbert. In many of his publications he has shown himself to be a tireless campaigner for Soviet Jewry and he has always been willing to assist the 35s when called upon. In October 1983 he formally launched the foundation of the Israeli branch of the 35s at the home of former Israeli Foreign Minister, Abba Eban, and in May 1986 he acted as the representative of the 35s in New York on the occasion of Solidarity Sunday, on behalf of Anatoly Sharansky. In their turn the 35s supplied biographies and other information to assist Gilbert in his regular newspaper columns on Soviet Jewry which appeared between 1983 and 1989. In December 1988 prior to his departure as a Delegate at the United Nations Human Rights Commission, he wrote to the 35s "...I will, of course, speak as forcefully as I can, particularly on behalf of our remaining refusenik friends... and I just want you to know that I will not let you (or them) down".

Over the years new groups have formed whilst others have disbanded, but since the early days there have always been about forty groups active in London, the provinces and abroad. Not all the groups were directly under the umbrella of the 35s but they all worked in close contact with it. There were also many other organisations working for a similar purpose, such as synagogues, youth groups, students, Amnesty International, the Association of Jewish Ex-Servicemen and B'nai B'rith[90] who cooperate with the 35s on occasions. It is sometimes difficult to draw the line between who is a 35er and who is not as there is no formalised membership, no official register and no defined hierarchical structure. Whilst there is no 35s group in Brighton and Hove or in Elstree, the 35s London office has been a constant source of information and assistance to them and other similar bodies. The work in Brighton and Hove is done by the Brighton and Hove Soviet Jewry Group which "incorporates the Women's Campaign for Soviet Jewry". Elstree was originally with the 35s but later became part of the Elstree and Radlett United Synagogue Soviet Jewry Committee which still works very closely with the 35s.

The 35s group is always happy to share their information and 'know-how' with anyone who is working towards the same goals as themselves, groups such as the United Synagogue Soviet Jewry Campaign, which now is mainly concerned with 'twinning' emergent Jewish communities in the CIS and the Baltic States, and with Jewish education in those communities. This organisation, which started in 1988, is run by Cynthia Jacobs and Ruth Urban[91]. A number of the synagogues which are 'twinned' with communities in the Former Soviet Union run their own campaigns. 'Visov', a young activist group in Chigwell, is typical of those which have worked together with the 35s. 'Exodus', the Soviet Jewry group of the Reform Synagogues and the Soviet Jewry committee of the Progressive Synagogues work towards similar ends. 'Prospekt', another young activist group, formed in the early 1980s and based in Chigwell, devoted itself mainly to fund-raising and had, since its inception, sent about ten thousand pounds to help Soviet Jewry.

There has always been very close contact with the students, mainly through their umbrella organisation, the Students' and Academics' Committee for Soviet Jewry. The 35s financed trips for a large number of student visitors to the USSR, who have, for many years, been amongst the most active participants in the campaign. "Refusenik" is an organisation mainly consisting of former students who wanted to continue to work for Soviet Jewry and to keep a

---

[90] A Jewish Fraternal Organisation. Literally 'Sons of the Covenant'
[91] Ruth Urban – a founder member of the 35s.

watching brief on Human Rights. From time to time they produce an excellent booklet, aptly entitled 'Watch'.

There are also many individuals throughout the British Isles who align themselves with the cause and work through the 35s, writing to refuseniks, sending them parcels and supporting the One-to-One scheme.

The expansion of the 35s into the provinces was largely due to the efforts of the Janners[92], who, from late 1971 onwards, spent several months visiting Jewish communities all over the British Isles. Myra recalls:

> We worked as a team. Greville would speak to the general community to try to interest them in the Soviet Jewry situation. I would address a meeting of women, perhaps in a private house, and pick out someone whom I felt would be a leader and encourage her to start a group. Zena Clayton[93] would then follow this up and that's how the national network of the 35s was created. We gave them our assurances that they would be backed up one hundred per cent by the office in London. We suggested that if London ran a campaign or held a demonstration, then Birmingham, Glasgow, etc. should do the same thing at the same time. In that way we could create a national impact.

The choice of Manchester and Ilford as examples of a provincial and a suburban campaign in no way denigrates the comparable and dogged hard work of any of the other groups. With a present total of about thirty groups it is impossible to do justice to them all. A similar story could be told about any one of them, but Manchester and Ilford, as well as being similar to, are just slightly different from the others as will be seen.

MANCHESTER – A PROVINCIAL CAMPAIGN

Manchester was different in that the city has a Friendship Agreement with St Petersburg[94], one of the most virulently

---

[92] The Hon. Greville Janner, MP, QC and his wife, Myra.
[93] Zena Clayton, a founder member of the 35s.
[94] Formerly Leningrad.

anti-Semitic cities of the former Soviet Union. There was a cultural, trade and commercial relationship between the two cities well before the inception of the 35s. Sylvia Sheff, the group's founder Chairman and current President, explained that:

> early on, outside of the 35s general campaign, we seized on the Friendship Agreement as being an excellent way of focusing attention on the problems of Soviet Jewry. We were very angry that delegates from Leningrad were coming here and being hosted by Manchester City Council on ratepayers' money. But Manchester had a left-wing Council and didn't take kindly to criticism of the Soviet Union. Initially our overtures were not met with much sympathy; Manchester not only seemed to be oblivious to our concerns, but was at times hostile to our approaches as they were primarily concerned with not upsetting the fragile agreement between the two cities and for years we had virtually no co-operation from the Town Hall. I used to say to them, 'The City Council should be assisting us in fighting on behalf of Human Rights instead of seeking to strengthen ties with a regime that practised such abuses'.
>
> Even Manchester's Jewish Lord Mayors, with one exception, were less than helpful; they saw their role as being Lord Mayor first. We tried to show them that it was not a Jewish issue but an issue of Human Rights. We found that we could get the message over more easily to the non-Jewish Mayors rather than to the Jewish ones. In fact, our fight was on two fronts, the Russians from without and the local Council from within, made even more difficult initially by the lack of co-operation from the British Jewish Establishment.

The Manchester Council for Soviet Jewry was often at loggerheads with the 35s over their method of campaigning, as described by Sylvia Sheff:

> We felt that the best way of getting our message across was to make our point publicly and defiantly. We decided that we would focus our campaign on Leningrad

refuseniks and Prisoners of Zion. We had a very heavy load to carry as we had to deal with the Leningrad so-called 'hijack' trials. At the same time, we tried to cultivate the Manchester/Leningrad relationship to open up a dialogue to discuss the issue.

But this offensive met with hostility from the Council Chamber of the Town Hall. She continued:

We knew we were getting through to them because we were called to the Town Hall and told that the Soviets would not come to Manchester on any more official visits unless the 35s stopped their activities. This was after the visit of the Mayor of Leningrad as Guest of Honour to the Manchester Festival. We followed him and his entourage wherever they went, flourishing our banners and handing out our leaflets. In the end they were taking avoiding action, going into the Town Hall on official visits by the back entrance – things like that. We had become *'personae non grata'*; they said they had taken the last insult they were prepared to take.

They were told by the Council that they, the 35s, were damaging the city and its industrial life and they asked her to promise that the 35s wouldn't demonstrate any more. She recalls:

I said, "This is a free and democratic country and these are spontaneous expressions of Jewish abhorrence of the suppression of Human Rights. I can't guarantee that they will be called off. I can give you a list of twenty activists in (Soviet) jails and Leningrad refuseniks. Let them give us a guarantee to free them..." In fact, four visits from Leningrad were cancelled but eventually they agreed to resume the relationship and another visit was arranged. Right up to the last minute the Council was begging us to call off our demonstration, but it took place. Shortly after that the Russians did release ten of the people on our list and gave them permission to emigrate.

By contrast not only was there no opposition towards them from the police, but they were actively sympathetic, knowing that they

Medallion made for Sylva Zalmanson campaign and worn by 35ers on demonstrations etc. Also presented to personalities who helped with the campaign.

Inscription on Medallion reads: Sylva Zalmanson (front), USSR Jewish Prisoner of Conscience (reverse).

could rely on the 35s to hold lawful and peaceful protests. Sylvia Sheff contrasted the 35s' behaviour to that of the Greenham Common women, who could be seen nightly on television being dragged away by the police.

Typical of their non-violent demonstrations was one held in the spring of 1973 during the visit of an eminent Judge of the Leningrad City Council, who was invited to sit with the presiding Judge during a session of the Manchester Crown Court.

> We were livid; you cannot allow a Russian Judge to sit in our Court when Jews were being thrown into prison for no other reason than that they wanted to go and live in Israel. There were thirty seats in the public gallery of the Court and we queued up and took them all. It did cross our minds – do thirty women dressed in black constitute a demonstration? We were wearing our Sylva Zalmanson medallions[95]. We raised our medallions and pointed them at the Russian Judge and stared at him. If he moved in his chair we followed him with our eyes; he just didn't know where to put himself. Thirty pairs of eyes fixed accusingly on him! The result was that in the recess he excused himself and left earlier than scheduled. The headlines in the local paper read: "Jewish women stare in protest".

On the occasion of visits by Russian artistes, the 35s placed notices in the Jewish newspapers asking the readers to stay away from the performances. It was a salutary method of expressing abhorrence of the abuses of Human Rights by the Soviet Union, and was an effective campaign as a large proportion of the local community heeded the requests.

The proximity of Blackpool, where many of the political party and TUC conferences were held, enabled the group to build up a good relationship with politicians and delegates of all parties, but especially with whichever party was currently in office. This was particularly so with the Conservative Party as they had been in office for a long period and also because Margaret Thatcher was so sympathetic to their

---

[95] As part of the Free Sylva Zalmanson Campaign the 35s issued a medallion inscribed 'Sylva Zalmanson' on one side and 'USSR Prisoner of Conscience' on the other.

150

aims. She gave a number of private interviews to Sylvia Sheff and when she lost office Sylvia wrote to her successor, John Major, hoping to continue the warm relationship. The result of this contact was a private meeting with the Foreign Minister, Douglas Hurd, at the Foreign Office in December 1992.

Despite the advent of 'glasnost' and 'perestroika', refuseniks and prisoners were still not free to leave the former Soviet Union, and anti-Semitism in St Petersburg) was more rife than ever. In February 1993 the group received a desperate appeal from the leader of the St Petersburg Jewish Association pleading for help as they were being unfairly evicted from their community centre, which consisted of a small rented room. The Manchester 35s responded immediately by bringing the matter to the attention of the authorities in Manchester and St Petersburg, and the decision was reversed.

In December 1992 Sylvia Sheff had a private meeting with the Foreign Secretary, Douglas Hurd, at the Foreign Office prior to his visit to Russia.

> I summarised what I saw as the current situation *vis-à-vis* anti-Semitism and the refuseniks. Douglas Hurd said that he found my arguments 'very convincing and utterly compelling' and asked what I thought the Government should be doing. I said that the British Government should put the refuseniks' Human Rights back on the agenda, nationally and internationally, as it was then chairing the European Parliament... I pointed out that the CIS wanted every form of help from us – we only want to see a democratic government upholding basic Human Rights and resolving the issue of the refuseniks once and for all. They have to pay the price of showing that they are actively working for Human Rights. The British Government can assist them but they have to deal with it. We should link our aid with Human Rights. Douglas Hurd promised that he would re-address the issue and give it high priority at all appropriate opportunities. He promised to explore every available channel to help the refuseniks.

As the years have gone by, the group has developed a very good relationship not only with the Manchester City Council but also with the St Petersburg City Council as well. They have now reached a position where, when a Russian visit is impending, the Manchester City Council automatically consults with them to arrange an official meeting with the delegation. On these occasions the 35s make sure that they (the Manchester Council) have up-to-date biographies of refuseniks. They are very proud of their biographies and claim that they are paradigms of what biographies should be. They are computerised and give the minutest details about each person, down to the name and telephone number of the director of the enterprise in which the refuseniks formerly worked. This enables the group to confront members of the St Petersburg City Council, who cannot then complain that they have insufficient information to look into the cases presented to them. The 35s can suggest that if St Petersburg wants to ratify a trade agreement with Manchester, it is in their interests to bring their influence to bear on the said director to stop blocking the visa application.

The co-operation between the Manchester 35s, the Manchester City Council, and the St Petersburg authorities was especially effective during visits made to St Petersburg by Sylvia Sheff and Linda Epstein, the treasurer of the group.

> The purpose of these visits was not only to take financial assistance, essential medicines and food items to the refuseniks and welfare groups, but also to interview as many refuseniks as possible in order to gather information both of a general and individual nature. Armed with extensive files we were able to argue their cases with great effect with the relevant authorities in St Petersburg, and to establish important personal relationships with the heads of departments there. It also gave us the opportunity to discuss the issue of anti-Semitism and ways of combating it. These meetings were backed by the Manchester City Council who initially assisted us in setting them up and who willingly supported a three way discussion between visits.

> But it wouldn't have happened unless we had pushed and pushed. The Manchester Council for Soviet Jewry said 'softly, softly', but we said 'push, push' loudly, publicly

and relentlessly. It is an exoneration of our policies in terms of how we conducted our campaign.

The group has been able to show the Manchester City Council that they must fight for Human Rights for Jews of the Former Soviet Union in accordance with the true tradition of the Manchester ethos. It is ironic that many of the 35s most emotional and effective meetings have taken place in that symbolic bastion of freedom – Manchester's Free Trade Hall. They are rightly proud of the close relationships built up with the Manchester City Council and with the St Petersburg City Council and of the personal relationship with Margaret Thatcher. They feel that over and above what they were able to do for the refuseniks and prisoners it was gratifying to know that they fought and did what was right at the time. History has now proved them to have been correct to have stood up against all their critics. "From day one we always said that we must meet force with force, the only language that the Russians understood is the 'Iron Fist'. Not until the last light goes out in the last Jewish home of the last Jewish person to be oppressed, do we give up".

Sylvia Sheff emphasised that none of this work could have been done without the solid support of her many colleagues, one of whom, founder member Betty Gouldman, was treasurer for over ten years and is still an active member.

In the 1995 New Year's Honours List, Sylvia Sheff was awarded the MBE for her many years of public service.

THE ILFORD-BASED FREEDOM FIGHTERS[96] – A SUBURBAN CAMPAIGN

The Essex campaign based in Ilford, is synonymous with the names of Dora and Sidney Gabrel, whose continuous dedication for over twenty five years has given the Ilford Campaign its distinctive character.

The Gabrels first became engaged in the fight for Soviet Jewry before the 35s was born; they were among the handful of individuals who foresaw the necessity for action by British Jews before this was belatedly recognised by the Establishment.

---

[96] A headline from the *Ilford Recorder*, 16 July 1981.

In 1969 they read an article in *The Daily Telegraph* about the unhappy situation of Georgi Minz, a Latvian refusenik architect from Riga. Sidney Gabrel, also an architect, felt a strong sense of personal commitment with this distant colleague. He wrote to other architects, his local Member of Parliament, church leaders and Latvian State officials in an effort to secure an exit visa for Minz. He and Dora campaigned for eighteen months and eventually their efforts bore fruit and Minz was given an exit visa and emigrated to Israel.

In the meantime, the fledgling 35s organisation, operating from its narrow north west London base, widened its scope and satellite groups were established in the suburbs and the provinces. Ilford became a substantial strand in the network. Dora and Sidney and their now diminishing band of colleagues work in close conjunction with the office, and their fertile brains have been responsible for many novel and successful ideas.

Five scrapbooks filled with press cuttings are the dry record of their campaigning years, but the column-inches are brought to life as Dora and Sidney recollect some of the exploits they devised in the hope of bringing the tragic situation of the refuseniks to local attention.

Dora recalls an episode when they hired a dove (to symbolise peace) from an Ilford pet shop at a cost of £5.

> We stood in the High Street asking for signatures to a petition which we were to take to the Soviet Embassy, when the dove escaped. We were frantic, rushing around chasing this blessed bird. Passers-by were joining in, and one of them, seeing us looking worried and upset and dressed in our customary black, asked sympathetically, "Have you lost someone, love?" – "Yes," we said, "a dove." It finally settled on a windowsill of the Town Hall and I managed to throw a coat over it. We did get to the Soviet Embassy eventually, together with the petition – and the dove.

At the height of the demonstration era, throughout the 70s and 80s, shoppers became accustomed to strange scenes on the streets of Ilford and its environs:- A table laid with the daily diet of a Potma prisoner containing six hundred calories per person; 35ers dressed in prison garb and shut inside a huge cage sewing gloves to focus attention on

Sylva Zalmanson's prison life. Again, dressed as prisoners they encouraged passers-by to send over twelve hundred postcards to their 'adopted' refuseniks. Attired in barristers' robes they stood outside the Ilford Crown Court to draw attention to the imprisonment of a Russian refusenik lawyer. In Southend, again in prison garb and chained together, they paraded in the High Street to emphasise the plight of forty Russian Jews held on fabricated charges in labour camps.

On one occasion Dora Gabrel dressed in the uniform of a waitress in order to deliver a letter to a visiting Russian official whilst he was attending a banquet.

No stunt was too outrageous for this group of mainly middle-aged, previously somewhat unremarkable, housewives.

They were accused of having CIA links by the local branch of the British Soviet Friendship Society. In truth their contacts were far less sinister yet infinitely more rewarding. The Gabrels recognised the value of the publicity that could be gained from liaison with local personalities and the press. They were tireless in their approaches to Members of Parliament, Bishops, local Churches and Synagogues, Councillors and the press. "If you don't keep up the pressure, you don't get anywhere" says Dora. "Because we were so responsible, we were respected by everyone".

The group has campaigned not only for the "famous ones" such as Sharansky, Nudel, Zalmanson, etc. but also for many "unknowns". In October 1976 it enlisted the support of the Fairlop Young Conservatives in an effort to free sixteen-year-old Dina Katzieva who was being held in a Soviet prison camp.

But most of the work of the group was far more pedestrian than that of the demonstrations. Over one thousand talks were given to schools and Church groups and many, many thousands of letters and postcards were written.

Dora Gabrel declared:

> The wonderful bunch of women who worked in our group over the years are too many to enumerate separately. They came out in full strength on every demonstration. They stayed in the group for many years until genuine circumstances such as ill health or bereavement forced them to quit. They were all superb.

The local Members of Parliament were always most co-operative, as shown by the following examples of their help. Human Rights, always on the agenda, was highlighted in June 1978 when MPs Arnold Shaw and Vivian Bendall joined a protest demonstration in Downing Street to coincide with a visit by Russian delegates. Both Bendall and another local MP, Tom Iremonger, also asked questions in the House regarding Prisoners of Conscience. In February 1979 Neil Thorne MP wrote to President Brezhnev on behalf of refusenik Emmanuel Smeliansky and in July 1980 Vivian Bendall and Neil Thorne were also active on behalf of the Rosenstein family who had fled from Moscow to Riga[97]. Sir John Biggs-Davison MP supported a 35s demonstration in Chigwell in January 1986, during the course of which he posted a card to prisoner Iosif Berenshtein.

A heartening feature of the Ilford campaign was the generous support by non-Jews. During the course of talks to Church groups, the 35s were frequently offered aid on both material and spiritual levels. "If I was short of people to go on a demonstration, I could always rally my non-Jewish friends," said Dora, "they never refused me".

The Ilford group have been particularly generous in their support of the Medical Committee of the 35s which provides aid to many acutely and chronically ill refuseniks. Throughout 1991 they took part in the Medical Committee's search[98] for a substitute bone marrow donor for eight-year-old Katya Macharet, who suffered from leukaemia. This project was supported by donations from local Church groups and from many individuals, and by the blessings of the Bishops of Chelmsford and Barking.

There was also support on a spiritual level. Prayers were said in local churches for Ida Nudel in September 1976, and in March 1977 a month of prayer was organised in support of Anatoly Sharansky.

In May 1975, Rene Kenley, a founder member of the group flew to Rome to appeal to the Pope for help in the fight for the release of Vladimir Lazarus.

After her release from prison, Sylva Zalmanson visited the Ilford group in 1975 to thank them personally for their efforts on her behalf.

---

[97] At the time of the "run-up" to the Moscow Olympic Games in 1980 the KGB were very active in arresting refuseniks and removing them from Moscow to minimise the possibility of their meeting visiting Westerners.

[98] Under the auspices of the Anthony Nolan Research Centre.

During her visit there was a symbolic burning of a huge pile of banners and leaflets which had been produced during the campaign. This took place in the front garden of 35er Audrey Cass and her husband, Frank. She was taken on a visit to Valentines Park, where she was shown the aptly-chosen weeping willow tree which had been planted in her name two years previously. This now mature tree, together with the one planted in 1985 to publicise the imprisonment of Iosif Berenshtein, are poignant living symbols of human sufferings under an inhuman regime.

A noteworthy feature of the Ilford contribution is the virtually one-woman postal campaign conducted by Gina Gerlis. At one time she was personally sending out up to ninety items of mail every week, and over a period of fourteen years she has posted over fourteen thousand postcards, birthday cards and letters. In addition she has arranged for twenty cards a week to be sent to prisoners and refuseniks by fellow members of the Wanstead and Woodford Liberal Synagogue. This congregation also had a stall outside a shop in Gants Hill and every Sunday, weather permitting, passers-by were encouraged to write a card. This resulted in an average yield of a further one hundred cards a week. Replies from Russia were very rare events. Gina Gerlis remembers receiving a mere fifty or so replies throughout the whole of her writing marathon.

Much faith and sense of purpose is required to pursue such activities in the face of silence – and rejection. Annually the group would send boxes of matzos[99] to Russia to enable refuseniks to celebrate the Passover, only to have them returned after several months, as a mass of crumbs. Only years later, when "their" refuseniks and ex-prisoners arrived in Israel, did the members of the Ilford 35s learn of the sustenance and hope that their efforts had afforded to the recipients[100]. Through the long, dark years of their refusal, the receipt of a message from the West, the knowledge that beyond the grim borders of the USSR people were fighting for them, was often the lifeline which saved them from depression and despair.

When Israel Zalmanson was liberated after serving an eight-year sentence of imprisonment, he visited the Ilford 35s to tell them "it was you who kept me alive".

---

[99] Matzos – unleavened bread, rather similar to water biscuits.

Perhaps even more praiseworthy were the efforts of the overseas groups. Detached from the umbilical cord of the London office, nevertheless they campaigned and demonstrated with an enthusiasm and ingenuity equal to that of the mother group. From nearby Luxembourg to distant New Zealand their efforts added substantially to the effectiveness of the overall work of the Women's Campaign for Soviet Jewry.

Brussels and Luxembourg had the added advantage of being centres of considerable international activity. For example, the Luxembourg 35s were able to take advantage of a meeting of the European Parliament in nearby Strasbourg to further their protest in May 1984.

The visit of a Russian Fisheries Minister to New Zealand was the opportunity for a 35s-style publicity stunt when they sent him a parcel of fish bearing the message, "Fishing Rights for the Soviet Union; Human Rights for Soviet Jews".

Three years after Ijo Rager had inspired the birth of the British 35s, his visit to Canada in 1975 led to the formation of a Toronto group. This was followed by the establishment of further groups in Montreal, Ottawa and Winnipeg. Details of the Canadian campaign can be found in Wendy Eisen's book. Affiliates in Australia, Italy, Switzerland, Holland and Denmark also added strength to the overseas campaign.

The 35s group in Israel was started by Doreen Gainsford in 1978. Little was achieved, however, until she revived it in 1985 when it was felt that the new immigrants from Russia were receiving insufficient support. To this end it was decided to help in the following ways:

- Assisting and informing immigrants who had been sent to hotels and other temporary accommodation.
- Recruiting volunteers to teach them Hebrew and English.
- Formation of the "Organisation of Russian Adoption Programme (ORAP) to encourage the "adoption" of new immigrants by overseas groups. This was targeted towards families with special needs, such as extra lessons, medical help, re-training, etc.

Much of this work is done through the "Keren Klita" and "One-to-One" organisations.

---

[100] This was the experience of all the 35s groups.

The value of the aid given by the Israeli 35s has been given official recognition by the conferring of the President's Award for Voluntary work for Soviet Immigrants on two of its members, Gladys Botwin of Haifa and Delysia Jason of Jerusalem.

Chapter Ten
The 35s and the Prisoners

Of all the functions of the 35s none was more urgent and fundamental than that of working for the prisoners. Sentenced on trumped-up charges, confined in harsh conditions and subjected to inhuman regimes, theirs was a situation warranting action of the utmost urgency. Whether for the victims of psychiatric abuse or for those suffering from malnutrition, beatings, and deprivation of the most basic necessities of life, the women lobbied and canvassed with an intensity born out of desperation. Perhaps the most blatant example of the abuse of Human Rights was the incarceration of mentally sound people in psychiatric hospitals. Psychiatric abuse in Russia was not new. The first recorded case of suppression of dissent by means of psychiatry occurred in 1836 when the philosopher, Pyotr Chaadayev, was labelled by Tsar Nicholas the First as suffering from 'derangement and insanity'. There were sporadic episodes until the Stalin era, when it became an established policy incorporated into the judicial system.

These illegal political repressions were a method of silencing dissenters without recourse to a major trial[101]. Far from being havens of care and cure, psychiatric hospitals became places where punishment was regularly meted out in the form of beatings, torture and the administration of mind-altering drugs. One of the most flagrant examples of this treatment was that of Semyon Gluzman, a psychiatrist who, after graduating from Kiev Medical Institute, declined the proffered position in a psychiatric hospital because mentally sound people were being kept there solely on account of their political views. From then on he was a marked man and after he

---

[101] From *Soviet Psychiatric Abuse* by Bloch and Redaway, Gollancz London 1984.

wrote a *Samizdat*[102] article criticising the political use of psychiatry, he was arrested and tried on a charge of "anti-Soviet agitation and propaganda", and in 1972 was sentenced to seven years strict-regime labour camp and three years exile. During those ten years he was harassed, beaten and confined for months on end in a special punishment cell.

At the end of 1980 he wrote[103] from exile:

> I work as a dispatcher in a Kolkhoz garage. There is no question of work in my speciality; all of us political exiles are forbidden to exercise their professions. Friends do not forget me; they help as they can. And letters from the West, even if they are rare, persuade me that evil and indifference do not completely reign in the world, that the prisoners of mental hospitals and camps are not forgotten.

Gluzman was the first known psychiatrist to denounce the barbarous practice of the use of psychiatry for political ends. He became a *cause célèbre* when psychiatrists worldwide took up his case, and in so doing opened a window on psychiatric abuse in the Soviet Union. He was listed as a political prisoner rather than a Prisoner of Conscience and was detained in a psychiatric hospital. The 35s conducted an intensive campaign on his behalf, involving doctors, Members of Parliament and lawyers, and succeeded in getting him reclassified in 1979. This campaign was of enormous importance to the issue of Human Rights.

Many of the 35s newsletters of the period record the personal elements, his suffering and his poor health. Newsletter No. 7 of 1978 reported: "...he is very depressed and is in desperate need of your support", and in Newsletter No. 15, two months later: "There is grave concern for his health. He has been recently moved to Camp 37 and is being held in solitary confinement in a punishment cell. Protest please to a) the Camp Commandant (address given) and b) the International Red Cross".[104]

---

[102] *SAMIZDAT* – underground circulated literature.
[103] In a letter to a friend.
[104] Unfortunately the International Red Cross were never able to help any of the Jewish Prisoners of Conscience.

SOUVENIR MENU

"BANQUET"

To celebrate the formation of the
All Party Committee for Soviet Jewry

at the

House of Commons, Room A

on

23 February, 1972

Presented by the 35's (Women's campaign for Soviet Jewry)

Prisoners' diet in USSR Labour Camp with 9 hours' hard labour

BREAKFAST	14 ozs. black bread (full days ration) 1 cup of hot water (no sugar allowed) 1 oz. herring
LUNCH	⅔rds cup of soup (cooked cabbage) ¼ medium size potato (no fat allowed)
DINNER	3½ - 5 ozs. potato (no fat allowed)

TOTAL CALORIES 1200. FOR HEALTH MAINTENANCE
UNDER PRISON CONDITIONS 2800 CALORIES REQUIRED

A part of the above diet was served at a "Banquet" in the House
of Commons. Professor John Yudkin, Emeritus Professor of
Nutrition, University of London commented:

"This diet will not sustain an inactive child
of three years old."

ARTICLE 123 OF THE SOVIET UNION'S CONSTITUTION
STATES: "ANY DIRECT OR INDIRECT RESTRICTION
OF THE RIGHTS OF CITIZENS ON ACCOUNT OF RACE
OR NATIONALITY ARE PUNISHABLE BY LAW."

BUT

THERE ARE 38 JEWISH PRISONERS OF
CONSCIENCE SUFFERING IN SOVIET JAILS
AND STRICT REGIME CAMPS BECAUSE THEY
WISH TO LIVE AS JEWS

Menu for 'Prisoners Luncheon' at the House of Commons, February
1982.

In Newsletter No. 77 of May 1979: "...he is due to be transferred via the notorious convict transport to Siberia on 11 May. Friends fear that his health suffered from two six-month periods of punishment and that he will not withstand the rigours of the train for criminals. An appeal has been issued by the Royal College of Psychiatrists and cables were sent to the Pope and to Mrs Rosalynn Carter[105], who was attending a conference on mental illness in Switzerland. Please protest to President Brezhnev and to the International Red Cross (address given)".

Evelyn Nohr met Dr Gluzman in Kiev in 1984, after his release. He told her that his "happiest" years were those spent in the Gulag[106]; there he knew who were his friends and who were his enemies.

A little known aspect of the Soviet prison system was the use of (slave) labour camps to produce goods for export. Articles such as cuckoo clocks, electric irons, binoculars, matches, and steering wheels for Lada cars were made by political prisoners who not only received no pay for their labour, but also worked under the worst of "sweatshop" conditions. These goods, produced in the cheapest possible manner, were an excellent source of the foreign currency so necessary for the crumbling Soviet economy.

Margaret Rigal recalls taking Anatoly Altman[107], after his release, to look round the "Russian shop" in Holborn, London, and he pointed out a number of items manufactured in the camps. They spoke to the owners of the shop on more than one occasion but they showed no concern.

A demonstration which made a huge impact and has long remained in the memory of all the participants'was the occasion of a "prisoners' luncheon" at the House of Commons to celebrate the formation of the All-Party Parliamentary Committee for the Release of Soviet Jewry. The diners were served a typical prison meal of cabbage soup, herring, black bread, and water. Sylvia Becker commented that the smell of herrings and cabbage soup must have remained long after the lunch was over.

---

[105] Wife of President Carter of the USA.
[106] GULAG – an acronym for Glavnoy Upravelyenye Lageryei. Literally – Head administration of the Camps.
[107] Sentenced to ten years imprisonment in 1970.

Rita Eker remembers that after the release of Edward Kuznetsov[108], when he and his wife Sylva Zalmanson visited her on their 'thank you' tour, she wanted to take them to a restaurant, but Edward begged not to go as he "had forgotten how to eat with a knife and fork".

A newsletter of October 1976 gave a list of Soviet Jewish Prisoners of Conscience. Each prisoner had been "adopted" by one or more 35s groups and one of more Members of Parliament. All 35ers were asked to write to the prisoners; all correspondence was to be sent to the central address for mail, when given, and if possible a copy sent to the camp address. There followed a list of twenty-four prisoners, ranging in age from Aleksander Slinin, aged twenty-one, sentenced to three years (adopted by Southampton 35s and Norman Lamont, MP for Kingston-upon-Thames) to Mikhail Shtern, aged fifty-eight, sentenced to eight years (adopted by the Leeds 35s and Edward Lyons, MP for Bradford West).

Rose Ellis was responsible for producing the meticulously compiled lists detailing each prisoner's name, home town, date of birth, occupation, marital status, date of arrest, nature of charge, sentence, prison address, central address for mail, adoptive 35s group and adoptive Member of Parliament and constituency.

A list circulated in 1984 gave details of searches, arrests and imprisonments during an eight month period from March to October involving the following refuseniks: Zakhar Zunshine, Tatiana Zunshine, Leonid Umansky, Alexander Balter, David Shekhter, Yakov Levin, Valery Lemelman, Svetlana Balter, Polina Balter, Yevgenia Lishchanskaya, Mikhail Vinaver, Victor Fulmakht, Yakov and Polina Gorodetsky, Alexander Kholmiansky, Vitaly Dyakteriev, Yuli Edelshtein, Yakov Mesh, Alexander Kushnir, Valery Pevsner, Mikhail Kholmiansky, Sofia Bukhbinder-Vitaver, Dan Shapira and Inna Brukhina.

The newsletter, with its wide circulation, was an invaluable tool for the marshalling of protest. Number 42 of September 1986 states:

> "In view of the forthcoming meeting between Edward Shevardnadze and George Bush at the United Nations and the probability of a summit meeting between Reagan and Gorbachev, we highlight below prisoners and

---

[108] Sentenced to fifteen years imprisonment in 1970.

ex-prisoners who should not be forgotten. Please write to the Soviet Ambassador, Mr Leonid Zamyatin, 18, Kensington Palace Gardens, London, W8, and remember to send us copies of your letters".

ABRAMOV, Moshe of Samarkand: Arrested 19 December 1983, charged with "malicious hooliganism", tried 24 January 1984 and sentenced to three years strict regime labour camp. Later changed to working for the National Economy following his appeal.

BEGUN, Iosif of Moscow: Leading Hebrew teacher, serving his third sentence. Arrested 4 November 1982, tried 12 October 1983 charged with "anti-Soviet propaganda" and sentenced to seven years labour camp plus five years exile. He is at the moment being held in Chistopol Prison under deplorable conditions. He has been hospitalised suffering from pneumonia and deprived of all family visits and letters.

BERENSHTEIN, Iosif of Kiev: Arrested 12 November 1984 charged with "resisting the police", tried and sentenced on 10 December 1984 to four years in a labour camp. He has suffered irreversible damage to one eye following a vicious attack by a fellow prisoner.[109]

BRAILOVSKY, Victor of Moscow: Arrested 13 November 1980. Tried and sentenced to five years internal exile for "defaming the Soviet Union". Released March 1984 – still waiting for an exit visa.

BRODSKY, Vladimir of Moscow: Arrested 16 July 1985, charged with 'hooliganism' tried 15 August 1985, sentenced to three years labour camp. Unconfirmed reports state that he was released on 14th September due to public pressure.

CHERNIAK, Alexander of Kiev: Arrested and tried 26 March 1984 for alleged "misuse of government

---

[109] Berenshtein and Chernobilsky are presently living in Israel and are helped by the One-to-One scheme.

property", sentenced to four years labour camp – changed to working for the National Economy in July 1986.

CHERNOBILSKY, Boris of Moscow: Arrested 26 November 1981 and charged with "striking a police officer", tried on 9 December 1981, sentenced to one year labour camp. Released December 1982 – still waiting for an exit visa.

EDELSHTEIN, Yuli of Moscow: Arrested 4 September 1984, charged with "possession of drugs", sentenced to three years labour camp. In 1986 Yuli 'met with an accident' resulting in a crushed femur and pelvis and a perforated urethra. Totally neglected due to primitive medical facilities in camp resulting in permanent disablement. Despite worldwide protests and contrary to labour camp regulations he has not been released.

ELBERT, Lev of Kiev: Arrested and then tried on 25 May 1983, charged with "refusing to report for military reserve duty", sentenced to one year in a labour camp. Released 20 June 1984 and still waiting for an exit visa.

The request for support for these victims of the Soviet prison system was reinforced by the message on the reverse side of the circular:

While we welcome on his first visit to London, Anatoly (Natan) Sharansky, ex Prisoner of Conscience, 'Hero of our Time', let us not forget all those still suffering in the dreadful prisons and slave labour camps of the Gulag Archipelago – Roald Zelichenok who will be fifty on 29 September. Please send greetings cards to his home and to the prison; and Boris Lifshitz, forced into the army in spite of his poor health who has now been admitted into the military hospital in Murmansk in the Arctic far north with a bleeding ulcer. He is nineteen. Please protest to the Minister for Health (address given).

In February 1986, the 35s were campaigning for eighteen Prisoners of Zion and twenty-four former Prisoners of Zion who were still refused exit visas. Every case involved hardship and deprivation, but none more so than Ida Nudel.

IDA NUDEL – "THE ANGEL OF MOSCOW"

Two miles from a remote Siberian village and a hundred miles from Tomsk, the nearest town, Ida Nudel was the only woman in a barracks reserved for criminals.

In June 1978 she was sentenced to four years exile in Siberia on a charge of "malicious hooliganism". Her crime was to have hung a placard from the balcony of her Moscow flat inscribed, "KGB give me my visa". This was a last desperate plea after trying to get to Israel through the normal channels. For this 'crime' she was condemned to live in a rat-infested room with only an outside toilet and washing facilities, in an area which was snowed-under for much of the year and with winter temperatures of minus fifty-eight Farenheit. She slept with a knife under her pillow, not to defend herself "from the drunken marauders and bandits who constantly attempt to break into my room" but to kill herself should she be attacked.

After her first application for an exit visa in 1971, Ida, a forty-seven-year-old economist, was dismissed from her post at the Moscow Institute of Planning and Production. Her application was refused on the grounds of secrecy although she had obtained a statement from the head of the Institute that her work was in no way secret. She wryly remarked that "the only secrets I have ever had access to have been where the rats and mice build their nests". Even before she was exiled to Siberia, and despite suffering from heart, kidney and stomach ailments, she was constantly beaten up, imprisoned and kept under round-the-clock surveillance by the KGB.

To the refuseniks and Prisoners of Conscience who adored her she became known as "the little angel", and "the angel of Moscow" for her dedication to their problems. Whenever they were in trouble she was the first to offer comfort despite the danger that this could entail to herself. She was often the only contact between the prisoners, the officials of the Potma, Vladimir, and Perm camps and the outside world. There are many printed testimonies to her devotion from those whom she helped during her seven years in refusal.[110] Ida took advantage of the Soviet authorities' regard for the letter of the law, which laid down that each category of prisoner was allowed a specified number of family visits per year, a specified number of parcels per year, etc. If a prisoner had no family she would get herself registered as family and visit them in distant camps many days journey from Moscow. If the authorities broke the slightest regulation she challenged them and insisted that they kept to the regulations.

Margaret Rigal: "She was like a gadfly buzzing around the officials; she wasn't frightened of them. She said to George (Rigal), 'I am the king's jester. I am permitted to see them all because I never go beyond the law'."

In a moving article outlining Ida's distressing situation, Bernard Levin posed his oft-asked question: "'Cui-bono?' I know, of course, why Ida Nudel has for more than six years been treated like this, 'pour decourager les autres'."[111]

One of the earliest messages received in the West from Ida in exile concerned her dog, a beautiful collie named Ssylka (translation – "exile"). The message said:

> He, too, is in need of food. Ida's only plea is that we organise some sort of regular supply of sustenance for her dog and that we should inform animal lovers of the conditions in which they are living. Animal lovers will understand that this is Ida's only source of comfort and her only companion.

This plea, published in the newsletter of 13 February 1979, brought an immediate response from an Ilford woman councillor who sent a parcel of dog biscuits for Ssylka. The idea was that if this got through it would be followed by nutritious human food in the shape of dog biscuits. The package was returned but the story received a good write-up in a local Ilford newspaper. The same newsletter told of Ida's awareness of the campaign being waged on her behalf. Throughout the period of her exile there were regular bulletins in the

---

[110] cf (a) *Our Ida Nudel* published by Israeli women for Ida Nudel, Tel Aviv, Israel 1980

(b) *Israel Year Book on Human Rights*, Vol. 9, Singer J. and Elkind I. Faculty of Law, Tel Aviv University, Israel.

[111] *The Times*, 14 October 1977.

newsletters, often weekly, on her health and living conditions, together with requests for readers to write both to her and to the appropriate Soviet authorities on her behalf.

One of the most distressing periods of her exile was that following publication of a vitriolic article about her in the local Tomsk newspaper, which added to the hostility already directed against her. Local shops and other public places in her nearest village displayed extracts from this article. In May 1979 she received the following letter:

> Dear Ida
>
> First of all it is not sufficient to say you are a political prostitute, you are simply a low person, you live in the soil of the motherland and you foul it. You should have been exiled not to the Tomsk region but out in the Tundra, so that with your yapping against the motherland you could frighten the white bears. May your parents and your future descendants be covered with shame by your life; may you be thrice cursed as the saying goes. It is a pity that we can't send you to Israel; that would be the best way of dealing with you.

That, of course, was what Ida wanted, and was the reason for her suffering. She had to endure two more years of exile, of living in this hostile atmosphere.

> For Ida Nudel – four years exile
> She had applied for a visa
> And now she's to freeze in Krivosheino;
> Not only from the cold
> But the age-old
> Snow drifts of hatred.
>
> She's going, and there's no knowing
> When she'll return
> And when she does return
> She'll have no home to return to.
>
> She's left the inhuman zoo
> And found the kind of treatment

Meted out to helpers of the helpless
By the unhelpful.
Neglecting herself
She protected other Lovers of Zion.

And this is her reward
The savage sword has cut at her
Injustice has butted her
With horns of steel
She says she feels no remorse
For she followed the course
She knew she had to.

She says she was glad to
Have led eight years of use.
Now she faces yet more abuse.
Four years exile
And so much more.

(Sylvia Lukeman, Liverpool 35s.)

Ida became a celebrity and a symbol. Well-known public figures, among them Harold Wilson, David Owen, Jane Fonda and Liv Ullman, as well as bodies such as the United States Congress, Amnesty International, both British Houses of Parliament and the International Women's Organisation campaigned on her behalf; Jane Moonman was a particularly active campaigner. In 1982 Ida was released from exile and returned to Moscow, but her troubles were far from over. She was forbidden to live in Moscow and whilst she was frantically travelling from city to city trying to find one which would grant her a residential permit, she ran from friend to friend, sleeping a few nights in one house and then moving on. At times she was driven to sleeping in railway station waiting rooms. The KGB harassment and the insecurity and stress of her life were such that the state of her health was giving rise for concern, and friends feared that she was losing the will to fight. She eventually found a job, painting fences in Bendery, in the Moldavian Republic and was able to take up residence there.

Finally, five and a half years after her return from Siberia she flew out to Israel in October 1987. Before long she was arousing the wrath of the Israeli Government and its supporters by criticising their handling of the refusenik and new immigrant situations. She was labelled a malingerer and a malcontent and the cruel taunt "it would have been better if you had stayed in Siberia" was flung at her.

The following extracts are taken from two letters from Ida Nudel[112]:

- "I read and heard (whilst in Russia) of the wonderful and special organisation and activities of brave women and women of influence who organised, and with much bravery, demonstrated over a long period until there really were results. About this extraordinary ability to get members of the British Parliament working on their behalf and to join their struggle and to cause the Prisoners of Zion to be anonymous no longer and turned them from being not just a number on a KGB list, but to people to whom one should relate."

- "The importance of the 35s group was in the forming of a new arm to come to terms with the problem, whether this was through multiple demonstrations or just that people wore prison clothing and chained themselves, the result was that they endangered themselves, and came to visit us in Moscow in the worst of times, when missions of this type positively endangered their lives".

- "I remember Jane Moonman who arrived in Moscow at the time when I was being held awaiting trial. She encouraged me both spiritually and materially. In the same way, during the whole period, representatives of the 35s came and helped my friends and myself over the dreadful period with the feeling that the world had not forgotten us".

- "I also remember Rita Eker and other women who neither kept quiet nor rested until they moved things and brought news of the distress of the Jews in Russia to the ears of the world. They did

---

[112] Written to the author, August 1994 (translated from Hebrew by Michael Alge).

this in a wise and effective way and thus brought the whole subject to a political level and not just a human one".

- "Many things have escaped my memory, for the memories are hard ones and have a way of being forgotten; one wants to keep one's strength for effective work, so urgent here in Israel".

- "It is very important to give publicity to all this period and the wonderful work that was done by the 35s group, that was pioneered in London and similar places throughout the world. These groups strengthened the conscience that we are responsible for one another. Russian Jewry owes the 35s a great debt".

The following extracts from the newsletters over a sample period of fifteen months will give some idea of the degree of involvement of the 35s in the long campaign for Ida Nudel which extended for several years, from the time of her arrest, imprisonment and exile until her final departure to Israel nine and a half years later:

12 March 1979, Liverpool
At a public demonstration a recording will be played of actress Dorothy Tutin telling of Ida Nudel's conditions in Siberia.

13 March 1979
Remember to be available to commemorate the anniversary of Ida's arrest and sentence on 21 June; the longest day for us but for Ida it is only one day out of one thousand, four hundred and sixty – every day is a long one for her.

27 March 1979
The 27th April will be Ida's forty-eighth birthday. Make sure a huge fan mail reaches her in exile.

Luxembourg – the 35s attempted to hand in a petition on behalf of Ida and others to the Soviet Embassy.

8 May 1979
Letter sent from the National Conference of Labour Women at Felixstowe to the Soviet Ambassador on behalf of Ida. 35s from Cambridge and elsewhere distributed leaflets outside the hall. As a result of the lobbying much interest has been shown, many members

have written to Ida and a letter will be sent on her behalf from the whole party to the Soviet authorities.

Rita Eker spoke on the BBC "World at One" programme (30 May) about the forthcoming Ida Nudel Day. A tape recording from Ida describing the appalling conditions in which she lived was played.

Instructions for Ida Nudel Day: Soviet officials must be inundated with cables and letters demanding Ida's freedom. Cars, decorated as for an election, with the slogan "VOTE FOR IDA NUDEL'S FREEDOM" will leave the office at 9.15 a.m. They will form a motorcade to the Soviet Embassy and then drive around in London. Demonstrators should assemble at 10.15 at the Soviet Embassy. Make this a mammoth demonstration of your concern for Ida.

There are printed postcards addressed to Soviet officials, on behalf of Ida, obtainable from Susan Lauder.

7 June 1979, Newcastle
The 35s had a stall at the Annual WIZO Bazaar. The film of Ida Nudel was shown continuously.

3 July 1979
The Luxembourg 35s produced a postcard with a photograph of Ida to be sent to her. They have collected a large number of signatures for their petition, including that of the Minister of Finance and many Parliamentarians.

Bournemouth held a meeting for Ida at which there was a dramatised reading and showing of the 'Ida Nudel in Exile' film. One hundred postcards for Ida and Sharansky were posted.

Brighton and Hove held an evening in support of Ida and Semyon Gluzman.

Newcastle 35s gave an interview on the local radio, had an article in the local paper and circulated petitions amongst women's groups.

10 July 1979, Liverpool
35s sent letters from the Annual Conference of the British Medical Association, on behalf of Ida Nudel, Sharansky and Slepak, to Soviet officials.

Birmingham 35s showed the 'Ida Nudel in Exile' film and obtained coverage on BBC Radio.

West Sussex 35s conducted a letter writing campaign.

Glasgow 35s attempted to send a letter to Ida via a Soviet tug which was in the King George Vth Docks. The tug was towing a cargo to Tomsk, the nearest city to Ida's place of exile. They were ordered to leave the docks.

17 July 1979, Newcastle
The local radio devoted its religious programme to Ida.

Luxembourg. On Ida Nudel Day, the 35s had a stand in the main square. A petition to Brezhnev was signed and a large number of postcards were sent to Ida including those from many tourists from all over the world. Television and press coverage was very good.

24 July 1979
The Ida Nudel Committee meeting was held in the House of Commons, chaired by Lynda Chalker MP. A Parliamentary petition is to be handed in to the Soviet Embassy in December. They agreed to ask the European Parliament to send a similar petition and to increase contacts with the House of Lords.

Brighton and Hove Soviet Jewry Group sold Ida Nudel postcards from door-to-door. Sister Josephine of Findon Convent posted over sixty cards.

18 September 1979
Brent 35s sent one hundred and fifty New Year cards to Ida and other refuseniks. Dr Rhodes Boyson MP visited the gathering in the main shopping street.

16 October 1979
An appeal was sent from the Trade Union Congress Conference to Mr Brezhnev which read: "We the undersigned British Trade Unionists request that a pardon be given to Vladimir Slepak and Ida Nudel, both of Moscow, exiled on a charge of 'malicious hooliganism' after peacefully displaying banners from their balconies requesting exit visas".

Sister Ann Gillen, a Roman Catholic nun, delivered a letter to the Soviet Embassy offering to serve the rest of Ida's sentence.

27 November 1979
The 35s sent a petition to the Secretary General of the United Nations, Kurt Waldheim.

South London 35s held a 'Focus on Ida Nudel' evening. Postcards were sent to her and to other refuseniks.

4 March 1980
Newcastle 35er Judy Lyons addressed fifty members of the Newcastle East Townswomen's Guild. Postcards were sent from the meeting.

15 April 1980
The newsletter carried a picture of Ida on the front page together with this message in bold print: "ON 27 APRIL IDA NUDEL WILL BE FORTY-NINE. ALONE, ISOLATED IN A HOSTILE ENVIRONMENT, TODAY SHE FACES TWO MORE YEARS OF HELL IN THE FROZEN WASTES OF SIBERIA... DO SEND HER A CARD FOR HER BIRTHDAY".

13 May 1980
35s lobbied the Women's Labour Party Conference at Malvern. Fifty delegates said they would write to the International Women's Conference Secretariat in New York, requesting them to put a resolution pledging support for Ida on the agenda.

24 June 1980
Liverpool 35s, together with WIZO, organised a 'Service of Solidarity with Soviet Jews'. A chair in Prince's Road Synagogue was dedicated to Ida Nudel.

London. The 35s held a demonstration outside the Russian shop. Leaflets were distributed on behalf of Ida Nudel and others.

Chapter Eleven

Risks, Rewards, and Achievements

Leaking roofs, dingy basements, and broken windows were minor discomforts compared to the hazards of being arrested, receiving hate-mail, personal abuse, sustaining injuries and being "taken for a ride".

Sylvia Sheff had a high profile in the Manchester group which placed her in the position of "fall guy" for the opposition to the 35s in that city. She was the recipient of abusive letters and had many anonymous phone calls during the night. On one occasion, at a demonstration during a visit of a delegation of Russian teachers, leaflets were knocked out of her hand, and when she bent down to pick them up someone deliberately stamped on her hand, necessitating hospital treatment.

Every 35er has the discomfort and misery of at least one demonstration engraved upon her memory. Great dedication was needed to leave one's family on a cold winter night and stand, often in a downpour of rain, only to be vilified and jostled. One such instance occurred in February 1980 whilst demonstrating outside the Round House Theatre in Camden Town, during the appearance of the Rustaveli Theatre Company. Members of the 35s were badly harassed by Turkish demonstrators who were in opposition to a pro-Armenian group and were chanting pro-Soviet and anti-Jewish slogans. They resented the presence of the women's group and the situation became so threatening that the 35ers decided to withdraw.

A bald statement such as "Leeds organised their tenth annual Chanukkah torchlight procession" can in no way convey the discomfort of a raw December evening spent assembling, slowly marching in a long procession and then listening to speeches from the Town Hall steps, whilst vainly attempting to keep warm in the bitter Northern winds, with ice and snow underfoot.

Even a summertime demonstration can bring discomfort. Standing around in blazing sunshine can be as demanding as two hours in a June cloudburst, which was experienced by the Manchester group during a demonstration in support of Ida Nudel on International Women's Day in June 1979. Together with the Manchester branches of the Women's International Zionist Organisation and Council for Soviet Jewry, they managed to collect over seven hundred signatures in the centre of the city despite being soaked to the skin in a torrential downpour.

It was even more disconcerting to be arrested and charged by the police. In July 1973 Annette Spiers was demonstrating outside Buckingham Palace, together with other 35ers, awaiting the arrival of the new Russian Ambassador, Mr Nikolai Lunkov, who was to present his credentials to the Queen Mother. On his approach they unfurled a banner bearing the slogan: "NIKOLAI LUNKOV, NEW SOVIET AMBASSADOR, STOP PERSECUTING GOLDSTEIN BROTHERS, INNOCENT JEWS FROM TBILISI".

Annette Spiers then threw into his horse-drawn carriage a bundle of three hundred letters which had been handed in to the Soviet Embassy during the previous two years but had not been accepted. Not surprisingly she was arrested and charged with threatening behaviour and was later bound over to keep the peace. She had the dubious honour of having her picture splashed on the front page of the *London Evening Standard*, as well as being reported in many daily newspapers.

The Jewish Chronicle of 2 July 1976 published the news of the arrest of Rochelle Duke, Rita Eker and Doreen Gainsford, who were charged with obstructing the highway during a proxy funeral they were holding for Colonel Yefim Davidovich (the first refusenik to die under house arrest). They had made the mistake of illegally demonstrating within a mile of Whitehall and to compound the felony had placed a coffin on the pavement. They were given a conditional discharge for one year.

However, life as a 35er was not without its lighter moments. In October 1973, South London group members June Kenton and Sandra Butcher ran across the ice at Streatham Ice Rink in order to present Sylva Zalmanson medallions to two competing Russian skaters. Unfortunately they slipped and fell flat on their backs. This resulted in "Whoops Goes a Demo" headline and pictures in *The Daily Express*.

June Kenton, together with other 35ers, was again in the news the following month when *The Croydon Advertiser* reported that she had pleaded guilty to obstructing the highway and was given a conditional discharge for one year.

Being arrested in one's own country was a relatively minor matter compared to the perils of arrest in countries behind the Iron Curtain, especially in pre-glasnost days. This very frightening situation was experienced by Joyce Simson and her husband in Kiev. Even more distressing was the experience of two tourists, Mr and Mrs Schneider, who were not members of the 35s. In November 1983, *The Jewish Chronicle* carried a report of the couple being held at the airport and refused admission to the Soviet Union on the grounds that "they had confessed that they were agents of the group". This was a complete fabrication but was an indication of how sensitive the Russians were about the 35s.

When Doreen Gainsford was arrested in Helsinki in 1975 together with five other women, they were taken away in a police van and their banners were confiscated. They were later released without charge but as a result of this incident they obtained a great deal of television and press coverage. On another occasion she was not only arrested but also deported. This happened in June 1975 in Belgrade, Yugoslavia, where there was a preparatory meeting for the forthcoming Helsinki Agreement Conference. Doreen Gainsford, Linda Isaacs, Pat Allin and others were gathered in a hotel foyer when the police arrested them in order to prevent their planned demonstration. When they were threatened with deportation they refused to move until they had seen representatives from their Embassies. They were then carried, kicking and screaming, to the rear of the hotel, bundled into a van and driven to the airport where they had a seven-hour wait until their passports were stamped, banning them from re-entering Yugoslavia for a year. They were then flown home.

These were some of the risks of life as a 35er – traumatic experiences indeed for women of their background. Nevertheless, having weighed up the situation, they were prepared for such eventualities. What they were not prepared for was the sense of betrayal which arose from deception. As early as the 1970s, it became apparent that the 35s had to check and double check their Russian sources after travellers started to bring back disturbing tales of deceit. Having been dismissed from their jobs, refuseniks had to try and make a living in a variety of ways. To this end some of them claimed that they needed expensive equipment such as cameras and tape-recorders and these were provided for them. But later travellers discovered that some refuseniks sold these gifts. There was a similar situation with drugs requested "for sick relatives". Whilst the group understood that economic circumstances may have led to this dishonesty by people accustomed to seventy years of "manipulating the system", they nevertheless could not allow it to continue. It was a bitter lesson but they rapidly learnt not to be exploited in this manner.

Travellers also returned with warnings about certain refuseniks who were suspected of working with the KGB. Disappointment was expressed also about the unhelpful attitude of some refuseniks for whom the organisation had worked incredibly hard over a period of many years; some whose names had become very well known in the West. After leaving Russia they were sometimes asked to assist in campaigns or even just to thank their protagonists: sadly to relate they were uncooperative.

Perhaps hardest of all to bear were the harsh criticisms heaped upon them, particularly during their most active years. Initially most of the 35ers were women typical of their background and period, and sticking one's neck out was not a common trait in such people. But so committed were they to their cause that they quickly became assertive, outspoken and unafraid of standing up for what they believed to be right. They were bound to attract criticism. From their first demonstration until the present day the 35ers have had to become accustomed to the condemnation of some of their methods of work. They were accused of being too high-profiled and over dramatic and were asked to be more discreet. It was said that they saw themselves as being the most important element of the Soviet Jewry campaign in this country, and that they felt that they had to act independently, which on occasions prejudiced the communal approach. They were accused of being publicity seekers and of endangering lives for their own glorification. Time and time again this accusation of risking the lives of refuseniks and prisoners was made, but they ignored such comments, refusing to believe that the effect of their work would be as catastrophic as the alarmists suggested (in fact there was no such effect whatsoever).

In the opinion of Rita Eker and Margaret Rigal, much of the hostility was due to the fact that the group did not treat the establishment with the degree of respect to which it thought it was entitled, that their success was resented and that "we didn't stop when they said we should. We did only what the Soviet Jews asked us to do and we said we would take our orders only from them, not from Tel Aviv or London. Our efficiency highlighted their inefficiency".

Engraved upon Rita's memory is a remark made about them by a leading member of the Anglo-Jewish Establishment: "They are spoilt little rich bitches who have nothing to do but stand on street corners".

Time has shown that the 35s were justified in what they did and the way in which they did it.

Over and above the *raison d'être* for the existence of the group, the rewards of being a 35er far outweigh the risks. From discovering a long lost branch of her family, to discovering herself, every 35er has had her life enriched. So many of them say how shy and diffident they had been previously. They have learnt that they possessed far more potential than they had ever realised.

Ros Gemal:

> I remember being in the office and one of the girls said, "There goes X. She's going to see a Member of Parliament, and three months ago she wouldn't even buy a pair of shoes without her husband." This happened to all of us. It widened our experiences and our lives; we found ourselves. I was the beneficiary. Apart from other things, I learnt to write; I learnt to 'sell' myself and I got a very good job on these new strengths.

Joyce Simson:

> I developed such 'chutzpah'. I used to telephone Makharov (the official who processed visas for

refuseniks in Moscow) and introduced myself as being from Mrs Thatcher's Helsinki Watchdog Committee and ask him how matters were progressing. He used to ask me how Mrs Thatcher was and I would say something like, "Oh, she's doing a tour up in the North of England". I managed to get away with that for a few weeks, but then he must have made enquiries as he wouldn't speak to me anymore.

Dora Gabrel of the Ilford group is typical of the many 35ers who marvelled at their own daring. In order to gain entry into the Masonic Hall where local dignitaries were dining with the Russian Trade Minister, she dressed herself as a waitress, walked into the dining room and coolly started handing out leaflets.

Rita Eker:

> I have met such wonderful people in this work, some of whom have become my very close friends... we've been to world conferences, summit meetings, we've nobbled world leaders. I remember once speaking on a satellite link-up with George Bush when he was a Presidential candidate and calling him "Mr President" and he said, "Not yet, honey, not yet".

Joyce Simson:

> The 35ers became the most important thing in my life – and I have to say 'hats off' to all the husbands who backed us up. The one wonderful thing about it is that I have received more friendship and satisfaction than I have given and it has transformed our lives.

Rachele Kalman:

> Although we were a group of very disparate women with different religions, financial and political backgrounds, Doreen made us into a cohesive group, she kept the lid on any personal antagonisms; she was quite incredible. There was a great cameraderie which I have never experienced anywhere else and a feeling of really working in unison.

An even greater reward for Rachele was the discovery of a previously unknown branch of her family. She had decided to work for refusenik Michael Magar (Magar being her maiden name). After his case had been publicised on American television, she was excited to receive a telephone call from a woman bearing the same name. Details and photographs (showing a strong family resemblance) were exchanged and so it was that she found her late father's cousins living in Washington DC.

Every 35er stressed that whatever 'risks' they may have taken and whatever inconveniences they may have encountered, faded into insignificance when compared with the knowledge that the freedom which they accepted as their birthright, was now being experienced by those for whom they had worked.

It was not only the individual members who felt some sort of emotional or "spiritual" reward. In many cases the whole community ethos was enhanced by the activities of the local 35s group, which gave them an added sense of purpose. As Doreen Gainsford put it, in respect of one example:

> They engendered a vibrancy into the Liverpool Jewish community; they stopped people being shy about being Jewish – they were very high profile. Before the 35s, Liverpool, and for that matter most provincial communities, didn't do 'that sort of thing'.

To the Committee of the 35s, London.   January 1981

For the first time for many years I am happy to reply to you myself personally, together with my family, from the land of our forefathers and the soil of our motherland, with deep-felt thanks.

Your tireless activity and your selfless colossal work is a wonderful help. We are happy and very, very thankful.

It is very difficult to estimate all that you did for my family and all that you do for the hundreds of other Prisoners of Zion. I hope that your efforts will lead to the release of our friends Sharansky, Slepak and Nudel.

The fate of the family of Professor Lerner who is living apart from his daughter, is very tragic

We are sure that your charitable activity will be appreciated by progressive thinking people for its true worth

I am ready to take part with you in your noble work as much as I can within my power and ability.

Yours with heartfelt sincerity,

Lev Roitburd. Ramat Gan, Israel

ACHIEVEMENTS

Sadly, as this is being written, the need still remains for the 35s to continue their twenty-five-year battle for the welfare of Soviet Jewry and against abuses of Human Rights. Latterly much of their efforts have been directed to the relief of poverty and illness both for Jews in the Former Soviet Union and for newly arrived immigrants in Israel, many of whom tragically have fallen through the overstretched net of the Israeli Social Services. Nevertheless, with understandable pride they can point to substantial achievements in their campaign up to the present time.

First and foremost is the hope which they afforded to the refuseniks and prisoners. On a more far-reaching basis is the influence which they contributed towards a change of attitude of the Foreign Office towards Jews. And thirdly, is their assault on Soviet sensitivity and the proposition that the Women's Campaign for Soviet Jewry helped to bring about the downfall of communism.

A number of former refuseniks and prisoners have written books describing their harrowing experiences. One theme, common to all of them, is that were it not for the knowledge that people in the West were campaigning for them, they would have been hard put to sustain their spirits to continue the fight for their freedom.

In his book *Refusenik*[113], Mark Azbel stated: "...it was only owing to such friends that we were able to survive during those years (of interrogation, persecution and refusal)".

[113] *Refusenik* by Mark Azbel, Hamish Hamilton, London 1982, page 360.

Victor Polsky, who was falsely accused of dangerous driving, is quoted as saying[114] "my case is a good example of pressure from the West affecting Soviet policy. Without it there is no doubt that I would have been imprisoned".

Margaret Rigal firmly believes that the 35s campaign changed the attitude of the Foreign Office towards Jews. Although not previously noted for its espousal of Jewish causes, it nevertheless supported the fight for Soviet Jewry under both Labour and Conservative governments.

> We pointed out that whether or not they supported Israel they should support Human Rights – and therefore Soviet Jewry. It was the British Government who pushed the Human Rights issue at Helsinki; we activists got the public to push the Foreign Office. On one occasion they told me that they had received hundreds of letters from supporters of the refuseniks, so much so that they had to get in extra staff. Did I think that this was a good way to spend the taxpayers' money? I pointed out that this wasn't just a Jewish issue, it was a Human Rights issue; there were Baptists, Germans and Ukrainians also suffering under this regime.

> ...There were many politicians who were anti-Israel but did not wish to be thought to be anti-Semitic. They became most active in their support of Human Rights and Soviet Jews. After all, there were no Jews coming to England, which made it easy for them to support the Campaign.

Ijo Rager, whose belief in the power of the women never wavered, remarked, "I have no doubt that if the Jewish women had demonstrated outside Anthony Eden's office in the 1940s, they would have forced Britain to bomb Auschwitz".

The Russians have always been extremely sensitive to world opinion and there is ample evidence that active protesting paid dividends.

Margaret Rigal recalled:

---

[114] *The Jewish Observer and Middle East Review*, July–August 1977.

Publicity was enemy No. 1 to the Soviets; they minded very much. They always needed to be respected. They felt adverse publicity was besmirching their international reputation and they couldn't bear it. So it was imperative throughout that the prisoners and refuseniks had to be the focus. So often the media wanted to base their stories on us, but we never allowed ourselves to become "the stars". We were the refuseniks and the prisoners who couldn't speak for themselves. We learnt that we had to push, push, push them all the time. Every story had to be about the refuseniks wherever possible, not about us. If they took pictures we always tried to have a banner in the background. We tried always to show the refuseniks' names somewhere.

In his book *Refusenik*, Mark Azbel reiterates the invaluable effect of publicity[115]:

I remember one (foreign) correspondent asked me if I didn't fear that the refuseniks would be in even greater danger if the papers made public their names and histories... we all felt strongly about the answer. 'Our only chance of survival lies in being known; once we are forgotten it will really be the end of us'.

Doreen Gainsford recalls an incident in 1975 which points to the powerful effect of demonstrations:

A Russian Trade Union leader called Shelepin was coming here. Those were early days and we weren't very good at getting information. I remember calling *The Daily Mail* (it was a very right-wing paper then) to see if they could tell us anything about the visit. We worked with them day and night, we found out when he was coming and we worked out a strategy.

It's funny how things turn out. We didn't want to be involved with other groups, but *The Daily Mail* had also given the information to the Ukrainian activists. Together, we staged this big demonstration at the Trade

Union headquarters. It was on the eve of Passover; I ask you, how many Jewish housewives could possibly be there? But the Ukrainians were there, so in the event it was a blessing.

Such was the crowd and the obvious publicity arising from it that the Russian delegation had to forego a dignified entrance and had to slip in through the back door.

Doreen said, "That was probably our greatest achievement! It was such a humiliation to the Soviets. It made people realise that we could get through to the Russians. We were visual and we were vocal. People power is such a dynamic tool"[116].

That the Russians regarded the 35s as a thorn in their flesh is clear from an article in *Pravda Ukrainy*[117] claiming that the 35s and the National Council for Soviet Jewry had sent people to the Soviet Union to promote Zionist propaganda. They called them "pseudo-tourists" and accused them of smuggling in hostile Zionist propaganda on weekly flights. And in July 1980, in a broadcast in English from Moscow, Victor Valentinov referred to – "the lady activists of the Zionist extremist committee 35, set up with Zionist money in 1968... the Zionist housewives club... are working their fingers to the bone for the Olympic Games with all kinds of punishment".[118]

In his book *The American Movement to Save Russian Jewry*, William Orbach states:

> responding in part to Soviet Jewish militance, in part to the international furore over its Leningrad blunder and in part to Brussels (the International Conferences), the Soviet Union drastically liberalised its emigration policy. By March 1971 the numbers of visas issued per month shot up to one thousand, in contrast to the previous peak

---

[116] Alexander Shelepin was, in fact, Head of the KGB at that time. He died in October 1994 and in his obituaries, in both *The Times* and *The Daily Telegraph*, it was recorded that because of massive protests from Jewish and Ukrainian groups his 1975 visit to this country was cut short after forty-eight hours and that this led to his resignation and the end of his political career.

[117] The main newspaper in Kiev about October 1978.

[118] Newsletter No. 41, 1980.

186

of two thousand a year in 1969, which was lowered to
one thousand a year in 1970.[119]

Three of the most informed members of the 35s – Rita Eker,
Doreen Gainsford, and Margaret Rigal – all maintain that the 35s
helped to open the first cracks in the Soviet edifice.

Margaret Rigal recalls:

> We supported these refuseniks who were the absolute
> spearheads. The refuseniks' campaign in the Soviet
> Union showed the KGB that it was not invincible, and
> once the gates had opened they couldn't cope with the
> situation.
>
> In the past, the KGB had used their odious methods to
> crush other revolts, but to their frustration they couldn't
> crush the Jews, mainly because of their support from the
> West. The 35s were the noisy end of the British
> campaign and this forced the campaign in the United
> States to become more vociferous and active than
> previously. After our demonstrations during
> Gorbachev's visit, he went back with the impression that
> we were a force to be reckoned with. At about that time
> the Red Army was brought back from Afghanistan and
> from Poland, the Berlin Wall was coming down – the
> Russian empire was not invulnerable. Baptists were
> campaigning, Germans and Ukrainians were leaving.
> The more that came out the more there were to put
> pressure on them from the West.

Doreen Gainsford supports this contention: "I believe that,
together with other Human Rights organisations, we changed the
course of history, years before it would have happened anyway".

These observations are reinforced by those of two journalists who
had often directed the spotlight of publicity on the work of the 35s
alongside their concern with Human Rights issues.

David Floyd was the Communist Affairs correspondent of *The
Daily Telegraph* in the early 1970s. He told the author that:

---

[119] Chapter 6, page 62.

the fact that a section of the (Russian) population acted jointly got people thinking. Many of them were people with relatively good jobs and yet they were prepared to give them up and go to Israel. This was something that was happening for the first time, the fact that a group of people was trying to move the regime... It certainly contributed to the downfall of communism.

John Simpson, Foreign Affairs Editor of the BBC expressed similar views on the role of the 35s:

I think the 35s played a distinguished part during the late 1970s and 1980s in the process which led to the collapse of communism. For one thing, they supported and drew attention to the one process which, more than all others, brought about change in the old Soviet Union: the discontent which most educated people there, a great many of them Jewish, felt towards the State itself. This made it inevitable that the State would have to change. By encouraging Soviet Jews to think about emigration, supporting their claims, I believe the Women's Campaign added significantly to this process.

Secondly, the 35s kept up an important and noticeable campaign in Britain after Gorbachev had come to power, prodding the consciences of politicians and journalists so that they would not forget what was still going on in the Soviet Union. Once Gorbachev had made his mark, it was very easy to think that everything was now all right with the Soviet Union, when it clearly wasn't. What the 35s did wasn't always popular at the time because people liked Gorbachev and wanted to believe that Moscow had changed. I think that by reminding us that it hadn't changed nearly enough, they did a great deal of good. And in the end the people of Russia themselves showed that they didn't feel things had changed enough either.

The 35s have got a great deal to be proud of in their campaign. Their approach to the media was always intelligent and they used us in exactly the right way. As for me, I am very glad to have been in contact with the 35s over the years. Of all the pressure groups I've dealt with I think they were the best and most effective.[120]

---

[120] Written to the author in 1994.

Chapter Twelve

The 35s Today

It is to be hoped that the harsh refusenik era is past and that the days of demonstrations are done. Nevertheless the Women's Campaign for Soviet Jewry dare not close its files. Over a century ago many of the grandparents of the 35ers left Russia to escape from its anti-Semitism and its poverty. At the present time[121], despite the optimistic assessments of some "Soviet"-watchers, Jews are continuing to leave the Former Soviet Union, mainly for Israel, at the rate of about one thousand per month. This figure increases whenever there is a regional conflict or tension with the Former Soviet Union, as in Chechnya at the end of 1994. Most of them give the same reasons for leaving as those of the previous century. The 35s, therefore, now see the alleviation of the problems of Israel's new immigrants as their most pressing mission.

Since 'glasnost' and 'perestroika' the restrictions in the Former Soviet Union have lessened. Nevertheless, the age-old fears remain, especially that of an anti-Semitic backlash in the wake of the lawlessness which has become entrenched in Soviet society. Raging inflation has caught many Jews in a poverty trap and some are unable to afford even basic necessities such as clothing and medicines. Today, the number of refuseniks, including prisoners and Poor Relatives[122] is but a fraction of that of the 1970s and 1980s. But they, together with needy Jews who wish to remain in the land of their

---

[121] This was written in the summer of 1994.

[122] "Poor Relatives". A name, given by themselves, of those who are unable to register an application for an exit visa because they cannot obtain the necessary notarised financial waiver from a close relative.

birth, and needy new immigrants in Israel, are benefiting from the expertise of the Women's Campaign.

The 35s has a network of known and trusted contacts in every major city throughout the Former Soviet Union and through them the group is able to distribute medicines, clothing, kosher food and money, taken in by visitors and tourists.

The finance for these items is raised by the 35s in their various activities, prominent amongst which is a Charity Shop in London. This was launched in 1992 and has become a major project. It is open five days a week and the physically demanding and tiring work required for its continued operation is effectively provided by a dedicated band of volunteers led by the indefatigable Lee Bash. As if to mirror the 35s office-moving saga, the Charity Shop is currently occupying its sixth premises. The constant moves into and out of dilapidated offices and shops have been both time-consuming and energy-draining, but the 35ers have always given this work top priority, preferring to spend money on the refuseniks, prisoners and new Israeli immigrants rather than on their creature comforts. It is a dream of Rita and Margaret that one day the 35s will have a permanent home – a shop with offices above. They are still awaiting a benefactor.

Sadly the problems of the new immigrants do not end with their arrival in Israel. Despite the manifold benefits provided by Israel's Social Services some applicants fall through the welfare net. A promising violinist whose studies could benefit from a better instrument, an applicant who needs extra Hebrew lessons in order to qualify for a promised job, a lone parent who cannot afford the fare for regular visits to her sick child in a distant hospital; these are some of the typical cases which are helped by the One-to-One scheme. This is a programme coordinated by the 35s which marries up individuals and groups in this country with needy new immigrants in Israel. The help given is usually financial and the applicants' needs are assessed by the Israeli 35s, Keren Klita and ESRA[123].

To hear Rita Eker debating the merits of case X against those of case Y with Joanna Aron and Judith Sheldon[124], is to glimpse a dilemma of Solomonic proportions. Only £300 is available this week: should it go to a diabetic child who could benefit from extra food, or

[123] English Speaking Residents Association
[124] Judith Sheldon, the One-to-One organiser.

to a lone parent suffering from cancer who needs money to help with caring for her children? Such agonising decisions have to be made with heartbreaking regularity.

One of the most ambitious fund-raising projects of the 35s was the "Mount Sinai to the Promised Land" trek in November 1994 in aid of the One-to-One scheme. One hundred and forty participants – doctors, solicitors, accountants, sisters, mothers and sons, sons and fathers, young and not-so-young – walked the sixty miles from Mount Sinai to Eilat. Each trekker was pledged to raise at least one thousand five hundred pounds in sponsorship, and the gruelling but inspiring "walk of a lifetime" resulted in two hundred and fifty thousand pounds being collected to help disadvantaged immigrants.

The logistics were mind-boggling, ranging from arrangements for the flight, first and last night hotels, Bedouin and Israeli guides, sanitation, camel baggage transportation, water, provisioning and catering, to a dawn service on Mount Sinai. These were impeccably masterminded by Rita Eker (herself one of the trekkers) aided by Joanna Aron and other 35ers.

The trek, brainchild of David Altschuler, had a life-enhancing effect on all the participants, many of whom immediately put their names down for the 1995 trek.

Here are but a few of the emotions expressed by some of the trekkers:

- "The experience was unique, the fulfilment of the ultimate challenge, unsurpassed – I'm sure I speak on behalf of those who took part in saying that I consider it an honour to have been one of the Children of Israel during the One-to-One trek".
- "I'd like to say how very moved I was by the spirit in which this walk was accomplished and the enormous satisfaction I felt in being able to participate in the collective sense of a singularly Jewish event, having remained so long on the periphery of Jewish culture".
- "A hearty Mazel Tov to you all and your team for the most wonderful and amazing week! I learnt and experienced many things that I will never forget, and which have therefore made me a different person".
- "I've already got you some trekkers for next year".
- "I have come home with a piece of the desert deep inside me".
- "An honour and a privilege to be part of such an historic trek".

A further rewarding aspect of the trek was the recruitment of hundreds of newcomers to the One-to-One scheme. There was a further completely unexpected bonus when the compulsory medical check for all would-be trekkers revealed that three of the volunteers had unsuspected cardiac problems and were thus enabled to receive the necessary treatment.

So successful was the first trek that the organisers have ambitiously undertaken to make this a bi-annual event. To this end extra office volunteers have been roped in and Sheila Gale, Ellane Isaac and Helen Shapiro can be found manoeuvring for desk space alongside the veteran regulars.

The Jerusalem-based Keren Klita is another organisation which depends upon the 35s for funds. Some indication of the scope of its work is given by the text of one of its pamphlets entitled "Some tips for volunteers working with new Russian immigrants".

- "When visiting your olim for the first time, don't be surprised if they look frightened! They really are not used to strangers taking such an interest in them. Try to visit or call weekly at least.
- "It is important to know that in Soviet society people are not used to displaying their feelings. It may take a long time before they will openly express their gratitude for your efforts. DON'T BE DISCOURAGED. Listen carefully to what they are trying to say. It won't be easy, but surely worthwhile. Don't forget that many of these olim came to escape anti-Semitism, although they often know little about Judaism.
- "Step 1. Greet your family with a WELCOME BASKET. Look carefully for things that they are lacking – be a good spy. Maybe what they need most of all is a hammer and some nails – or some hangers.
- "Show them where the local grocery is, but explain to them that there are cheaper places to shop.
- "Help them to read the telephone directory – it is very informative. Explain to them the importance of carrying some spare phone tokens (assimonim) for their street phone calls. Give them your phone number and tell them to feel free to call you whenever they have a question. Let them feel they are important people. They really are! And if they offer you something, accept it kindly.

- "Check with your area representative or Shirley Cahn at 637674 or Jane Klitsner at 660860 concerning 'adopting' a family, or any related questions.
- "Welcome basket – Keren Klita funds a 'welcome basket' for each new family, to be given to them by the volunteer".

In 1991 Delysia Jason, in her capacity as organiser of Keren Klita and as a 35s representative in Israel, was awarded the President's Award, for work in the absorption of immigrants.

The following letter (published in the *Jerusalem Post*, 8 May 1991) testifies to the practical and humane work which is the hallmark of Keren Klita and the Women's Campaign for Soviet Jewry.

"Sir, I am an immigrant from the Soviet Union who arrived in January 1991 with my large family of four generations, from eight to eighty-six years of age, ten people in all. From the first day of our arrival in Israel, we were overwhelmed by the help offered to us by our Israeli neighbours in Beit Hakerem. Not only was material help offered us, such as money and furniture, but what we most appreciated was the outstretched hand of friendship.

Especially during the war, my family and I appreciated the support and caring of our new friends who, as members of the Keren Klita organisation, went all out to provide for our every need, including that most needed item – a transistor radio – without which we would probably still be in our sealed room!

I am sure my fellow immigrants join me in thanking Keren Klita for their thoughtful gifts which helped us to thoroughly enjoy this, our first Pesach in freedom in the land of our fathers.

Yitzhak Skorokhod"

The English Speaking Residents Association or ESRA[125] is another Israeli group which receives support from the 35s, and again much care is taken to ensure that the claims of the new immigrants are genuine. It is a remarkable grass-roots organisation which operates all over the Sharon area of Israel and has a vast range of activities to help

---

[125] ESRA also means 'help' in Hebrew.

new immigrants. In general it is the settlers from western countries who volunteer to give help to the less privileged newcomers.[126]

The 35s also work in co-operation with the Central British Fund for World Jewish Relief (CBF), whose objective, as its title demonstrates, is concerned with assisting Jews with their social, religious and educational activities. The Glasgow branch of the 35s in particular, has been active for some time in supporting the work of the CBF by sending medicines, food and clothing to needy Jewish families.

Another facet of the co-operation between the two organisations is the exchange of up-to-date information about Jewish communities and individuals in the Former Soviet Union. The raising of the emigration barriers has resulted in the Fund being deluged with requests for help. In 1994, for example, they contacted the 35s regarding a letter they had received from an organisation in St Petersburg, written on impressively printed headed notepaper, which was most "official-looking". This letter recommended a Jewish man who wished to settle in this country. The Women's Campaign for Soviet Jewry informed the CBF that they had no knowledge of the existence of this organisation.

On occasions emergencies arise which are outside the direct remit of the 35s, but given the humanitarian nature of their work, aid is willingly provided. Their stocks of medicines and clothes were considerably depleted following the Armenian earthquakes and again during the ongoing conflict in the former Yugoslavia. In 1994 clothes and medicines were sent via a visiting group from the Ealing (United) Synagogue to the ageing eight-hundred-strong Lithuanian community of Kaunas.[127]

The provincial and suburban groups reinforce this current work. As well as supporting the One-to-One scheme by adopting individual cases, they sustain links with their own adoptees who are still living in the Former Soviet Union or who have emigrated to Israel, giving material help wherever they can.

A circular listing plans for future activities is sent regularly to all groups both in Britain and abroad, and the 35s continue to work in

---

[126] *Jerusalem Post*, 12 September 1994.
[127] Kaunas – formerly Kovno, where before the 1939 war there were over forty thousand Jews.

close co-operation with the (American) Union of Councils and with the Soviet Jewry groups in several European countries.[128]

The fortnightly newsletter, now in its twenty-fifth year, also continues to inform the hundreds of people to whom it is sent. Some of the contents are still depressing but now there is also more cheerful news than in previous years. This is demonstrated by the following extracts from two letters published in 1992.

- From Emil Kunin, now living in Jerusalem (Newsletter No. 17, May 1992)

  "...Our greetings to Rita Eker and to all members of the 35s. Today we received a letter from the Music Academy that Stanislav is admitted to the Academy as a student. Irena works as a dressmaker and she began to study in special courses on 'How to Open Businesses in Israel'. She dreams to open her own dressmaking establishment. I've organised a small new ensemble and for the last two months we are spending lunchtime rehearsing for concerts. We will be very happy to see you in Jerusalem".

- From Vladimir Goldshtein of Dnieprepetrovsk, now released from prison (Newsletter No. 18, June 1992).

  "To Rita Eker, Chairman of the Jewish Association (sic) and the company of the 35s.

  Dear Mrs Eker, I send you all every good wish, may you have bright and joyful days in your life. May all your dreams and desires be realised – I wait impatiently to receive letters from you. I am now at liberty thanks to such people as you, for which I am extremely grateful".

Whilst the 35s do not see it as their role to encourage Jews to stay in the Former Soviet Union they recognise the need to assist those who are still there. To this end they support some of the many cultural groups that have sprung up there by sending in teaching materials and text books. They also send kosher food as there are

---

[128] The Union of Councils is the American counterpart of the National Council for Soviet Jewry (NCSJ).

now many more families who are trying to follow an orthodox way of life.

A visitor to the office today will no longer find the pressurised atmosphere of previous years as the immediacy of the campaign no longer applies. But the work continues.

Chapter Thirteen

The Future

It would be nice to think that in the approach to the millennium the work of the 35s could be wound up. It would be even nicer to think that fifty years after the revelation of the most horrendous manifestation of anti-Semitism ever perpetrated, Jews could go freely about their lives.

Sadly, such hopes are futile. History has shown that where there are Jews, more often than not, there is anti-Semitism, and where there is anti-Semitism, organisations such as the 35s will always be needed. There are still refuseniks and prisoners in the CIS who live in fear of attack, and there is still hardship amongst new immigrants in Israel. So the work goes on.

There is much controversy over the advisability of encouraging Jews to remain in the CIS. Whilst communal leaders, aided by overseas religious organisations, are encouraging the establishment of communities together with the necessary back-up facilities, the 35s (and others) believe that there is no long-term future there for Jews. They cite evidence of increasing anti-Semitic activity and propaganda, and maintain that every Russian Jew should be encouraged to emigrate without delay.

However, a leader in *The Jewish Chronicle* (21 February 1994) questioned the 35s' justification for this contention and suggested that they have a tendency "to speak out on the needs and interests of Jews there without taking full account of local views and conditions". In a vigorous reply the following week, Margaret Rigal wrote:

> ...our comments are based solely on letters and phone-calls received from Russian, Ukrainian and other

Jews of the CIS and from experienced visitors who are appalled by the deteriorating situation. We believe that every Russian Jew should be encouraged to emigrate without delay. Our history is full of communities who have allowed hope of better times in the future to delay their departure until, for some of them at least, it was too late... No Jew in Russia, Ukraine or any other part of the world should be denied a Jewish education if one can be offered, but sinking vast sums of money into buildings and non-transferable assets should be reconsidered.

Her views were echoed in a *Times* article (29 March 1994) by Bernard Levin entitled WAS IT REALLY ALL IN VAIN? He describes present-day Russian anti-Semitism as at least the worst since Stalin, "so that another exodus may yet be needed". He continues:

Did I, did the dear untiring ladies, optimists every one, waste all that time and energy, only to see the filthy ghosts of Brezhnev and his kind, go by, laughing?... Imagine the ladies and me waking up and realising that it really is happening – countless freed men and women are voting to put the communists back into power... The dear ladies with whom I worked, when they read this, will try to lift my spirits. It will tax even them, I fear.

Nevertheless, in an article in *The Jewish Chronicle* (26 August 1994), its East European correspondent, Zev Ben Shlomo, maintained that anti-Semitism in the CIS was not a serious threat. He went on to say:

The campaigners for Soviet Jewry achieved successes of historical importance. To all intents and purposes their mission has been accomplished. And yet a mind-set remains in place, which fails to adjust to changed circumstances and can see in modern Russia, only dangers and demons.

One year on, a glance through the newsletters of 1995 reveals that, contrary to Ben Shlomo's assertions, there *is* hard evidence of what the 35s see as a very genuine threat. On 5 January, the newsletter carried three pages of extracts from anti-Semitic papers and tracts openly distributed on the streets of Moscow and St Petersburg. The vicious passages range from excerpts from the notorious political forgery *The Protocols of the Learned Elders of Zion* to a tortuous explanation "of how the Jews killed Stalin"! On 25 March 1995, Boris Yeltsin issued an anti-fascist decree condemning "incidents involving the fanning of social, racial, national and religious discord". However, as no specific sanctions were outlined, the decree would appear to be toothless. Yet a month after this decree was issued "a shop selling mainly blatantly racist, anti-Semitic and right-wing literature was operating about a mile from the very walls of the Kremlin in Moscow. Much of the material is printed at a press belonging to the Russian Ministry of Defence and under the direct control of the General Staff. Leaflets put out by the 'Union of Rightist Publishers' are disseminated throughout the city publicising the bookshop and listing the items for sale and their exceptionally low prices" (Newsletter, 28 May 1995).

Furthermore, one has only to read current newspapers in this country to see that there is growing disorder and violence in the Former Soviet Union; a fertile field indeed for its endemic anti-Semitism.

In an article in *The Jerusalem Report* (22nd February 1996) Natan Sharansky underlines the need for the continuing work of the Liason Bureau (Israel). Despite opposition from officials such as Jewish Agency Chief, Avraham Burg, he views the current situation in the former Soviet Union with foreboding. Politically, nationalist and pro-Communist forces are on the rise which could easily lead to a deterioration in policy, not only to emigration but to the Jews in general.

With elections looming at the end of 1995, there is a very real threat of a return to authoritarianism. Whichever way the elections go it bodes ill for the future of the Jews of that region. It is obvious, therefore, that there is an ever-present need for organisations which are experienced in, and ready for rescue, should the need arise.

During the 1995 hostilities in Chechnya, Sally Becker (dubbed the Angel of Mostar for her humanitarian work in war-torn Bosnia), acting as a voluntary emissary for the Jewish Agency, travelled to Grozny to assess the situation of the Jews in the breakaway Chechen Republic. Between forty to one hundred members of this small community are missing (*The Jewish Chronicle*, March 1995). The 35s helped to finance her trip and also handled the donations from an appeal for her work which was made in the newsletter. In May 1995 she wrote to the 35s that she had found forty-five remaining elderly members of the Jewish community still struggling to hold on... without the support of the 35s none of this operation would have been possible.

The current work of the 35s in supporting the new immigrants in Israel has already been recounted. As yet, there is no end in sight for the continuing call on its resources and expertise.

It is interesting to note that the dire predictions of the Anglo-Jewish establishment expressed during the 35s' more active campaigning years were without foundation, and events have shown that the ends most certainly justified the means. The strengths which they discovered then have stood them in good stead in the ensuing fulfilling years. Today, the women are twenty-five years older, and the buggies which they now push are those of their grandchildren. They are no longer as energetic as they were, some are in ill-health, some have died. But the remaining workers are as determined as ever they were to continue in their mission.

The 35ers of the 1970s were women of their time. The movement grew out of an imperative for immediate action, and the women, although unprepared, gave their all, and in return were rewarded one thousand-fold. Today, they are still giving.

Epilogue

The following comment was made to Sharansky by KGB Colonel Volodin during an interrogation: "That's enough! What do you think, that your fate is in the hands of these people and not ours? They're nothing more than students and housewives".

Sharansky observes[129]: "Students and housewives. Thank you Citizen Colonel, for providing me with such an excellent formulation. Today, whenever I appear before an audience in Jerusalem and New York, in Paris, London, and many other cities where people demonstrated on my behalf, I thank them for their efforts, and I remind them of their strength and their power. And I always remember to tell them what Volodin said, for in the end the army of students and housewives turned out to be mightier than the army of the KGB".

[129] *Fear No Evil* by Natan Sharansky, p.170.

All past and present members of
THE 35's WOMEN'S CAMPAIGN FOR SOVIET JEWRY
in the United Kingdom and beyond
are deeply shocked and terribly saddened
by the tragic death on 3rd October 1995 of

RAIZA PALATNIK

Our organisation was founded in May 1971 on behalf of Raiza Palatnik when we heard that she had been falsely arrested and imprisoned by the Odessa KGB. The entire Soviet Jewry Campaign in the U.K. was initiated as a result. Her outstanding heroism and deep love of Zion were an inspiration to all of us.

We extend our deepest condolences to her sister KATYA and to her family and her very large circle of friends and admirers.

Newsletter, October 1995.

Appendix 1

The Testimony of George Samoilovich

George Samoilovich applied to leave the Soviet Union in 1979 but was refused permission on the grounds that his occupation as a Senior Scientific Lecturer in Applied Mathematics had given him access to state "secrets". It was ten years before he was allowed to leave and this was only after an intensive international campaign brought about by the onset of a grave illness. These bare facts conceal an intensely moving story in which the 35s are proud to have had a role, a story which is told here by George in his own words.

OUR EXODUS

Perhaps it sounds strange but the time which I spent in refusal was, maybe, one of the happiest in my life because I was lucky to know people who I can characterise only with one word – "wonderful". Many of them became a part of my life and we remember them and meet them now. We are obliged to them for our lives in the very literal sense of the word and some of them I am proud to name as our friends.

That was in spite of my last time in refusal being darkened by illness.

That summer, the summer of 1988 (our ninth summer in refusal), was unusually hot in Moscow. It was also a period of great tension for refuseniks who were united in different seminars and groups. At the beginning of June an International Juridicial Seminar was held in

Moscow and just before that the President of the United States, Ronald Reagan, visited the Soviet Union.

Refuseniks had prepared for these events; discussed and elaborated an appeal for passing on to the President and prepared for meetings with foreign lawyers coming to Moscow (we had several of them). I took part in this work, using some material from our symposium "Refusal to Grant Permission to Emigrate for Consideration of State", which was held last year, where I made a report..)

In the middle of June I fell ill with a heavy cough, fever and a sore throat. In spite of treatment (including that of my wife, Vera), my illness lasted a very long time and after some weeks a tumour appeared on my neck near the throat. Vera insisted on showing this to a specialist. After examination the doctor became very serious and called a second doctor and then they sent me to another hospital where there was 'a specialist in this field' as they told me. As I left them I asked if I could take a shower. "Certainly" was the reply – "it is not a cold after all". I began to guess what sort of illness I had, but tried to fight back these thoughts.

A polyclinic, where this specialist received patients was near our home. After he had examined me the doctor sent me to a 'special hospital' and gave me his opinion, in a sealed envelope to be passed on. (There is a Soviet rule that people sick with cancer should not be told of the diagnosis).

Sometimes our memory keeps some events like pictures during the whole of life. So vividly do I see our shady street when I came home after that visit. I passed our house, wishing to think about the news which I had guessed. When I returned, I saw Vera from afar. I understand that she had returned home from her work, and finding that I was not at home she went to the polyclinic, spoke with the doctor and knew my diagnosis. She did not see me and I shall never forget the impression of horror and confusion on her dear face. I will never forget this picture; our shady empty street and her coming to me with this awful face.

So I became a patient of the Central Oncological Hospital in Moscow. It was located far from the centre of the town in a new, grey, huge building named by Muscovites "Blokhinwald" – the word combining the name of the Nazis' concentration camp "Buckenwald", with its ominous appearance and content, and the surname of the director of the hospital, Academician Blokhin. The hospital was full of sick people of all ages and among them I have seen many children (mostly from the south) with sore eyes, together with their mothers. There were long lines to see doctors, long lines for examinations and long lines to have a place in the hospital.

Although my veteran's status gave me privileges I was told that it would take at least one or two months before it would be my turn to go into that hospital, but before then many examinations had to be done, as there was a long line to do them it would be better if I could (arrange to) have them done myself, etc., etc.

But there was one more thing which I knew from some doctor friends; there was no confidence in successful treatment. That was not the fault of the Russian doctors; the medicine there was out of date. In other words, lymphoma – that was my diagnosis – can only be suppressed for some time. That means to delay the end. No more.

Now I must go back a little in my narration. For a long time there was a vast steady campaign among Western Jewish organisations to support refuseniks. In this activity some English and American doctors came periodically to the Soviet Union to test ill refuseniks and give them advice and medicine. At the end of 1987 four American doctors came from the United States. This group was led by Dr Richard Rosenbluth, an oncologist, a person with a very uncommon soul, a particular specialist in lymphatic and blood oncological diseases.

Our family had gathered oncologically ill Jews, not only refuseniks, in our small apartment. Victor, my son, brought doctors to us and we made there a one-day clinic. I remember how these poor people came to our tiny rooms. Doctors made reception in two of them, anxious relatives thronged in the kitchen and a small antechamber where there was space for no more than two persons, encumbered with coats (it was in winter).

As some people left, reassured or perturbed, new ones arrived. Vera helped the doctors and Victor served as a translator and we were happy that we could give some small help to these ill people.

We became friends with these doctors and Richard Rosenbluth became especially close to us. After he left we started to be in correspondence, so it was natural for Vera to send a long telegram to Richard when I received this diagnosis.

After less than one week the whole Rosenbluth family arrived in Moscow; Richard, his wife Susan – a journalist publishing a Jewish magazine, whose energy can be measured only in terms of an atomic bomb – and three nice children, Jonathan, Benjy and Rachel. Richard had brought an invitation for me to be treated free of charge in the Hackensack Medical Centre, where he was director of the oncological department.

While my paper for leaving was being prepared they wanted to visit Leningrad and Israel and on the way back to take me to the USA. Nice and naïve Western people! They thought that my illness and this invitation were enough to let me out. They had never come face to face with Soviet principles.

First of all, officials wanted to have an official certificate about my illness, but Soviet law prohibits the giving of such certificates to private persons. Next day, Richard, Vera and Victor went to the oncological centre. Later they told me about the alarm that was caused when they asked for such a certificate. This alarm was doubled when the authorities of the centre realised that this paper was needed to take me abroad for treatment. There was a long wrangle but at last they agreed to give such a certificate but only in exchange for a receipt that I refused to be treated in that centre, signed by Vera.

Everybody who has acquaintance with Soviet rules understands that there was no confidence that the authorities would give me permission to leave. To sign such a receipt would mean that I lose a possibility for treatment in this case. Of course, Vera refused to give this paper and after some consultation with somebody they gave the certificate we needed. It was successful only thanks to the pressure of Richard – an American professor.

Nevertheless I was expelled from the Cancer Centre. When I attended after some days I was not accepted there. A nurse showed me a list of patients, with my family crossed out. But this was later.

Getting this paper, we then went to OVIR.[130] For Richard and Susan that was an unusual experience, which, I suppose, did not happen to any foreign person, and we all got satisfaction in seeing how put out was the OVIR's officer. This officer tried to behave friendly and said that if I wanted to receive the permission sooner, the best way is to apply not for treatment, but for a temporary visit (that was wrong, as we have seen). But that would take time to get such an invitation because it could only be made in Washington.

---

[130] OVIR: Office of Visas and Registration.

It was a very cunning step. First, this procedure will take time, they will get rid of the Rosenbluths and think out something else to obstacle me. The second – in this case 'a reason' for my refusal – remained. But we realised this was OVIR's last word and, while this officer went for a lunch break, we hurried to the American Embassy. Richard and Susan went in and we three stayed anxiously in the car. After a half hour they came back with an official invitation to visit them in the United States.

It is impossible to depict the face of the officer when I put the paper which he had asked for on his desk just after his lunch.

While the Rosenbluths visited Leningrad, one of Vera's friends made a puncture to take some of my tumour. The tissue was divided into two parts; one was analysed in Moscow by another of Vera's friends (in another hospital), the second Richard took to America. (It was a big risk to take a test-tube through the customs). After testing this tissue Richard made a legalised medical statement about my illness and situation.

At the beginning of autumn I received a refusal to go for a visit to the United States, and at the end of 1988 my family was anxious with two tasks, how to get me abroad and how to get treatment here to prevent the spread of my illness. My status could be known by a CAT scan test but it could only be done in Moscow in special clinics for "special" people, (in London I had this test on the next day after my arrival), although amongst Vera's patients there were many good doctors and academicians. Nevertheless she arranged for me to have medical attention, and all this time I have seen on her and Victor's faces worry, anxiety and love, but at what cost to their strength and nerves. I have to thank Vera's colleagues, who gave me injections and tests. Richard had sent a modern treatment plan and a latest medicine but it couldn't be used by Russian doctors and in my situation especially. Because of all these problems I had not time to think about my future, but only on today's troubles. I could only apply again by asking to go, not for a visit but for treatment. But in this case OVIR demands approval from the Ministry of Public Health. All Vera's attempts to get into her Ministry and discuss the question with the authorities were unsuccessful.

As usual, the help came from abroad. In Moscow arrived Linda Opper, director of the International Physicians Commission, with Marilyn Tallman, director of the Chicago Council for Soviet Jews.

They made an appointment with the deputy Minister and after almost the same conversation as was in OVIR, they promised to give the certificate that OVIR needed. I received a paper on which it was written that the Ministry of Public Health "don't object to me to go for treatment abroad". A very funny formula, but OVIR was satisfied and I gave up my papers.

After one month I received again a refusal. This was catastrophic because, according to the law I could make a next attempt only after six months. An exception is only if I will apply to go to another country (i.e. not the USA).

A popularity in the West helped and supported refuseniks very much and gave them a kind of warranty – the person will not vanish without any sign in KGB's prisons, camps or mental hospitals. For me there was an additional reason; it helped me get permission for treatment, it rescued me. Richard, Union of Councils for Soviet Jews, 35s Women's Campaign for Soviet Jewry (where not only women participated), Medical Campaign for Soviet Jewry, International Physicians Commission and the student's organisation, "VISOV", launched a vast campaign on my behalf, with demonstrations in front of Soviet Consulates and Embassies. Richard and several doctors were arrested demonstrating in New York; Naomi Samuelson passed a petition with many signatures to the Soviet Ambassador in London during a demonstration organised by "Visov"; there were simultaneous demonstrations in London, New York and Philadelphia; Micah Naftalin organised a meeting in Washington; the Union of Councils for Soviet Jews worked with the State Department and Mr Shifter (whom I met several times in Moscow; he had promised to get us out). The 35s raised the campaign not only in England but involved Jewish organisations in France and Luxembourg and also in the European Parliament; my case was put in its resolution of 19 September 1988; Lord Plumb[131] made a statement on his visit to Moscow and discussed this topic with Gromyko.

Most important and decisive was the involvement of British Members of Parliament, the Office of the Prime Minister, and the Foreign and Commonwealth Office, and Mr Geoffrey Howe and Mr William Waldegrave personally. Without all this restless activity

---

[131] Lord Plumb. A member of the European Parliament.

Arrival of Sylva Zalmanson at Heathrow after her release from prison in September 1974, greeted by (from left to right) Margaret Rigal, Edward Kuznetsov, Sylva Zalmanson, Rita Eker.

Arrival of Sharansky at Heathrow after his release from prison in February 1986.
Left to right: Lynn Singer, Rita Eker, Natan Sharansky, Martin Gilbert.

South London 35ers demonstrate at 'the strongest man in the world' competition at Crystal Palace, November 1974.

35ers invade pitch and present Russian footballers with petition for Sylva Zalmanson, December 1972.

Wearing only a body-stocking and a wig, seventeen year-old Maryanne Ellis, dressed as Lady Godiva, rode through London streets to demonstrate with 35ers before a Soviet parliamentary delegation outside the Barbican.

35ers mount a demonstration outside the Soviet Embassy in support of Alexander Feldman, a twenty-seven year old Kiev engineer on trial for alleged hooliganism, November 1973.

South London 35ers together with local MPs gather to celebrate the release of Sylva Zalmanson.
Left to right: John Moore MP, June Kenton, Ruth Urban, Bernard Weatherill MP, Rita Horowitz, September 1974.

from strong people in Britain and the US my fate would be much more glum.

The Netherlands Ambassador, Mr Peter Buwalde, made some statement to the Soviet authorities. He and his staff were in constant contact with me, so were the American and British Embassies. Susan Vagner from the American Embassy became our good friend. It is a great pity and I am very sorry that I have lost a lady from the political department of the British Embassy and do not know her name. We are very obliged to her and her chief. She has helped us very kindly, phoned us and met several times.

Refuseniks have known that among Jewish organisations abroad there are only the 35s and the Union of Councils for Soviet Jews, who really understand their aims, who supported them and struggled for them. After I fell ill the flow of letters, telephone calls and visitors grew tremendously, not only from the USA and Great Britain, but from many other countries. We were very moved when Nellie Hewspear from Birmingham explained in her letter that she could not come to see me because her husband was ill. I tried to answer all people and it took a lot of time, but with some people we established a correspondence and they became our friends.

All this was as a beam of light in a kingdom of darkness, a gleam of hope. When I spoke over the telephone or opened a letter with a foreign stamp, my personal feeling was as if I was breathing a fresh and clean air. After that it was easier to live, the life was not pictured so utterly dark. At the same time I could not shake off an impression that we live in different worlds, on different planets, because it was impossible to imagine the existence of another life and it was as impossible to reach countries with this different life as to reach another planet.

Although telephone reception was better than when I spoke with Leningrad or Rostov-on-Don, sometimes it was interrupted so you can hear only some sounds, some parts of a word and can hardly understand the sense. During my illness the telephone was seldom disconnected, much less than before. (There was a funny occasion not long before my illness. There was a call from a public phone, a person had come to Moscow and wanted to see us. She told us that she didn't know her schedule and would call again to fix the visit. Just after that my telephone became deaf and dumb. I went to the telephone exchange, which was near us. There I was told that a line is out of order and could be fixed only after a couple of days, but at the same time my neighbour's telephone was good... Nevertheless we met with our visitors).

I have met leaders of the Union of Councils for Soviet Jews sometimes when they came to Moscow; Pamela Cohen and Micah Naftalin, David Waxberg and Linda Opper with Marilyn Tallman, but I never saw anybody from the 35s who have phoned me many times. The explanation was very simple – because of their activity the Soviets (of course the KGB) have refused the activists and leaders of this organisation permission to come to the USSR. Because of that I knew them only by names and by voices.

When there was a call from London, I heard most often a strong woman's voice – that was Rita – which made me confident that we had a firm support in her person. After a couple of words she called, "Michael, Michael, it is George". (Later she would call Michael just after hearing my voice – it was, and perhaps is, not so easy to speak with me in English!). And then I heard an optimistic voice in Russian, "But we are brothers". It was so touching. What was good was that Vera could also speak with him. Then I heard the voices of Joyce Simson and Liz Phillips, which I could distinguish very soon, and I was happy to hear them. Michael Isaacs[132], the calm, soft voice of Lionel Salama[133], Michael Chissick[134] and Jonathan Morris[135] who have visited us and whom we came to love very much, Myra Lauder whom I have seen in 1987 and who came in 1989 and visited us with Paul Lauder – many voices, a lot of friends. When Vera heard Naomi Samuelson telling us about their activities (Naomi and Albert Samuelson visited us later), she couldn't help crying, "What people! They don't know you, but what an enthusiasm", which she repeated many times.

There was also a flow of visitors from England and America. Sometimes we arranged to meet them on the platform of the metro-station "Airport" (one small block from our house) and then return together to our home. It was very easy to recognise foreigners by their unconstrained behaviour, a little different appearance and absolutely different faces. Sometimes the people came to us directly

---

[132]) Members of "Refusenik" (A Soviet Jewry Group).
[133])
[134]) Members of "Visov" (a group of young activists for Soviet Jewry.
[135])

and also unexpectedly. Sometimes there were misunderstandings but with lucky endings. We missed each other with Jonny Morris and Michael Chissick, as our metro-station has two exits. I waited a very long time and came home grieved. What a joy it was to see two young people near our door. I recognised them faultlessly and we greeted each other cheerfully. I was very upset when Edward Mack became frozen near his hotel when we were both waiting for each other in different places. He and Patricia Mack had visited us the past evening and agreed to take an important letter which I promised to pass to them the next evening. But we were very happy to find each other.

Each visit of people from abroad was an event, a holiday.

Sometimes we had guests three or four times a week and twice in a day. They have embarrassed us a little by bringing different gifts. We understood them but it was much more important to see them and to speak with them. After they left us we felt stunned and remembered all the details – we have seen the people from another world. It was something special in their eyes, their faces. I don't know why but we became more confident. They gave us hope and strength to withstand the system, which we hated, the State which we wanted to leave. And, of course, there was a special hope for me – a hope for treatment, for rescue.

How could we thank them? Vera tried to prepare best meals, but we shared with them our news, told them about our fellow refuseniks, tried to explain the absurdity of life in that country and its features. If they had any time and wished to do so, Victor took them on a tour of the city and showed them places which they would never see with an official guide or excursion.

So passed the time. We were completely upset after getting the second refusal to go to the United States, when unexpectedly, on 18 January 1989 there was a telegram from Professor Daniel Catovsky of the Royal Marsden Hospital, London, inviting me to be treated by him personally. Efforts of the 35s and the Medical Campaign for Soviet Jewry made this possibility successful. I applied immediately and on 21 February received again a refusal, this time to go to London. Things turned to absolute gloom.

After that the contacts with the British Embassy became especially intensive. Rita, Liz, Joyce, and other friends called almost every day, asking me about my situation, telling me what they are undertaking and assuring me not to abandon hope. Could you imagine Vera's and Victor's feelings at that period. I have written to Gorbachev and Shevardnadze and tried to pass my application to them, but all in vain. I know that my application didn't reach them at all. Vera also sent a long telegram to Gorbachev, she applied to the Commission for Human Rights of the Supreme Soviet (using writers of her acquaintance), a very official organisation (without doubt under the bearing of the KGB), with the same result.

Rita and Joyce advised me to appeal to Mrs Thatcher, who was held in high respect in Russia, but I hesitated. If I ventured to trouble her there was a risk; the Soviet authorities would not forgive me for this step and there will be no hope at all to get permission if she will not support me very firmly. But after some reflection we decided that it was, apparently, the last hope. Just at that time we were visited by Patricia and Edward Mack, a nice couple from Leeds, who agreed to take the letter and give it to Rita.

That was a salvation step and Mrs Thatcher became the most honoured person to our family. Later it was made known to me (by Joyce – a "foreign Minister") that she had sent word to Moscow that my case must be cleared up before Gorbachev's arrival in London. Their summit was planned for the beginning of April. He was in Cuba and had to leave there for England on April the fifth. On Sunday evening, 2nd April, I heard from Pamela in Washington. She was very agitated and told me that Mr Shifter phoned; by diplomatic channels he had known that my restriction was lifted and I could go to London.

I could not believe it, so wonderful it was. At that time we had guests from abroad who had heard our conversation and after us had to go to see another refusenik. I asked them not to tell anybody this news; I was afraid it was not true. But next morning a joyful and excited Rita's voice confirmed this news. That was more than success. That was salvation and I was completely stunned. This state remained during all my last days in Moscow. I lived like a dream.

Then there was a call from OVIR; Vera took the call. Karakulko, a deputy chief (and practically a chief of this organisation), asked how I was feeling. (Vera wondered if he was interested in if I am still alive) and he very politely informed us that after the lunchbreak I could come, take a foreign passport, and go to London for treatment.

After that the television men arrived from the BBC, and at the same time came Lord Bethell. He didn't know my news and I didn't know who he was. It was only later that we knew that we had received a real British lord in our modest apartment.

After the lunchbreak I went to OVIR. It was not a reception day; Karakulko received me in his private study and again very politely asked me if I still want to emigrate. "Why have I struggled for ten years?" I answered. Karakulko started to tell me that they give me a five-year foreign passport, I can go for treatment, then come back, and at any time may go abroad and see my friends, etc., etc. so I do not need to emigrate!

"Why do you persuade me?" I asked. "I don't persuade you at all," he answered and continued more formally. If I wanted to have my family abroad, I must leave a legal document that I do not object to them doing this. They must fill in a new form (which was changed recently) and give it with my certificate. I asked him if they needed a new invitation (I had one at home) but he answered in the negative. "And could they leave with no obstacles?" I asked. "And they can leave" he answered.

The whole next day I spent preparing and legalising this certificate (I could only do this with my interior passport). When I came on Wednesday and showed Karakulko this paper, he said it was good and they could join me abroad as soon as they want. After that he took my foreign passport from his safe and passed it to me in exchange for my interior one. I looked at it and smiled; my birthdate and birthplace were wrong. In the hurry they did not see my file, when the order came from high up to let me out. My restriction was lifted without any procedure – was it real before? They corrected my birthdate but the incorrect birthplace remains: Moscow, instead of Rostov-on-Don.

The next step was to buy a ticket, which was never simple in that country, and of course there was a long line in front of the booking office for foreign trips. I went to the top, as a veteran, and asked for a ticket to London and was told that I could get it only by buying a return ticket also. I insisted, and the line behind me started to shout, as usual. The cashier called for her chief and he confirmed that they could sell me only a round-trip ticket. "But it is my right to buy what I like," I said. "And if you are deported, what will you do? We bear the responsibility for you – you are a Soviet citizen," he said. "If they deport me, I go on foot from London," I joked. He looked at me with hate and said "Confirm this in writing". The earliest time for which they could sell me the ticket was 9 April, the following Sunday at 10 o'clock in the morning, and I only had one working day – tomorrow, to complete all my affairs.

On Friday Victor took a day off and went everywhere with me. Vera rushed between her patients, whom she must visit, and home, preparing for my journey. In the British Embassy we were met by the nice lady from the political department of whom I have told earlier. She took my passport and said that it will be ready in a couple of hours. Without wasting time we hurried to the bank where people going abroad exchanged roubles for hard currency. Of course there was a line also.

When we went back to the Embassy we were asked to wait in a hall finished with wood in an old style (The British Embassy is located in an old and rich house). After some time we were invited into a second hall where a person from the Embassy staff and a Deputy Ambassador (the Ambassador was in London on the summit meeting with Gorbachev at that time). It was a short, solemn procedure. He congratulated me, hoped that I would have a good treatment and all the best in the free world. I don't remember what I answered. I was too agitated and I also felt very solemn. It was a significant moment for me.

When we returned to the bank and I reached the teller, the officer looked at my passport and said that according to an order from the Ministry of Finance, from April the first of this year they don't change money for people who go abroad for treatment. There were several hours left until the end of the working day, so we hurried to this ministry. I don't know how we eventually succeeded to get to a Deputy Minister. Perhaps our worried and upset appearance helped and it was lucky for us that he was there. After some discussion ("How can I go for treatment if I have no money even to smoke?"), he wrote a permit for me to change a hundred roubles, which was equal to approximately £75. It was our good luck that when we came back to the bank it was still open. All my affairs were now completed and now I can fly. We breathed with relief.

All Saturday I was busy sorting out my papers, my archives, my things and answering numerous calls. One of them grieved me; Liz Phillips phoned to say that she was in Israel and could not meet me in London (I had phoned Rita to let her know when I would arrive). I knew that she had done very much for me and, of course, I wanted to thank her as soon as I arrived. Victor helped me. Vera, Tanya (Victor's wife) and her sister prepared a party which had to be held that evening. My farewell party.

The first friends came at about six o'clock. The people came and left, and other friends arrived. I saw all of them that evening and promised that I would not forget that they, my fellow refuseniks, still remain in that country. There was also the Netherland's Ambassador and his wife, Peter and Vilma Buwalde, a chief of the political department of the British Embassy with that nice lady who took care of me, Susan Vagner (her colleague from the American Embassy) with her husband Stephen – all people to whom I was so obliged.

At two o'clock the last people left our apartment and I returned to the packing of my two suitcases. At four o'clock we took a short sleep to be at the airport at eight a.m. – we knew how long it takes to go through the customs.

There was little sleep. We were tired, but I talked with Vera, fell asleep for a moment, awoke, talked again, fell asleep and awoke again. We had to separate and our future was very unclear. Am I in the state where my illness is curable? When will we meet (we knew that OVIR can change its mind)? Will we see each other at all? All was uncertain.

At six a.m. we were up. (Victor and Tanya slept on a sofa bed in the second room). A shower, a cup of coffee and the four of us are sitting in a car riding to Sheremetevo 2 – Moscow International Airport which was a distance of one hour from our home. There was no line at the customs for my flight. "Why do you go to London?" a customs officer asked me nastily. I did not have to answer but I told him, also nastily, "for treatment". – "What is your disease? Why could you not be treated here?" he said. I didn't want to make him angry as I was under his power, but I could not hold back my hatred. "Because my cancer cannot be treated here," I answered, looking into his evil eyes, and we didn't exchange another word while he finished his long search.

Last words, which cannot express our feelings, last kisses, last embraces – and I cross the line which separates me from my dear ones, from my past. It is so difficult to take this step, only one step. But I must do that, and I do, and I try not to hesitate like when diving into cold water. My feet are heavy, they are leaden, they stick to the floor, but I must go onward and they become further and further away. We wave to each other; we send blow-kisses; I see tears on their dear faces, but I must go – and my heart tears in pieces...

My plane was half empty. I took a place near a window. Outside was a wet flying field and the usual aerodrome life so familiar to me from my youth. The plane took off and from on high I saw a dirty melting snow, grey wet buildings. I tried to look for familiar places, the centre of Moscow, which I loved and which I know that I will never see again. But nothing except grey wet roofs, grey buildings and wet dirty earth could be seen. And I try to press this picture in my heart. I left the place where I was born and lived the whole of my life – for ever. I left my dearest and was not sure to see them again. (The same day, at six p.m. my dear Vera was taken to hospital with a severe heart attack).

When the plane gained height, I fell into a troubled slumber and when I awoke I saw in the window a green water with several small ships. There was a line of shore and, at last, green fields with lots of red roofs. All this was lit up with bright sunshine. That was England.

I have not mentioned how we landed at Heathrow. All was unfamiliar and strange around me. I guessed that they would meet me but I could not hurry. I had to accommodate these conditions and surroundings. Also, my two suitcases didn't allow me to hurry – they were heavy, as if there were bricks inside; but there were no bricks, but books.

When I approached the passport control, a man came to the officer, called my name and asked him if I had passed already or not. Passing the control after some minutes, I saw a crowd of people meeting passengers and a group of women on one side. A tall energetic lady with a beautiful strong face separated from them and came to meet me. That was Rita Eker.

Rita Eker recalls meeting this "gaunt stranger" at Heathrow: "We embraced each other with tears streaming down our faces. I took him home and after a meal we went into the garden; he looked around and said "Who owns this park?""

George's treatment at the Royal Marsden Hospital, London, was successful and he went to live in retirement in New Jersey, USA. His wife and son followed him a little while later, but it was not until 1993 that his daughter-in-law, Tanya, was given an exit visa. George was given a clean bill of health in February 1990.

Appendix 2
Statistics And Campaigns

STAFF RESOURCES

Frontliners – July 1977

Name*	Address	Tel. No.
Becker, Sylvia*	The addresses and telephone numbers of all the frontliners were supplied on this list.	
Birkin, Martin		
Burns, Rhoda*		
Clayton, Zena*		
Conrich, Carol		
Cumber, Leila*		
Duke, Rochelle		
Eker, Rita		
Gainsford, Doreen*		
Gamse, Hinda		
Gemal, Rosalind		
Goldfarb, Simone		
Green, Valerie*		
Harris, Zelda*		
Isaacs, Linda*		
Janner, Myra*		
Kalman, Rachele*		
Kennard, Celia		
Lader, Phyllis		
Levine, Sylvia		
Linden, Minnie		
Lowy, Joy		

* These frontliners are willing to speak at meetings – always to be accompanied by a Provincial or London Group Leader.

Millet, Janet
O'Hana, Genia
Owen, Phyllis
Perkin, Marcia
Phillips, Liz
Rigal, Margaret*
Satin, Mona
Schofield, Mary
Shaw, Judy
Sherry, Enid
Simson, Joyce
Sosnow, Jennifer
Spelman, Marcella
Usiskin, Sue
Vice, Elizabeth

Telephoners
In charge: Carol Conrich, Liz Phillips, Janet Millet, Rhoda Burns.

Each of the following holds individual telephone lists for demos:
Cumber, Leila
Goldfarb, Simone
Graham, Herta
Greenby, Molly
Herold, Susan
Janner, Myra
Kut, Zena
Sherry, Enid
Urban, Ruth
Witte, Rosalind

Office Staff
Chalfen, Diane; Ellis, Rose; Frank, Hilda; Gilmont, Rina; Hylkema
(now Aron), Joanne; Israel, Frank; Gabay, Jacob; Lyons, Barbara;
Paul, Joy

JOB/STAFF	NAME	OFFICE
Assistance *General Administration*	Doreen Gainsford	Diane/Joanna

Office Administration	Rita Eker	Diane
Demonstration organisers	Sylvia Levine	Joy
	Rochelle Duke	
Jewellery Sales		
Overall admin and ordering	Rochelle Duke	Joanna
Sales/delivery to 35s groups	Marcella Spelman	
Sales/delivery to all other groups and shops	Valerie Green	
Key rings	Sylvia Levine	
Telephoners		
Overall charge	Carole Conrich	Diane
	Liz Phillips	
	Rhoda Burns	
Membership		
Lists and files	Linda Isaacs	Diane
	Liz Phillips	
Minutes of Meetings	Liz Phillips	Diane
London 35s Groups organisers	Zelda Harris	Diane
	Linda Isaacs	
	Myra Janner	
Provincial 35s Groups organisers	Zena Clayton	Joy
	Sylvia Becker	
	Phyllis Lader	
Adopt-A-Prisoner Campaign	(Rita Eker	Joy
	(Rachele Kalman	
	(Phyllis Owen	
Adopt-A-Refusenik	Barbara Lyons	
	Sue Usiskin	
	Liz Phillips	
National MP Contact	Margaret Rigal	Rose
Trade Union Contact	Rosalind Gemal	Rose

Helsinki Watchdog Committee	Doreen Gainsford Enid Sherry	Hilda/Rina
Schools/University/Youth Groups	Rachele Kalman	Joanna
Organising letter writing to Press	Leila Cumber	Diane
Visiting Soviet Delegations, Soviet Officials, Radio phone-in	Liz Phillips Simone Goldfarb	
Non-governmental organisations	Elizabeth Vice Hilda Gamse	Joanna/Diane
Contact with Jewish and Gentile Religious Leaders	Mary Schofield Linda Isaacs	Rose
Maintenance of Press Cuttings Books	Joy Lowy	Joy
Sending Letters/Press cuttings to Refuseniks and Soviet Officials	Margaret Rigal Genia O'Hana	
Embassy Letters *(twice weekly)*	Marcia Perkin	
Travel to USSR co-ordinator	Rhoda Burns	
VIP correspondence	Mona Satin	Diane

Newspaper Reading
1. Future activities for attention of demo organisers
2. Articles/letters which need reply for attention of letter-writers
3. Information
All cuttings will be available on Joy's desk for all to see.

The following will read their press early a.m. and pass for attention immediately:

DAILIES (Monday to Saturday)	*SUNDAYS*
Mail .... Rochelle Duke	Mirror .... Linda Isaacs
Express .... Genia O'Hara	Express and Times . Leila Cumber
Times .... Leila Cumber	Observer .... Celia Kennard
Guardian .... Martin Birkin	Telegraph .... Sylvia Levine
Telegraph ...... Celia Kennard	
Fin. Times	
(Sat. only) ... R. Duke	
Evening News. Rhoda Burns	

Distribution of this list to the following:
35s Frontliners, London Group Leaders, Provincial Group Leaders, Overseas Groups, British Soviet Jewry Groups, Cyril Stein, Michael Sherbourne, Nan Griefer.

CAMPAIGNS AND DEMONSTRATIONS (PROTESTS)

These lists are by no means comprehensive but serve to give a picture of the wide range and variety of the work of some of the groups, and typical of the work of all of them.

Specific groups such as Brent (Wembley Conference Centre and Arena), Bournemouth, Brighton and Hove, Leeds, Liverpool, Manchester, etc. (TUC and political party conferences), Luxembourg and Brussels (European meeting centres) had extra responsibilities.

Some groups described their activities as demonstrations and some as protests.

As most of these references were taken from the newsletters, they were sometimes reported one or two months after the event, hence occasional discrepancies in dates.

LONDON AND THE SUBURBS

Where no specific group is mentioned, the demonstration was organised by the office, but was supported by members from many different groups.

1971

May
A 24-hour hunger strike[136] on May Day for Raiza Palatnik by 28 women, who made a vain attempt to hand a letter to Madame Smirnovskaya, wife of the Soviet Ambassador at the Embassy. The letter, taken by Barbara Oberman, Myra Janner and Sylvia Wallis, and signed on behalf of all 35-year-old Jewish women in Britain called upon her to use her good offices to stop the KGB from torturing Raiza. This demonstration attracted much publicity on BBC radio and in the national press.

May
Demonstration outside the Soviet Embassy on behalf of Palatnik and Ruth Alexandrovich.

July
A table spread with a typical prisoner's meal, outside the Soviet Embassy.

August
A vain attempt to deliver the 64th daily letter to the Soviet Embassy.

August
Brent and others; on three separate evenings broadcast to crowds attending the Moscow State Circus.

November
Demonstration for Sylva Zalmanson.

November
Demonstration by the wives of Jewish and non-Jewish MPs, for Sylva Zalmanson, outside the Soviet Embassy.

December
South London and others; demonstration during reception for three Russian delegates outside Lambeth Town Hall.

December
Demonstration on the first anniversary of the Leningrad trial, outside the Soviet Embassy. Attended by over two hundred participants. The Chanukkah candles were lit by the Chief Rabbi.

1972

February
Prisoner's 'banquet' at the House of Commons.

[136] The First Demonstration

June	South London; (a) sent a parcel of matzo to Smeliansky family in Moscow. (b) held a 24-hour hunger strike in sympathy with six Russian scientists. (c) Bouquet containing message about Sylva Zalmanson handed to Russian tennis star Olga Morozova at Beckenham tournament.
July	Demonstration outside Buckingham Palace as Soviet Ambassador Nikolai Lunkov arrived in horse-drawn carriage to present his credentials to the Queen Mother. Banners and umbrellas bearing slogan "NIKOLAI LUNKOV STOP PERSECUTING INNOCENT GOLDSTEIN BROTHERS, INNOCENT JEWS FROM TBILISI" displayed. A file containing three hundred letters which had been sent to the Soviet Embassy during the previous year and remained unanswered was thrown into the carriage by Annette Spiers, who was arrested and charged with threatening behaviour. The incident received extensive press coverage.
December	Dressed as Santa Claus, 35ers handed out roubles to passers-by outside the Narodny Bank.

1973

June	At the Coliseum Theatre during a performance of the Georgia State Dance Company, a hunting horn was blown from a box occupied by 35ers, six members rushed on stage and opened black umbrellas bearing the slogan "USSR FREE JEWS", whilst twenty women opened similar umbrellas in other parts of the auditorium. Doreen Gainsford appealed to the audience not to forget Russia's persecuted Jews whilst watching the performance. Demonstrations continued outside the theatre for three weeks.
July	Demonstration outside the Soviet Embassy for the release of the Goldstein brothers. Twenty mothers (including Hayley Mills and her baby) with babies in buggies displayed banners with the slogan "WILL THIS MAN EVER SEE HIS BABY?" (Isai Goldstein's wife was expecting a baby.)

July	Demonstration for Isaac Skolnik (serving ten years hard labour for applying for an exit visa) outside the Soviet Embassy. A large replica of Brezhnev's head was paraded.
July	Demonstration for Yevgeny Levich (conscripted when in ill-health). Outside the Soviet Embassy, two 35ers dressed as nurses carrying stretchers, and one 35er beating on a drum.
September	Demonstration at Crystal Palace during the World Modern Pentathlon Games, in reply to an attack on Jewish competitors and spectators at the Moscow World Student Games. Placards were displayed from the balcony.
October	Actress Janet Suzman cut symbolic cake on Sylva Zalmanson's 29th birthday outside the Soviet Embassy.
October	South London members June Kenton and Sandra Butcher presented Sylva Zalmanson medallions to Russian skaters at the International Ice Dancing Championships, Streatham Ice Rink.

1974

January	South London: prisoners' luncheon in Croydon attended by clergymen of different denominations.
January	Protest on behalf of Sylva Zalmanson outside the Soviet Embassy. Thirty 35ers took part in a 'sew-in' (Zalmanson's prison work was sewing tough fabric). Actress Yvonne Mitchell attempted to deliver a letter on Zalmanson's behalf.
January	Demonstration outside the Intourist Office, Regent Street on behalf of Alexander Feldman (sentenced to three and a half years' hard labour, on a trumped-up charge of knocking a cake out of a woman's hand).
January	Presented a chess set to Soviet chess Grand Master Mikhail Tal, together with a letter seeking the release of Alexander Feldman.
January	Bromley: together, clergymen of different denominations met with Second Secretary Subolov at the Soviet Embassy on behalf of Sylva Zalmanson and

others. He refused to accept the petition of several hundred signatures.

February	A birthday cake with three and a half candles handed in on behalf of Feldman, at the Intourist office, on the occasion of President Podgorny's birthday. (Feldman had been removed to solitary confinement).
February	A two-hour vigil outside the Soviet Embassy for hunger strikers Rubin, Azbel, Galatsky and Nudel, who were "striking for all Jews in refusal".
February	Greeted Russian delegation as they entered the Machine Tool Trade Association in Bayswater. Handed crutches to head of delegation on behalf of Yankel Khansis, crippled by maltreatment in Soviet labour camp.
February	Presented a lifebelt at Soviet Naval Attache's reception at the Soviet Embassy, symbolising the need to save Alexander Feldman's life.
March	Demonstration outside Hampstead post office for Professor D. Azbel and Ida Nudel.
March	Demonstration at Ideal Home Exhibition; put up tourist posters at the Intourist stand "VISIT RUSSIA – VISIT INNOCENT JEWISH PRISONER, ALEXANDER FELDMAN".
March	Posted Passover prayer books and matzo from Trafalgar Square post office.
April	35ers followed thirty-two visiting Russian doctors during their week-long visit (to study the British hospital system). When the doctors left the hotel to return to the airport, they were confronted by heavily bandaged 35ers protesting on behalf of Maximillian Kessler and his wife, and Poltinnikov and family, all medically employed and refused visas.
May	Demonstration at Highgate Cemetery during the visit of Russian tourists to tomb of Karl Marx; they were confronted by 35ers dressed as 'ghosts'.
May	Demonstration outside the London Coliseum during the visit of the Bolshoi Ballet. To the slow beat of a drum, 35ers paraded on behalf of ballet dancers Panovs.

May	Dressed as British Lions bearing placards asking why the rugby tour of South Africa was banned, whilst allowing the Bolshoi Ballet to perform.
June	Demonstration during Bolshoi rehearsal, dressed in flowered hats and white gloves, and equipped with dust carts and brooms 35ers swept St Martin's Lane (to highlight Russian 'clean-up campaign' of Jews during President Nixon's visit to Moscow).
June	Further Bolshoi protest – drove a car carrying a cage containing a life-size model of a ballerina on the roof continuously around Grosvenor Square (home of the US Embassy), to protest at the mass arrest of Jews during President Nixon's visit.
June	Demonstration outside the US Embassy. 35ers formed a 'chain-gang' dressed in prison garb.
July	Protest to Russian participants in International Conference on High Energy Physics on behalf of Victor Polsky (about to face a show trial on trumped-up KGB evidence).
July	Demonstration during the visit of Soviet Ambassador Lunkov to Greenwich, attending a birthday dinner for the Queen.
July	Demonstration outside Carlton House Terrace during a reception for the Bolshoi Ballet and the Foreign Press Association, who were handed flowers by 35ers dressed as ballet dancers.
August	Demonstration by Panovs and 35ers outside the Soviet Embassy. Motorcade demonstration along Regent Street to the Intourist Office and on to the Soviet Embassy, displaying banners: "DON'T DRIVE IN MOSCOW IF YOU ARE JEWISH" (for Polsky, during his trial on a trumped-up driving charge).
October	At the Motor Show, on the Russian stand, 35ers locked themselves into Russian cars, displaying placards at the windows, for Polsky.
October	Demonstration outside the British Olympic Association, dressed as babies, for Dr Mikhail Shtern, also as part of the campaign for the run-up to the Moscow Olympics. Banners read: "NO 1980 OLYMPICS IN

MOSCOW WHILE KGB PERSECUTES JEWS LIKE DR SHTERN".

November	35ers dressed as workmen carrying ladder and builders' gear, outside Soviet Embassy, for Shtern.
November	Funeral procession to Intourist Office with a girl in the coffin and accompanied by twenty 35ers dressed in mourning carrying placards: "LIUBOCHKA BELINSKAYA IS ALIVE. WHY IS DR SHTERN ON TRIAL FOR HER MURDER?"
December	Demonstration outside the Soviet Embassy on Human Rights Day, with mothers and babies in a play pen.
December	Demonstration outside the Thai Embassy during a visit there of the Soviet Ambassador; for Dr Shtern.
December	Demonstration outside Novosti, the Soviet News Agency, for Shtern.
December	Demonstration outside Congress House, during a visit of a Soviet Trade Union delegation; for Dr Shtern.

1975

March	Hunger strikes and demonstrations held during the visit of former KGB chief, Alexander Shelepin, head of the Russian Trade Union delegation.
June	Belgrade; demonstrations.
August	Helsinki; demonstrations
November	Six 35ers dressed in football kit tried to present the Yerevan football team (who ran away from the women) with a new football inscribed with the names of thirty-one Prisoners of Conscience.

1976

July	Proxy funeral service for Colonel Yefim Davidovich. 35ers were charged with obstructing the highway.
October	Demonstration outside the Savoy Hotel during the Woman of the Year Luncheon, the Duchess of Gloucester accepted a petition on behalf of Nudel.
November	Demonstrations during the visit of Boris Ponomariev, Secretary of the Central Committee of the Communist Party: a) outside Transport House b) at the Cenotaph

c) outside his hotel. 35ers dressed as butchers carrying placards accusing Soviets of having butchered the Helsinki Agreement.

December   Demonstration outside the Aeroflot Office, Piccadilly, to commemorate the sixth anniversary of the Leningrad trials.

December   A week of protest outside the Gaumont Cinema in Notting Hill Gate during the Soviet Film Week.

December   Demonstration outside the Soviet Embassy, 35ers and children demonstrate for two young Russian refuseniks carrying banners: "WE HAVE OUR DADDIES".

December   Demonstration at Camden Arts Centre, during an exhibition attended by the Soviet Ambassador. Banners read: "HUMAN RIGHTS FOR RUSSIAN JEWS".

1977

January   Vladimir Bukovsky eats a 'prison meal' on his release, in homage to all Prisoners of Conscience.

February   The 35s contribution to International Women's Year was a petition signed by over ten thousand women, entitled "HAVEN'T ALL HUMAN BEINGS THE RIGHT TO FREEDOM?" It was piled into a supermarket trolley and wheeled to the Soviet Embassy by Margaret Drabble, Doris Hare, Helene Hayman, Cleo Laine, and Lady Rhys Williams. The Cultural Attaché refused to accept it as he said that it was political. (A picture of this demonstration is in *The British Encyclopaedia*, under Human Rights).

March   Demonstration outside Aeroflot Office during Jewish Festival of Purim. Hamantaschen (Purim cakes) were handed out to passers-by, by David Kossof.

March   During a wreath-laying ceremony at the Tomb of the Unknown Warrior in Westminster Abbey, by members of the Soviet army, 35ers displayed placards "HUMAN RIGHTS FOR SOVIET JEWS", and appealed in Russian and English for Sharansky.

March   Doreen Gainsford gave members of the Soviet Badminton Team a lift to London in her car, as there was no one to meet them at Heathrow!

March	A large advertisement in *The Daily Telegraph* placed by the Helsinki Watchdog Committee (which was organised by the 35s). Signed by Beilin, Nudel, Chernobilsky, Kremen, Lerner, Sharansky and Slepak protesting about the escalation of anti-Semitism in the USSR.
April	Demonstration outside the Intourist office, protesting against the lack of Passover facilities for Soviet Jews.
April	Outside Aeroflot, a prayer service for Sharansky, conducted by Rabbi Bernstein and the Rev. Freilich.
May	Brent and others: outside the Wembley Conference Centre. A banner demonstration against Jewish persecution to coincide with the opening of a Russian Film Week attended by Soviet Ambassador Lunkov.
May	Bromley and others: a letter handed in at Bromley Magistrate's Court to protest at the harassment of Iosif Begun.
May	Brent and others: outside the Soviet Embassy, Brent MP, Dr Rhodes Boyson handed in a protest letter for Professor Benjamin Fein (Brent group adoptee).
May	Outside Aeroflot Office, Sonia Davis of Finchley, impersonating Lady Godiva, rode a horse past the offices, protesting at the unjust imprisonment of Iosif Begun.
June	Simone Goldfarb and other 35ers chained themselves to a pillar inside Aeroflot and threw away the key, during the visit of Ponomariev. (As well as good coverage in London papers, this demonstration was also reported in the *Hong Kong Standard*).
December	Outside the Soviet Embassy, a two-hour vigil on behalf of Ida Milgrom (mother of Sharansky).

1978

April	Demonstration outside the Soviet Embassy, on behalf of Vladimir Slepak. Many public figures, including the Secretary of State for Energy, Tony Benn, were present.
April	Southgate: Communal postcard 'write-in'.
May	Bromley and others: outside St Martin-in-the-Fields on May Day for Sharansky.

July	Children's march for Misha Voikhansky.
October	Demonstration outside the Royal Festival Hall during the visit of the Leningrad Philharmonic Orchestra.
October	Brent: New Year card 'write-in' in Kingsbury attended by Dr Rhodes Boyson and his wife.
November	Hendon: letter sent to President Brezhnev. Signed by local MP John Gorst, on behalf of the Rosenstein family. Public signing outside the Edgware post office.
November	Brent: Demonstration for Professor A. Lerner and Sharansky during a display by Russian gymnasts at Wembley Conference Centre.
November	Demonstration outside Shaftesbury Theatre during a meeting of the Britain/USSR Friendship Society on Guy Fawkes night. Displayed giant guy bearing head of Brezhnev. Banners proclaimed: "GUY FAWKES TRIED TO DESTROY PARLIAMENT. DON'T LET BREZHNEV DESTROY HUMAN RIGHTS".
November	Demonstration outside the Soviet Embassy on the eve of Barbara Oberman's departure for Israel.
November	Demonstration on the steps of the British Museum during the visit of the Soviet Deputy Minister of Culture, Vladimir Popov.
December	Bromley: 'write-in' by 35ers and members of Bromley Reform Synagogue Soviet Jewry Committee. Attended by local MP John Hunt, who adopted a refusenik family.
December	Hendon: Books sent to adoptee Gregory Rosenstein, and a petition on his behalf sent to President Brezhnev, signed by local MP John Gorst and many eminent international scientists.
December	Edgware: Sends letters and books regularly to Gregory Rosenstein.

1979

February	Women's World Day of Prayer attended by 35ers and women from many different religious groups and denominations, at St Margaret's, Westminster. Prayers were said for the Moscow Women's Refusenik Groups.

June	At the USSR National Exhibition at Earls Court. Soviet officials distributed leaflets unaware that they were the 35s version of the original leaflet. They were placed next to the official leaflet but bore the message: "The real truth not on show at the USSR National Exhibition".
June	At the National Women's Labour Party Conference, Felixstowe. Lobbying and leafleting resulted in many delegates writing to Ida Nudel, and a letter on her behalf from the Conference was sent to Soviet officials.
July	Brent: At the Wembley Conference Centre, leaflets were handed out at a display by international gymnasts on behalf of Goldshtein and Gluzman.
August	A letter delivered to the USA Embassy on behalf of Sharansky, by Margaret Rigal and Rita Eker.
August	Brent: outside Wembley Jewish shopping area, a New Year card 'write-in' for Ida Nudel and others.
August	A New Year card 'write-in' by 35s and Exodus group in Golders Green Jewish shopping area.
August	South London: left a three-foot-high brown bear and a letter for a team of Soviet athletes at their Croydon hotel, on behalf of Nudel and Sharansky. One hundred and five letters delivered to the rooms of the athletes.
September	Brent: at the Wembley Conference Centre. Delegates (Soviet) to the International Computer Conference confronted by 35ers, on behalf of Professor Lerner.
September	At the Liberal Party Conference, Margate. A warm reception was given to four London 35ers. Delegates signed a petition on behalf of Sharansky and others.
October	Southgate: members of a correspondence circle regularly write to Slepak and Isabella Novikova.
October	Roman Catholic nun, Sister Ann Gillen, delivered a letter to the Soviet Embassy offering to serve the remainder of Nudel's exile in Siberia. She was accompanied by Margaret Rigal who presented a personal appeal for the release of a Russian Orthodox nun, Sister Makeyeva.

October	Rita Eker interviewed on the radio programme "You don't have to be Jewish" regarding the arrests of twelve Kiev activists.
October	Demonstration outside the Connaught Rooms, during a meeting of the British and Soviet Chambers of Commerce delegates.
October	Southgate: public 'write-in' and posting of one hundred and fifty birthday cards for Slepak.
November	Bromley: "Focus on Ida Nudel Evening" attended by many non-Jews. Postcards sent to Nudel, Sharansky and Mendelevich.
November	Demonstration outside Drury Lane Theatre during a rehearsal of the Royal Command Performance Variety Show where two members of the Bolshoi Ballet were performing.
November	St Albans: bombarded the Soviet Embassy with telephone calls for Riva Feldman
December	Demonstration and march from the Aeroflot Office to the Intourist office on Human Rights Day.
December	Brent: organised a showing of the film *Prisonland*.
November	Produced a booklet entitled *The Year of the Child, Soviet Style*, during the Year of the Child.
December	St Albans: sold postcards in the main street for Riva Feldman.

1980

January	Demonstration outside the Soviet Embassy for Sharansky, on his thirty-second birthday, the public was asked to sign a giant birthday card.
February	Demonstration outside the Roundhouse, during the appearance of the Rustaveli Theatre Company. 35ers were harassed by Turkish demonstrators.
March	Wembley and Bushey Heath: demonstration at Bushey Heath for Prisoner of Conscience Yaakov Kandinov.
March	Southgate: 'write-in' for Slepak and Novikova in the local shopping centre.
March	Brent: sold over two hundred passover cards in the Jewish shopping area, attended by local MP Dr Rhodes Boyson.
March	Attended International Seminar on Soviet Jewry.

March	Demonstration outside the Soviet Embassy on the third anniversary of Sharansky's arrest.
May	35ers lobbied on behalf of Ida Nudel at the Women's Labour Party Conference, Malvern. Delegates promised to write to Nudel and agreed to send a resolution to the International Women's Conference Secretariat pledging support for her.
June	Demonstration outside the Aeroflot Office on Human Rights violations. Over one thousand appeals were signed by passers-by.
June	Stanmore; during Stanmore Carnival Week 35ers participated in the parade, demonstrating on a lorry float with banners and posters for Sharansky and others.
June	Demonstration outside the Russian shop in Holborn. Distributed leaflets on behalf of Nudel, Slepak and Leningrad prisoners.
July	Bushey: 'knit-in' for Soviet Jewry. Scarves were sent to refuseniks.
June	Held daily protests outside Aeroflot Office (except weekends) during the Moscow Olympics.
December	Demonstration outside the Russian shop against the sale of goods made in 'slave' labour camps.

1981

January	Demonstration outside the Queen Elizabeth Hall during a performance by the Kasatzka Cossaks.
May	Demonstration outside the Festival Hall for Sharansky.
May	With other groups, a three-thousand-strong rally in Hyde Park for Sharansky.
October	Helped to organise the Camden Exhibition on Nudel, Prisoner of Conscience.
December	Mass Chanukkah card posting at Trafalgar Square post office.

1982

November	During the Miss World contest, 35ers, dressed as beauty queens, delivered Helsinki Packs to thirty-five representatives of signatories to the Agreement.

November	Demonstration at a concert at the Festival Hall given by the Philharmonia Orchestra and Russian-trained singer, Inna Arkhipova, during a performance of Prokofiev's *Alexander Nevsky*.
November	Mounted an exhibition highlighting the plight of Sharansky at the Save Our Sharansky shop in Bayswater (immediately opposite the Soviet Consulate office).
December	Edgware: organised a children's Chanukkah torchlight procession.

1983

January	Chained themselves to pillars inside the Aeroflot Office on behalf of Sharansky who was on a prolonged hunger strike.
February	Haggadoth (Passover prayer books), translated into Russian, sent to Soviet Union. Mailed in assorted sized envelopes to avoid suspicion of a mass mailing.
March	With others, including Chief Rabbi Jakobovits, and Greville Janner, MP: march to Hyde Park on behalf of Sharansky.
April	Kenton and Wembley: send thrice-yearly greetings, Haggadoth and kosher food to their adopted refuseniks.
April	South London: reported on the International Seminar on Soviet Jewry, Jerusalem, to the local papers.
May	Kenton and Wembley: organised sponsored silence on Lag B'Omer (Jewish festival).
November	Edgware: organised a Chanukkah torchlight procession.
November	Brent: demonstration for the Goldsteins at the Wembley Arena during a display by Russian gymnasts.
November	Demonstration outside the Festival Hall during the visit of the USSR State Symphony Orchestra.
November	Demonstration outside the Great Eastern Hotel during the chess semi-finals.
November	Demonstration outside the Soviet Embassy for Sakharov.
November	Organised March of the Refuseniks.

1984

May   Demonstration outside the Dominion Theatre during a performance by the Moscow Classical Ballet, on behalf of Andrei Sakharov.

October   Mass phone-in to jam the Soviet Embassy, Intourist and Aeroflot switchboards on behalf of Alexander Kholmiansky.

November   Organised an emergency meeting at the Adolf Tuck Hall to 'match-up' protesters with refuseniks.

December   Organised a series of demonstrations during the visit of Gorbachev.

1985

March   Organised "Second Festival of Music for Soviet Jewry" concert.

April   Demonstration outside the Soviet Embassy. 35ers demanded a list of long-term refuseniks (who, it was reported, had been given permission to leave). For the first time since the campaign had begun, a Soviet official came out and discussed the situation 'in a civilised manner'.

August   Demonstration outside the Dominion Theatre during a visit of the Moscow Circus, demonstrators dressed as clowns.

1986

January   Together with students and Baptists: outside Aeroflot Office, demonstration for Sharansky, causing the office to be closed.

March   Brent: demonstration outside the Wembley Arena during a visit of Russian gymnasts.

May   Bromley: meeting for Sakharov and the Zunshines.

May   Demonstration outside the Prince Edward Theatre for chess champion Boris Gulko, during the premiere of the musical *Chess*.

June   Brent: organised a sponsored parachute jump.

July   Demonstration outside the Royal Opera House during a visit of the Bolshoi Ballet. Nightly protests continued for two weeks.

August	Demonstration outside Downing Street, on behalf of Alexei Magarik, Prisoner of Zion, during the visit of Soviet Foreign Minister, Edward Shevardnadze.
November	Barnet: ongoing campaign for Nudel.
November	Demonstration outside the Aeroflot Office. 35ers played musical instruments in protest for musician Magarik.
December	Reported a heartwarming response to an appeal to all denominations of churches to remember Prisoners of Zion in their Christmas services.
December	Demonstration outside the Soviet Embassy. 35ers managed to speak to Embassy officials during a protest on Solidarity Day With Prisoners of Zion, on behalf of the Begun family.
December	Organised a letter-writing campaign to the Foreign Office at the time of the review of the Helsinki Accords.
December	Edgware: at local post office, a big 'post-in' by children who had made their own Chanukkah cards.

1987

January	Bromley: ongoing campaign for Cherna Goldort.
February	Held a ceremony on the first anniversary of Sharansky's release, at the oak tree planted on his birthday.
February	Letters sent to Raisa Gorbachev on International Women's Day.
March	Special Passover letters sent to refuseniks.
June	Organised a film show of *No Exit*. Bernard Levin introduced Dima Joffe, son of Professor Joffe.
June	Elstree and Radlett: Derek Praag MP spoke on his recent visit to the Soviet Union.
July	With others: attended Hyde Park Rally on Refusenik Sunday.
August	Demonstration outside the Royal Opera House during a visit of the Kirov Opera, for Magarik and others.
October	Demonstration outside the Soviet Embassy where Maisie Moscow 'launched' her new novel.
December	During the Thatcher/Gorbachev meeting, a lorry, bearing a huge placard in English and Russian: "LET MY PEOPLE GO", was driven from Golders Green to Whitehall.

| December | 35s groups countrywide wrote letters, sent telegrams, demonstrated, etc. during the Superpower talks. |

1988

February	35s meeting with Foreign Secretary, Geoffrey Howe, to discuss the refusenik situation, prior to his Moscow visit. He subsequently met four refuseniks at the British Embassy in Moscow.
March	Phoned Jewish 'sisters' in USSR on International Women's Day.
March	Demonstration during a performance of the Moscow State Circus in Battersea.
May	Demonstration outside the Albert Hall during a performance of the Red Army Ensemble choir.
July	Organised the sending of New Year greetings.
August	Demonstration outside the Coliseum Theatre during a visit of the Kirov Ballet.
October	On the fiftieth anniversary of Kristallnacht, organised the dispatch of Jewish books to the USSR to demonstrate that Jewish culture will not be allowed to perish.

1989

| April | Sent Haggadoth (Passover prayer books). |

1990

| December | At the Soviet Embassy, Margaret Rigal and Rita Eker had meeting with Ambassador Zamyatin on International Human Rights Day. (Margaret Rigal contrasted this meeting during which they were served tea, with previous 'turnings-away' at the door). |

1991

| December | Protest for prisoners Felix and Roman Bodner, 35ers delivered two hundred letters from MPs to the Soviet Embassy. |

SOUTHGATE

During the high activity period of the seventies and eighties, under the chairmanship of Lindy Grant, Southgate's main adoptees Vladimir

Slepak and Mark Dymshitz were supported by many local demonstrations. Visits by Slepak's sons gave added impetus to the campaign, which culminated in a huge meeting attended, amongst others, by the local MPs and the Mayor of Southgate.

The group also twinned two Bar-Mitzvot and organised numerous card signings at the three main festival periods of Passover, the New Year and Chanukah.

Together with their sister groups they joined in the larger demos, lobbied their MPs and other people of influence.

A collection of twenty thousand signatures was organised by Pearl Venit on behalf of Yuri Orlov, a member of the Helsinki Watchdog Committee exiled from Moscow during the run-up to the Olympic Games.

Many local churches were particularly helpful with this petition which was presented to Anthony Berry MP, outside the House of Commons.

From its inception the group was vitalised by the unstinting work of Anna Pliskin.

BIRMINGHAM

1977

May	35s, in conjunction with other Human Rights groups at Our Lady of the Wayside Convent. They felt that their protests had contributed to the release of two prisoners, scientists Alexander Feldman and Professor Yuli Tartakovsky.
June	Lobbied five Birmingham MPs at Westminster, to coincide with the Belgrade Review of the Helsinki Agreement on Human Rights.

1978

November	Demonstration on behalf of Slepak and Kim Fridman during visit of Russian Trade Unionists.
December	'Write-in' for Vladimir Slepak.

1979

January	Public meeting addressed by Israel Zalmanson.
April	Talk on psychiatric abuse in Soviet Union with particular reference to Semyon Gluzman.

April	'Write-in' supported by local churches, Bible college, Amnesty International, and the local Jewish community.
July	Publicity in the *Birmingham Evening Mail* about Ida Nudel. Church groups working for her. One hundred and fifty cards sent to her and protests sent to Brezhnev. Good coverage on BBC local radio.
July	Presentation of flowers and letters to Soviet visitors by local Young Farmer's Union in Mayor's Parlour. Publicity in local press.
November	Stand at B'nai B'rith Book Fair. Ted Willis spoke on behalf of Soviet Jewry. Books and Chanukkah cards sent to refuseniks.

1980

February to May	Write-up in local paper about difficulty of 35s attempting to telephone USSR. Example: it took two full evenings, twelve hours in all, to get through to Kiev.
May	Organised "Freedom Games" (reference to Moscow Olympics). Opened by the Duke of Devonshire. Jewish youth groups from all over British Isles participated.
August	Telegrams sent to the President of the International Olympics Committee calling on his help to free Vladimir Kislik who was jailed on the eve of the Olympics. Help also asked from the Royal College of Psychiatrists and from local MPs.

1983

January	Protests at Great Britain/USSR Athletics competitions.
November	Protests at Soviet State Symphony Orchestra concert.

1986

February	Talk on local radio on the day of Anatoly Sharansky's release.
December	Chanukkah candle-lighting ceremony attended by the Mayor, MPs and clergy.

1989

March	Meeting with the Lord Mayor and other dignitaries during the campaign for George Samoilovich.

BOURNEMOUTH

1973

October   Mass New Year card posting. Protest in the grounds of Beaulieu House when the Mayor of Moscow and party were guests of Lord Montagu.

1977

November   Twenty-four-hour hunger strike by Linda White in Bournemouth shopping centre to publicise case of Lev Furman, victimised for teaching Hebrew.

1978

May   (With others), handed protest letters and flowers to cyclists during Milk Race regarding Orlov, Ginsburg and Sharansky.

September   Handed protest letters and red roses to crew of Russian ship, on Weymouth beach, during World Sailing Championships.

1979

January   Meeting, together with B'nai B'rith Youth Organisation and Association of Jewish Ex-Servicemen. Bournemouth and Christchurch Trade Union Council passed a resolution condemning the persecution of Jews and other dissidents in the USSR. Write-in for Sharansky's birthday, attended by Mrs Sue Atkinson, wife of the local MP.

April   Protest meeting outside the Winter Gardens during a performance by the Bolshoi String Ensemble, for Nudel.

May   Brains Trust phone-in for Sharansky on local radio.

July   Meeting for Nudel and Sharansky – one hundred postcards sent.

October   Two hundred cards sent to Sharansky from outside Poole Arts Centre.

November   Protest outside Kings Theatre during a performance by the Russian Song and Dance Group.

November   Protest outside a meeting attended by Vladimir Propokov, member of Moscow Olympics Committee. He refused to accept a letter.

1980

March   Visit by Avital Sharansky who made many local appearances.

1982

December   Fund-raising and publicity lunch.

1983

January   Vigil in city centre for Sharansky. Members each fasted for twenty-four hours.

1984

October   Publicity meeting with David Steel (Leader of the Liberal Party).

1985

September   Meeting with Neil Kinnock (Leader of the Labour Party) at Labour Party Conference, who made reference to Soviet Jewry in his speech.

1986

December   Campaigned for release of Magarik.

1987

December   Presented sticks of Bournemouth rock for Gorbachev and Regain at Soviet and USA Embassies. Lettering inside rock spelt FREE SOVIET JEWS.

1988

October   During the TUC Conference members obtained over three hundred signatures on a petition to Soviet Trade Unionists requesting facilitation of exit visas.

BRIGHTON AND HOVE SOVIET JEWRY GROUP
(Affiliated to the 35s)

1972

August   Children of group members saved pocket money to help Leonid Slepak (who was celebrating his Bar-Mitzvah by proxy).

1973

June   A prison lunch, consisting of a hunk of black bread, 2oz. herring, and one potato was eaten to publicise the situation of Sylva Zalmanson. Actress Dora Bryan, to whom a Sylva Zalmanson medallion was presented, joined in the meal.

July   Letter-writing campaign launched on behalf of Olga and Michael Rijika.

1974

September Prime Minister Harold Wilson gave interview to Cecily Woolf during the Labour Party Conference. She asked him to speak on behalf of war hero, Mila Felzenstein.

1975

November Visit by Raiza Palatnik. She called on the two local newspapers to thank them for their support. Excellent coverage. Headline read: "FREEDOM IS WALKING IN TO SAY 'THANK YOU'".

November Ongoing campaign during 1975 for twin violinists Leonid and Arcady Wainman, involving many prominent musicians. A touching message was sent to them from Yehudi Menuhin.

1976

                  Adopted Alexander Paritsky and family, supporting them during his three-year prison term, and until they left for Israel in 1988. Partook in synchronised international write-ins and a phone-in, which jammed all lines to Kharkov.

May   Actor Jeremy Hawk joined in wreath-laying ceremony for Colonel Davidovich, who had died in refusal.

October   The group broke the Communist monopoly on the local Trades Council after intensive lobbying.

September Lobbying at TUC Conference.

1978

April   Mrs Anna Weiss launched a one-woman campaign for Lev Roitburd.

July	Wrote a song for the Slepaks which was broadcast on local radio. Later used for Sharansky and Sylva Zalmanson.
September	Lobbied the TUC Conference.
October	Picketed the Conservative Party Conference.
December	Helped to organise a programme of readings at Radio Brighton on United Nations Human Rights Day. Anthony Quayle read Sharansky's trial speech, and David Markham, Margaret Lockwood, and Phyllis Calvert also participated.

1979

January	Cable sent to Ida Nudel, good local press coverage. Horsham members held a coffee evening to raise money to visit their adopted refusenik Lev Roitburd.
June	A spectacular demonstration during the Milk Race. David Fifer, husband of the chairman, encased in strait-jacket to highlight Semyon Gluzman's plight. Featured on local and national TV.
August	Sixty-four cards sent to Soviet officials on behalf of Sharansky and Nudel.
October	Delegates to the Labour Party Conference were lobbied on behalf of Sharansky and others. Six hundred signatures were collected. Soviet officials at conference were presented with flowers and letters on behalf of Iosif Begun and Baptist Nikolaus Radom.
December	At write-in for Paritsky, three hundred cards were sent to Colonel Davidov, Head of Karkhov Ovir, asking to grant exit visa for Paritsky.
December	Children's letter-writing competition to Semyon Gluzman in labour camp. Entries were judged by novelist Madeleine Duke.

1980

January	'Thank you' visit by Boris Penson. Excellent coverage on BBC TV. An exhibition of his work had been organised and shown at Brighton Museum in 1977, which was opened by cartoonist Ralph Sallon and author Alan Sillitoe.

March	Following a campaign 'cocktail party', local Euro MP Sir Jack Stewart-Clark took up cases of Sharansky, Gluzman and Paritsky.
November	Demonstration at Confederation of British Industries Conference to coincide with the opening of the Madrid Review. Two hundred signatures obtained on behalf of Paritsky and Raoul Wallenberg.

1981

January	Adoptee Dr Semyon Gluzman made honorary member of The Royal College of Psychiatrists, through the efforts of Dr Peter Sainsbury.
January	Party for elderly members of local Jewish community to mark the thirty-third birthday of Sharansky.
February	During a reception for the Mayor and Mayoress, eighty guests wrote postcards and signed petitions in support of Prisoners of Conscience. Alan Sillitoe spoke on recent visit to Russia.
February	Campaign launched to send books to dissidents.

1981

May	Demonstration to protest at the visit of Moscow Philharmonic Orchestra, with presentation of letters and flowers, appealing against the persecution of Soviet musicians.

1983

September	Cecily Woolf spoke on BBC *Woman's Hour* on the work of the group.

1985

	Demonstrators dressed as clowns during the visit of the Moscow State Circus, on behalf of persecuted Hebrew teachers. Banners in Russian and English read: "STOP CLOWNING WITH HUMAN RIGHTS". Received good BBC and ITV coverage.

This group worked for non-Jews wherever possible, e.g. Pastor Vins (imprisoned for his Baptist beliefs), Dr Anatoly Koryugin in conjunction with Campaign Against Psychiatric Abuse), Veronica Rostropovich (sister of the famous cellist) and Raoul Wallenberg.

At the head of the campaign was their interpreter, Mrs Sonia Knufken. Thanks to her, letters and banners aimed at visiting Russians were written in their native language as well as in English.

DUBLIN AND BELFAST

(As Dublin was always included in the provincial section of the 35s, it is to be hoped that an international incident will not be provoked by continuing to regard them as such).

The following resumé of their work is from Lynn Jackson of the Dublin 35s.

"...I would like to say how great it was to work with Rita and Margaret, Joyce and many others in the 35s office during my time as chairman of our group.

The efficiently run office always provided us with up-to-date information and there was good rapport and enthusiasm between us all. We even had fun – working for such a serious matter.

Ireland joined the Campaign for Soviet Jewry in 1972 (we were called The Dublin 35s, Women's Campaign for Soviet Jewry) and demonstrated in support of the refuseniks in many different ways. Naturally, all the big names were at the forefront, including the first – Raiza Palatnik – for whom the 35s were founded, also Nudel, Sharansky, Zelichenok, Essas, Zunshine, Kosharovsky, Kholmiansky, Edelshtein and so on. We found an excellent way of highlighting the plight of the refuseniks at any public event. For instance, if the Bolshoi Ballet, opera or musical events were taking place, we presented every patron with a flower as they entered the venue. Attached to each flower was a note saying "Enjoy the performance, but please do spare a thought for the thousands of Soviet Jews (or the specific refusenik's name) who are suffering persecution because they wish to leave their country". This proved to be an excellent way to protest because it did not prevent people from going to the show – but it made them think. We got a very positive response from this.

When the Moscow State Circus hit town, we presented everyone with a gas filled balloon with a note attached, and this particular protest was screened on BBC News at 9 p.m. with our balloons gaily floating to the top of the Big Top! We also had large golf umbrellas printed with RIGHTS FOR SOVIET JEWS emblazoned on them. We had Soviet Jewry pins made which often provoked an enquiry, thus highlighting the plight in another way. These were very useful.

We organised, and coordinated sometimes through Europe, the telegram showers and phone-ins to the Soviet Embassies on behalf of individuals whose cases were urgent at the time.

The marches, demonstrations, vigils and fasts all drew attention. The most successful of these was the Roll Call for Soviet Jews which we did with the Dublin Jewish Student's Union in the city centre. The names of thousands of refuseniks were read out continuously throughout the day and many personalities participated in this. It was acknowledged in *The Dail* proceedings!

In 1982, we formed the Irish Council for Soviet Jewry, which a lot of men joined. Many were from the professional, business and religious world and we used this committee to liaise with the Government. A large number of people from the Dublin Jewish community visited refuseniks during the 1980s. In 1989, we amalgamated both committees to form the Irish Council for Soviet Jewry.

We now work mainly as a fund-raising body for Soviet Jews. We have a major Passover appeal and produce New Year cards. We raise money for Keren Klita and for the Children of Chernobyl, and are happy to say that although we are a very small community with very limited resources, we send off a nice cheque to Delysia Jason at Keren Klita at least once a year".

1977

| February | Held meeting together with Amnesty International. Addressed by Viktor Shtern for his father, Dr Mikhail Shtern. |
| February | Demonstration outside the Soviet Embassy, dressed in prison garb. |

1978

| December | Public meeting for Lev Gendin. |

1979

| February | Demonstration outside the Soviet Embassy on behalf of Igor Gutz separated from his wife and child. |
| February | Picketed the International Stand at the Travel Fair. 35s banners were ripped up by the Russians. |

March	Prayer vigil and proxy Bar-Mitzvah held outside the Soviet Embassy. Participation by Christian and other Jewish organisations.
June	Approached Irish parliamentarians on behalf of Soviet Jewry. They were very sympathetic.

1980

February	A Moscow Olympic protest at the Royal Dublin Society on the occasion of a government-sponsored sports exhibition.

1983

November	Demonstrations during the visit of the Soviet State Symphony Orchestra.
December	Demonstration outside the Royal Dublin Society Soviet Trade show. Sold notelets and Chanukkah cards. Helped by non-Jewish schoolchildren.

1984

December	One thousand seven hundred and fifty telephone calls made to the Soviet Embassy on behalf of Jewish prisoners
December	Silent Chanukkah demonstration outside the Soviet Embassy.
December	Annual Chanukkah procession.

1985

May	At the National Concert Hall, bouquets were thrown on the stage during a performance by the Georgian State Dancers.

1986

July	Demonstrations during the visit of the Bolshoi Ballet.

1987

May	Demonstrations during the visit of the Georgian Dance Ensemble.

GLASGOW AND EDINBURGH

1973

October — Held silent protest outside the main post office for Sylva Zalmanson. Hundreds of postcards sent.

1976

October — Demonstration at Glasgow Airport at the visit of Boris Ponomariev. 35ers wore white coats and face masks to recall Stalin's infamous Doctor's Plot.

1977

November — At the request of the 35s, the local District Council unanimously agreed to contact the Foreign Secretary, David Owen, (during his visit to Scotland) in an effort to secure the release of Jewish refuseniks.

1978

December — Demonstration outside the City Chambers when the Russian Ambassador lunched with the Lord Provost.

1979

April — 35ers gave talks to Jewish children during their withdrawal classes.

June — 35ers marched to the King George Dock in a vain attempt to deliver a letter to be sent to Ida Nudel via the captain of a Soviet tug ship.

July — Demonstration for Ida Nudel.

September — Together with Amnesty International, organised "Gulag 79" exhibition as part of the Edinburgh Fringe Festival. Over one thousand attended. Many wrote cards to Nudel, Sharansky and Soviet officials.

November — Demonstration for Sharansky and others outside theatre during the visit of the Russian Song and Dance Group.

1980

July — Demonstration during the visit of the former 1970 Leningrad trial prisoner Anatoly Altman. The Lord Provost of Glasgow promised to work for the release of others imprisoned at the same time.

September Exhibition organised in front of St Giles Cathedral. One thousand one hundred postcards were sent to Prisoners of Conscience during the Edinburgh Festival.

1984
April Broadcast on Radio Scotland on the work of the Glasgow and Edinburgh 35s.

1985
March Talk given on BBC local radio on the plight of Soviet Jewry.

1986
December Held Chanukkah card posting session.

ILFORD

Starting in 1969, since when Dora and Sydney Gabrel have given numerous talks throughout the campaign.

1972
May Demonstrations during the visit of Russian delegates to Newham. Local MP Arthur Lewis refused to attend a reception for the Moscow October Region, twinned with the borough.
June 35ers fasted for David Markish.
July Collected old brushes in the main street of Gants Hill to highlight the situation of Jewish professors who had been reduced to sweeping streets in the Soviet Union.
August Adopted an impoverished family.
November Demonstration at Harlow New Theatre at a performance during the Soviet Festival of Music.
November Wrote to the Soviet Minister of Education and to local councillors as part of an ongoing campaign.
November Organised a torchlight procession to the Town Hall for Sylva Zalmanson.

1973
February Torchlight procession to Dagenham Civic Centre for Sylva Zalmanson.

February	Organised articles in the local papers highlighting Sylva Zalmanson's situation.
April	Campaigned for fifteen-year-old Marina Temkin.
April	Demonstration outside Southend post office for Sylva Zalmanson to whom they posted a parcel.
June	Organised petitions for Sylva Zalmanson outside local factories.
November	Planted a weeping willow tree for Sylva Zalmanson in local Valentines Park.
December	Demonstrated the Potma prison camp 600-calorie diet in the main shopping centre, for Sylva Zalmanson.

1974

February	Glove sewing demonstration (her prison task), for Sylva Zalmanson outside Barking railway station.
April	Demonstration in Ilford shopping centre attended by local MP Arnold Shaw. Money was collected to send matzot to the USSR.
June	Demonstration in Ilford High Road, where 35ers, inside a cage, sewed gloves, for Sylva Zalmanson.
July	Demonstrations in Greenwich during a visit of the Bolshoi Ballet to Greenwich Observatory.
August	Sylva Zalmanson is released, but the campaign for her husband and brother continued.
September	Organised petition for Edward Kuznetsov and Zalmansons (*see above*) signed by local MP Arnold Shaw and others.
November	35ers visited local hospitals and handed letters on behalf of Dr Mikhail Shtern to the medical staff. A letter was handed to Russian delegates visiting Hackney, from the Architects, Engineers and Building Trades Committee for the Release of Soviet Jewry, on behalf of the Smeliansky family.

1975

January	Sylva Zalmanson visited 'her' tree in Valentines Park.
March	Partook in a demonstration at the visit of Alexander Shelepin, Russian Trade Union official who had been invited by the TUC. 35ers launched a petition against the visit outside a local factory.

April	This group was accused of being linked with "rich Jews of New York and the CIA" by the local branch of the British/Soviet Friendship Society!
May	Founder member Rene Kenley flew to Rome to appeal for the Pope's help in the fight for the release of Vladimir Lazarus.
May	Demonstration in Chelmsford for the seriously ill child of Vladimir Lazarus. Organised a petition signing in the shopping precinct.
July	Delivered the above petition to the Prime Minister.
August	Posted eight hundred Jewish New Year cards.
October	Marched to Harley Street on behalf of Dr Mikhail Shtern.
November	Demonstrated in prison garb in Ilford High Road. Shoppers signed one thousand two hundred cards to be sent to prisoners.

1976

January	Demonstrated together with local church officials for prisoners.
March	Members attended the World Conference on Soviet Jewry in Brussels.
June	Demonstration in Southend. Dressed in prison garb and chained together, 35ers paraded in the High Street to draw attention to the plight of forty Russian Jews imprisoned on trumped-up charges.
October	Following a talk by Dora Gabrel, Fairlop Young Conservatives adopted sixteen-year-old Dina Katzieva, who was being held in a prison camp.
October	Demonstration in Ilford, supported by local MP Arnold Shaw, appealing to the Prime Minister to ignore the visit of Boris Ponomariev (Secretary of the Central Committee of the Communist Party).
October	During the campaign for Ida Nudel, the group persuaded local churches to pray for her in their services.
December	Dressed as barristers, demonstrated outside Ilford Crown Court, on behalf of lawyer Lazarus.

1977

March   During ongoing campaign for Sharansky, prayers were recited in many churches throughout the month.

September   Telegrams were sent to Downing Street, the White House and President Brezhnev on behalf of Iosif Begun.

December   A card signing demonstration was attended by the Bishop of Barking.

December   A local paper, *The Ilford Recorder*, adopted Pavel Abramovich, who was trying to join his wife and son in Israel.

1978

June   Organised a Human Rights protest to Downing Street. Attended by local MPs Arnold Shaw and Vivian Bendall. This was to coincide with a visit by a Russian delegation.

June   Local MP Vivian Bendall asked a question on prisoners in the House of Commons.

August   MP Vivian Bendall attended a protest and petition-signing at Barkingside.

1979

February   Local MP Neil Thorne wrote to President Brezhnev on behalf of Emmanuel Smeliansky.

June   MP Neil Thorne took petition on behalf of Nudel to the Soviet Embassy.

1980

March   MP Vivian Bendall and 35ers made a vain attempt to deliver Bibles to the Soviet Embassy.

June   MPs Neil Thorne and Vivian Bendall press for the release of the Rosenstein family.

November   Sydney Gabrel supplied information to the Madrid Conference on Soviet interference with the mail – an infringement of Human Rights.

December   The group adopted Karl Grunberg, who was separated from his wife and children.

December   Held "send-a-postcard-to-prisoners" demonstration in Ilford High Road.

1983

March   A "blitz" of three hundred and twenty cards sent to Sharansky.

July   Demonstration during the visit of the Mayor of Moscow to Newham Town Hall.

1984

July   Organised campaign in attempt to get a sick baby to Israel.

1985

February   Planted a weeping willow tree in Valentines Park for prisoner Iosif Berenshtein.

September   Leaflets were distributed to four hundred Russian visitors to Grays, on behalf of Berenshtein.

1986

January   In Chigwell town centre, local MP Sir John Biggs-Davison sent postcard to Berenshtein.

March   Organised prison breakfast demonstration in Ilford High Road, attended by MP Neil Thorne.

March   Organised campaign for brothers of Pavel Abramovich.

1989

December   Organised campaign for Adolf Gorvich in Siberian labour camp.

1990

December   Dora Gabrel and other 35ers introduced to Soviet Ambassador Zamyatin at Soviet Embassy.

1992

March   Organised campaign for leukaemia victim Katya Macharet.

LEEDS

1973

December   Protest for Leonid Zabelishensky outside Leeds City Station on the arrival of three Russian guests of the Great Britain and USSR Friendship Society.

1975

September   Passers-by outside Holy Trinity Church in the city centre were asked to sign a protest petition for Lev Roitburd.

1976

December   Together with the Bradford Jewish communities, protest outside the Alhambra Theatre, Bradford during the visit of the Tschaika Cossacks, handed out leaflets. Coverage by local press and radio.

1977

June   Twelve 35ers attempted to present letters to Russian cyclists partaking in the Milk Race as they passed near Leeds.

August   Protest in shopping precinct for Iosif Begun.

1978

January   Greetings cards posted to Sharansky on his thirtieth birthday, at city centre post office.

December   Annual Chanukkah torchlight march by over five hundred participants. Addressed by Israel Zalmanson, Colin Shindler and attended by clergy of all denominations and MPs of all parties.

1979

February   Weeping birch tree planted in the grounds of the Deborah Taylor Nursery School (which is twinned with the Moscow Jewish Kindergarten).

May   Visit by Yanella Gutz (whose husband was in a camp). Publicity on local radio and in press.

July   Telegram sent to TGWU Conference at Scarborough protesting at Russian Trade Unions' lack of interest in Sharansky's plight.

November   Produced T-shirts with slogan "LET MY PEOPLE GO".

1980

March   Visit from Avital Sharansky who made many public appearances. Good media coverage.

April   Protest outside the international swimming pool during the visit of a Soviet swimming squad.

1981
> Tree planted for Sharansky.

1982
December   Annual calendar produced.

1983
November   Protests during the visit of the Soviet State Symphony Orchestra.

1984
January   Tied a yellow ribbon on the tree planted for Sharansky in 1981.

1985
March   Sponsored Sydney Levine in a Marathon run for Soviet Jewry.

December   Awarded a scholarship to Louisa Skolnik, daughter of an ex-Prisoner of Zion. Protest at the Town Hall at the visit of the Moscow Radio Orchestra.

1988

March   Partook in a nationwide campaign for the Kremen family and Chernobilsky

1990

March   Passover food collection outside Jewish stores; to be sent to Soviet Jews.

1993

March   Visit to Leningrad by Norma Weinberg and Susan Appleton, who took money, food, and clothing for the needy.

LIVERPOOL

1971

November   Silent demonstration held outside the Town Hall by newly-formed 35s. They planned to collect five thousand signatures for Raiza Palatnik to send to the Mayor of Odessa.

1973

June   Held one-day hunger strike in sympathy with six Moscow hunger-striking scientists.

July   Three banner-carrying 35ers gave a protest letter to Russian singer Alexander Vedernikov, (together with Manchester 35s). Demonstration at the visit of the Georgian State Dance Company at St Helens, displayed banners and prison rations, (together with Manchester 35s). Climbed Mount Snowdon together with mountaineer Don Whillans to leave a banner for Sylva Zalmanson.

September   (Together with Southport 35s), held a symbolic prison "banquet" to draw attention of delegates to the Liberal Party Association conference, at the conditions for prisoners in the USSR.

1977

January   Demonstration in the city centre during "Focus on Soviet Jewry Week".

March   Together with Merseyside Inter-denominational Committee for Soviet Jewry held a Forum on Soviet Jewry. The Duke of Devonshire praised the 35s for their efforts for Jewry and for "the enormous comfort you give to these people". The meeting was also addressed by MP Lynda Chalker.

June   Lobbied delegates at the TGWU Conference at Southport.

June   Organised "The Interview" by Alan Sillitoe, with Janet Suzman, for Ida Nudel.

July   Presented flowers and letters to visiting Russian transport delegates. The Soviets denied the lack of freedom to travel.

November   Demonstration on the sixtieth anniversary of the Russian Revolution.

1978

January   Held blood donating session. Donors included comedian Ken Dodd and two local MPs, Richard Crawshaw and Anthony Steen, to draw attention to the plight of Sharansky.

January	Held twenty-four-hour fast to protest at the treatment of Edward Kuznetsov (who had vowed to starve himself to death in a Siberian camp).
March	Lobbied delegates to the NUT Conference at Blackpool on behalf of Pavel Abramovich.
May	Street birthday party for Nudel. Children from the King David School and others from the Jewish community participated and sent birthday cards.
October	Demonstration at the visit of the Leningrad Philharmonic Orchestra, organised together with Amnesty International and Inter-denominational Council for Soviet Jewry. The Bishop of Liverpool, the Rt Rev. David Sheppard and his wife, Grace, participated.
	Action protest meeting for Nudel and Slepak. Petition sent to Mr and Mrs James Callaghan and President Jimmy Carter.

1978

October	Demonstration at the Labour Party Conference at Blackpool. 35ers dressed as pregnant women and carried banner "HELP US TO LABOUR FOR HUMAN RIGHTS".
December	Organised meeting for Nudel.

1979

January	Demonstration during "International Year of the Child".
March	Public signing of cards to President Brezhnev on behalf of Sharansky.
	Demonstration depicting Jewish heroines, Queen Esther and modern day, Ida Nudel. Reading by Dorothy Tutin on Nudel.
April	Organised Teddy Bears' Picnic for children.
May	Question asked in the House of Commons by local MP David Alton re Igor Gutz. Visit of Yanella Gutz and her baby.
	On Human Rights Day twelve nuns ate typical prison meal in foyer of Catholic Cathedral.
June	Demonstration "Vote for Freedom for Ida Nudel".

July	Visit by Slepak who made many public appearances, wide media coverage.
August	Demonstration in the city centre for Iosif Mendelevich, cards were sent to him on his thirty-second birthday.
August	Demonstration for Sharansky.
September	Demonstration for Nudel, Sharansky and Slepak attended by MP David Alton, authoress Lynne Banks and Jane Moonman, director of BIPAC(British Israel Public Affairs Committee)

1979

September	Collected six hundred and seventy-two signatures for Sharansky at the Conservative Party Conference at Blackpool. Visit by Wolf Zalmanson, with many public appearances.
October	35er interviewed on local radio re Elena Oleynik. Organised a petition for Mendelevich.

1980

February	More than one hundred pints of blood donated by 35ers and others at the annual blood-donating session. It was regarded as a symbolic giving of blood to Prisoners of Conscience and refuseniks.
March	Visit of Avital Sharansky to launch her book *Next Year in Jerusalem*.
June	(Together with WIZO) dedicated a chair in the Princes Road Synagogue to Nudel, during Service of Solidarity with Soviet Jewry.
December	(Together with WIZO) held an Open Forum on Soviet Jewry for the community. Visit by Hillel Butman. Chanukkah cards mailed to Prisoners of Conscience refuseniks.

1982

December	On Jewish Child's Day organised a day on the theme of Refusenik Children. Chanukkah candles were lit for Soviet Jewry.

1983

January	Tree planted for Sharansky at the King David School.

Avital Sharansky tape played on local radio.

September Organised a series of protests during the visit of Mr Promyslov, Mayor of Moscow.

1984

June Demonstration during the visit of the Moscow Classical Ballet Company.

1985

April Five hundred balloons released at Speke Airport for Nudel and others.

1986

June Alan Sillitoe spoke at "Evening of Solidarity with Nudel".

December Knit-in of baby clothes for refusenik children.

1987

June Postcard campaign for Nudel.

1989

May Hebrew teachers sent to Moscow.

1990

February Petition sent to President Gorbachev on resurgence of anti-Semitism.

Throughout the Liverpool campaign, 35ers Sylvia Lukeman and Debby Lazarus wrote a series of poems, some of which were set to music, articulating the plight of Soviet Jewry. Proceeds of the sale of some of this work was donated to the campaign.

MANCHESTER

1972

May In St Peter's Square, collected over one thousand signatures to a petition for the Markishes. This was also signed by the Mayors of Prestwich, Whitefield and Bury.

June City centre. Collected signatures to the Markishes petition outside Marks and Spencer's store.

June	Presented a two-foot-long key to the Leningrad speedway team. This was inscribed "To the Jews of Leningrad expressing the hope that this key will be used to open the door of freedom."
July	Parcels of brushes and broom-heads sent to the Soviet Ambassador in London to protest against the assignment of menial tasks to Jewish scientist refuseniks. Also held a "sweep-in" street demonstration.
September	"Auction" for the Levich family to protest against a £41,000 visa tax. (This was a protest demonstration not a fund-raising activity).
October	The Soviet Embassy refused to accept the six thousand signature petition for the Markishes.
November	The 35s, Herut members and students together held a silent protest during the visit of Russian musicians. The 35s left twenty-four toy musical instruments in the conductor's room with a letter explaining that they were a symbolic gift for twenty-four Jewish musicians who had been dismissed from their posts.
December	Participated in the annual Chanukkah torchlight procession.
1973	
January	Demonstration outside Chester Crown Court against show trial of Lazar Lubarsky in Rostov-on-Don.
February	During "Teitelbaum Week", three thousand five hundred cards were distributed to Manchester women's groups; these were printed and ready for signing and posting to the Soviet Ambassador in London. One thousand children in north-west England sent cards and presents to four-year-old Sonja Teitelbaum, the daughter of the Leningrad refuseniks.
April	Bouquets presented to two visiting Soviet women Trade Unionists, together with welcoming letters urging them to help improve conditions for Soviet Jews, especially the Panovs.
May	Demonstration, together with other groups, in front of Soviet officials from Leningrad, protesting against the forthcoming visit of the Leningrad Kirov Ballet.

May	Demonstration at Manchester Airport on the arrival of the Leningrad Kirov Ballet.
May	Demonstration at Manchester, '73 Festival, at tree planting by special guest Mr E. Gogolev, First Vice-Chairman of Leningrad City Council.
May	Parade and motorcade in support of Sylva Zalmanson.
May	Headline in *The Sunday Telegraph*, 20 May 1973, "Boycott hits Kirov Ballet, only fifty-five percent capacity bookings".
May	Leaflets handed out at Kirov Ballet performance: "Apology for non-appearance of Valery and Galina Panov".
May	When the Soviet national anthem was played at the beginning of the ballet performance, eighty members of the 35s, in three rows of the stalls, walked out, displaying placards and a long banner bearing the name of Valery Panov.
May	Demonstration outside Manchester Crown Court in protest of the visit of senior Leningrad Criminal Court Judge (cf "stare" protest).
June	Manchester and Liverpool 35s, supported by twenty members of St Helens Baptist Church, demonstrated outside the St Helens Theatre Royal in protest of the visit of the Russian Georgian State Dance Company.
July	35s "Climb for Sylva Zalmanson" led by Everest climber Don Whillans, his wife Audrey and wrestler Adrian Street.
	A birch tree, bearing a plaque, was planted on the three thousand foot summit of Tryfan, in North Wales.
October	Demonstration in Blackpool for Sylva Zalmanson's twenty-ninth birthday, in the presence of Mary Wilson, wife of the Prime Minister. They displayed two tables, one showing Western birthday food and the other showing Potma-camp style food – salted herring and dry black bread. Mrs Wilson sent a copy of her book of poems to Sylva Zalmanson. *(This demonstration took place during the annual Labour Party Conference.)*

November	Ten 35s on hunger strike outside Manchester Central Library, on behalf of the Goldstein brothers of Tbilisi.
December	"Prisoners of Conscience" exhibition at Whitefield Synagogue.

1974

March	Passover demonstration on behalf of the Gorman family, to whom a box of matzos was sent.
May	Dressed in academic gowns and mortar boards in protest at the downgrading of Jewish academic refuseniks to cleaners. *(On the occasion of the visit by the Chief Education Officer of Leningrad.)*
June	A delegation of visiting Soviet teachers and youth leaders was greeted with roses bearing a message demanding an end to anti-Jewish discrimination.
August	A giant chocolate box was presented to the Leningrad speedway team. Inside was a letter about the plight of refuseniks in jail together with a typical day's prison diet.
October	Protest at exhibition of Russian art at Whitworth Art Gallery.

1975

March	Demonstration protesting against the visit of Alexander Shelepin, head of the Soviet Trade Union movement. (He was a former KGB chief.)
March	Sylvia Sheff joins protest in Geneva on the occasion of International Women's Year at the Conference on Security and Co-operation in Europe.
April	Demonstration for the release of fifteen Jewish scientists. A tableau depicting a Russian bear savaging Jewish scientists was displayed on a lorry.
May	Demonstration in conjunction with the Manchester and Salford Council for Soviet Jewry during the visit of a delegation from the City of Leningrad.
June	During an athletic meeting at Bolton, in which four Russian athletes were competing, four 35ers in tracksuits ran round the track bearing placards... "Race for Soviet Jewish Freedom".

June	Demonstration during the visit of a delegation of Soviet teachers. There was a clash with the British Soviet Friendship Society.
September	Demonstration against the arrest and trial of Lev Roitburd.
September	Demonstration at the TUC Conference in Blackpool. A petition on behalf of refuseniks was presented and Soviet delegates were lobbied and interviewed.

1976

February	Nine members of the Manchester 35s attended an International Conference on Soviet Jewry in Brussels.
March	Joined with Manchester Jewish youth groups in a "Mother and Youth" rally and march on Mother's Day.
May	Organised a memorial service for the Soviet Jewish hero Col Yefim Davidovich.
September	Lobbied Prime Minister James Callaghan during his visit to a Trade Union and industrial officials luncheon.
October	Lobbied MPs and delegates to the Labour Party Conference at Blackpool.
December	Nightly protest demonstrations outside a cinema during the showing of a series of Russian films.

1977

January	Unsuccessful attempt to persuade the Manchester City Council to pressurise a visiting delegation from Leningrad to secure the release of Soviet Jewish prisoners.
February	Valentine's Day demonstration. The 35s, dressed in black, carried a large "broken heart" and the slogan "Stop breaking the Helsinki Agreement and Jewish hearts".
February	A 35s group was formed in North Cheshire.
May	A two-hundred-strong Silent Vigil was held outside the Town Hall during a reception for a delegation from Leningrad. As the guests entered the Town Hall they were greeted by blasts from eight shofarim (ram's horns) blown by eight Rabbis. There was a tableau with twelve members dressed in prison garb,

representing the twelve tribes of Israel. Two drummers sounded symbolic funereal beats.

July   Series of meetings organised during the visit of Prof. Benjamin Fain.

September   During the TUC Conference at Blackpool, they dressed as clowns and displayed banners with the slogan "Don't clown around with human lives". They distributed lists of Soviet workers who had been dismissed from their jobs after applying for emigration visas. *(This demonstration was held in conjunction with the Liverpool 35s.)*

October   At the Conservative Party Conference in Blackpool, the Prime Minister, Margaret Thatcher, was presented with a basket containing twenty-seven roses, each of which represented a Jewish Prisoner of Conscience.

November   Demonstration outside the Free Trade Hall during a British Soviet Friendship Society concert. A mock programme was distributed.

December   An outsize Chanukkah card (three feet by two feet) was left at the Soviet Embassy, but no one would accept it on behalf of the Ambassador. The card had been signed by Manchester citizens at a public lighting ceremony of a menorah (symbolic candelabrum).

December   Series of meetings organised during the visit of Prof. Eugeny Reinberg.

1978

April   Series of public meetings arranged for the visit of Prof. Herman Shapiro.

April   Eve of Passover "Let My People Go" meeting with the Duke of Devonshire and Baroness Hornsby-Smith as guest speakers.

April   Meetings arranged for visit of Vladimir Slepak.

June   Demonstration in support of Ida Nudel. Copies of letters on her behalf were handed to judges at the Manchester Crown Court.

July   In conjunction with the Manchester Council for Soviet Jewry, a twenty-four-hour vigil and fast was held in a silent demonstration outside the Law Courts, on behalf of Ginsburg and Sharansky.

September	Demonstration outside the Town Hall during a civic reception for a visiting delegation from Leningrad.
September	Annual New Year greetings sent to refusenik families and prisoners via the local Jewish newspapers.
October	In conjunction with the 35s of Southport and St Anne's, the delegates to the Labour Party Conference at Blackpool were lobbied and urged to sign a petition against the holding of the Olympic Games in Moscow.
October	Prior to a visit of the Leningrad Philharmonic Orchestra, the 35s launched a campaign urging intending patrons not to attend the concerts. A large demonstration was held outside the Town Hall during a civic reception for the orchestra. Twelve members attended the concert, dressed in black and wearing Sylva Zalmanson medallions. During the playing of the Russian national anthem they displayed banners inscribed "Leningrad – Stop Playing with Jewish Lives". They left before the concert began. *(They were later complimented on their dignified demonstration.)*
December	Letters of protest on behalf of refuseniks were handed to the Russian Ambassador. These had been written by Jews and non-Jews on the anniversary of the signing of the Declaration of Human Rights.
December	Series of meetings organised during the visit of Sonia Lerner, whose parents were refuseniks.
December	Together with two local MPs, Frank White and Jim Callaghan, 35ers attempted to deliver protest letters to the Soviet Embassy on behalf of the Taratuta and Gorman families. Although there was a pre-arranged appointment no one was available to receive them and they were refused admission. The MPs complained of the discourtesy shown to them.
1979	
March	Non-Jewish members of the 35s obtained a promise from the Lord Mayor, Cllr Trevor Thomas, to plead on behalf of Boris Kalandarev during his forthcoming visit to Moscow.

April	Manchester City Council was persuaded to pass a motion deploring the lack of Human Rights and they agreed to limit grants or subsidies related to exchange visits.
May	Delegation from Leningrad refused to accept leaflets from the 35s.
August	MP Frank White visited the Soviet Embassy to plead on behalf of refuseniks. He took six case histories with him but the second secretary refused to accept them. They were later posted to the Embassy.
September	Meetings organised for the visit of Wolf Zalmanson.
October	Prime Minister Margaret Thatcher received a delegation of 35s during the Conservative Party Conference at Blackpool. She was presented with a framed painting by eighteen-year-old Leningrad refusenik Mischa Taratuta.

1980

February	Demonstration in support of Sakharov in the City Centre.
February	Demonstration at visit of Russian Trade Unionists.
February	Demonstration outside meeting of British Soviet Friendship Society.
February	In conjunction with youth groups, there was a one thousand strong silent torchlight procession on behalf of Anatoly Sharansky.
March	Demonstration outside the Town Hall during a visit of the head of Intourist from Moscow.
April	Many meetings arranged for the visit of Avital Sharansky.
May	The "Freedom Olympics" opened by the Duke of Devonshire. This was organised in conjunction with the Manchester Council of Christians and Jews. Jewish youth groups from all over Britain competed.
June	Demonstration in conjunction with WIZO and the Manchester Council of Christians and Jews on International Ida Nudel Day. This was held in torrential rain, but over two hundred signatures were obtained.
October	Two hundred postcards sent to Anatoly Sharansky.

1981

February	The Lord Mayor, Cllr Mrs Winnie Smith, wrote to the Chairman of Leningrad City Council, Mr Kazakov, on behalf of the Taratuta family.
March	A seven-hundred-and-fifty strong torchlight procession.
September	"Missing Relatives in the USSR" campaign linking members of the local Jewish community to refuseniks in the USSR with the same or similar surnames.
September	The Lord Mayor, Cllr Hugh Lee, addressed a personal appeal to the Russian Ambassador on behalf of refusenik families.
September	Demonstration outside the Central Library in protest at the exhibition of Russian books. An alternative book exhibition was staged to publicise the banning of many Jewish books inside the Soviet Union.
September	A half page New Year greeting in the *Jewish Telegraph* and the *Jewish Gazette* listed the names of all Jewish refuseniks and prisoners.
September	Visits by Bronia Gimpilson and Dina Beilin, who met the Lord Mayor and other officials.
December	Campaign on behalf of the Taratuta family, supported by the Mayor of Bury.

1982

January	Demonstration at Snooker Classic in Oldham. (This was sponsored by Lada cars, components of which are made in Soviet prison camps.)
January	Demonstration in support of the Taratuta family during the visit of a Russian conductor to the Hallé Orchestra.
February	Letters and telegrams sent to visiting Soviet Trade Unionists.
March	Organised "Children for Freedom for Soviet Jewry" competition.
April	Demonstration outside the Free Trade Hall during the visit of the Moscow Balalaika Orchestra.
May	On the tenth anniversary of the 35s, they marked the tenth year of their adoption of the Taratuta family and noted their severe harassment.
June	Demonstration objecting to the reception of a party of visitors from Leningrad by the Jewish Lord Mayor.

July	A delegation of Soviet students tried to avoid the demonstrating 35ers by using the back door of the Town Hall.
September	Sponsored a tree planting in the grounds of the Broughton Jewish Junior School in the name of Anatoly Sharansky. The City Council had rejected a request to plant a tree in the city centre at that time.
October	Sylvia Sheff had a private meeting with the Prime Minister Margaret Thatcher, during the Conservative Party Conference at Blackpool. She presented her with the book *Exit Visa* (by Colin Shindler) and a bouquet of flowers.
November	The Manchester 35s participated in a London rally for Soviet Jewry.
December	Demonstration on the arrival of a delegation from Leningrad. Later there was a meeting in the Mayor's Parlour between the Russians and a Jewish delegation which included Sylvia Sheff and the President of the Jewish Representative Council. Following a "full and frank discussion" six refuseniks were granted exit visas as a goodwill gesture.

1984

February	Organised "Dreams of Freedom" concert at Whitefield Synagogue.
March	Seven hundred strong annual torchlight procession to the city centre, together with the Manchester, Jewish Youth Council.
March	Tree planting ceremony in Piccadilly Gardens by the Lord Mayor and Lady Mayoress, in the name of Anatoly Sharansky.
September	Daily vigils held at "Sharansky" tree during the Ten Days of Penitence (a period of Jewish religious observance). A different Jewish organisation was in attendance on each of the days and there were silent prayers and soundings of the Shofar (ram's horn).
November	Sylvia Sheff met the Prime Minister's personal secretary at 10 Downing Street.
December	Mass "post-in of two thousand cards to the Soviet Embassy on the occasion of the visit of President

Gorbachev. (Twenty-five thousand cards were sent nationally.)

1985

February Fig tree planted in the Soviet Jewry Biblical Garden of Broughton Jewish Junior School in the name of refusenik Iosif Begun.

June Demonstration during the visit of a Russian peace delegation. The attempted presentation of a white floral bouquet, symbolising peace, and a letter was thwarted by a TUC official.

July Demonstration outside the Palace Theatre during a visit of the Moscow State Circus.

October Sylvia Sheff had private meetings with Prime Minister Margaret Thatcher at 10 Downing Street and at the Conservative Party Conference in Blackpool.

1986

February Sylvia Sheff travelled to Israel to be amongst the welcoming crowd for the arrival of Anatoly Sharansky at Ben Gurion Airport.

May "Prayer Vigil and Symbolic Lunch" to celebrate Sharansky's release.

July Meetings arranged for the visit of Dr Yaacov Gorodetsky.

August Demonstrations outside the Palace Theatre during the visit of the Bolshoi Ballet.

August Many meetings arranged for the visit of Sharansky including a huge public meeting in the Free Trade Hall and a press conference.

August Demonstrations during the visit of the Kirov OperaCompany.

1987

May Demonstration outside the Palace Theatre during the visit of the Georgian State Dance Company. A mock programme was distributed.

May Demonstration outside the Intourist office in support of a group of "Moscow Women against Refusal" (a group of Jewish women whose families had been split up).

October	Visit of Mischa Taratuta after his fifteen years in refusal. He had tea with the Prime Minister during the Conservative Party Conference in Blackpool.
December	Demonstration to coincide with the visit of President Gorbachev. A float containing a caged Jew, representing the refuseniks, toured the city centre.

1988

February	Visit of the Taratuta family, Manchester 35s special family who had been in refusal for fifteen years.
April	Picketed the Red Army Ensemble concert outside a Stockport Theatre.
June	Demonstration at the visit of the Moscow State Circus. A mock programme was distributed.

1989

October	Sylvia Sheff met the Prime Minister Margaret Thatcher during the Conservative Party Conference and they discussed the continuing plight of the refuseniks.

1990

March	Petition sent to Mrs Thatcher requesting that pressure be put on the Soviet Government to enforce its constitutional ban on Pamyat (the right wing extremist group).
May	The Prime Minister and MPs were lobbied about the increase of Soviet anti-Semitism.
May	Meeting with Soviet Embassy second secretary who admitted that anti-Semitism did exist in the Soviet Union and that the plight of long-term refuseniks would be resolved by the end of the year.
May	Meeting with Frazer Wheeler of the Soviet department of the Foreign Office, who promised that the Foreign Office would urge that new laws should be introduced in the Soviet Union.
May	A petition was handed in at 10 Downing Street urging the Government to refuse to participate in the 1991 Human Rights Conference until the Soviet Government guaranteed the Human Rights of Soviet Jews.
June	Delegates attend the Conference on Security and Co-operation in Europe at Copenhagen.

June	Meeting with top Soviet officials to put the case for Soviet Jewry in view of the threat from Pamyat. They admitted that anti-Semitism was a serious problem in the USSR. The meeting was instrumental in the granting of exit visas for two refuseniks.
December	Took part in a national delegation of 35ers in a meeting with Soviet Ambassador Leonid Zamyatin on Human Rights Day.
December	Launch of campaign to send food to the Soviet Union. Sixty large packing cases of food were sent.

1991

July	Visit to Leningrad.
July	Meeting with the Lord Mayor of Manchester, Cllr George Chadwick, following the visit to Leningrad to apprise him of the problems facing Jews in the Soviet Union.
August	Sylvia Sheff visited St Petersburg and apart from visiting refuseniks she also saw St Petersburg officials. The head of emigration, Leonid Savitsky said that they would be considering the refuseniks' applications more sympathetically.

1992

January	Following a visit by a delegation from Manchester City Council, four long-term refuseniks received exit visas, due to representations by the 35s.
October	Visit to St Petersburg by Sylvia Sheff to assess the refusenik situation prior to the visit by a St Petersburg civic delegation to Manchester. She had a meeting with Alexander Belyaev, Chief of the St Petersburg City Council, armed with first-hand knowledge of a group of seventy refuseniks and poor relations.
December	Meeting with Foreign Minister Douglas Hurd at the Foreign Office in London.

NEWCASTLE-ON-TYNE

1977

May President Carter, on a visit to Newcastle, accepted flowers and a letter applauding his stand on Human Rights from Chairman Melanie Mark. Demonstration on behalf of Sharansky and Begun.

December Week-long activities during "Worldwide Solidarity Week for Soviet Jewry", ranging from interview on local BBC Radio to services in synagogues.

1978

February Visit of Sylva Zalmanson, many public appearances.

March Showing of film *Prisonland* (together with Gosforth Christian Fellowship).

November Address to Union of Jewish Students at Newcastle University. Students adopted Igor Korchnoi.

1979

March Demonstration outside St Nicholas Cathedral attended by local rabbis and the Provost, The Very Rev. Christopher Spofford. Two hundred postcards sent by passers-by.

Organised "prisoners lunch" outside St Thomas to commemorate the second anniversary of Sharansky's arrest.

April Talk given to Youth Council, postcards sent.

May Write-in for Semyon Gluzman. Forty members on a letter-writing rota.

Visit by Yanella Gutz, much media publicity.

June Manned a stall at the WIZO Bazaar with publicity for Nudel.

July Local radio devoted their religious programme to Nudel.

October Articles in the local press re Yanella Gutz.

November Gave talk at Round Table meeting.

December Chanukkah party "protest", Chanukkah cards were sold.

1980

January Protest against a civic reception for the crew of a Russian ship, outside South Shields Town Hall.

February	(Together with Scientific and Technical Committee), letter and petition campaign organised for Andrei Sakharov.
March	Visit by Avital Sharansky.
	Protest at meeting of British Soviet Friendship Society.
	Gave talk at Townswomen's Guild, postcards sent to Nudel.
June	Presented bouquet and protest letter on behalf of Sharansky and Nudel to visiting Russian cyclist in Milk Race, by Melanie Mark.
November	Questions asked of Russian poet guests at Tyneside Poets Association meeting re Gluzman.
December	One hundred Chanukkah cards sent during Hebrew school prize-giving.

1981

January	The Provost of St Nicholas Cathedral agreed to read a 'psalm' written by Gluzman at a service.
	Talks given at schools re Gluzman.
	Action for Gluzman at Methodist church.

1983

January	Day-long fast and vigil in city centre which was attended by the Lord Mayor and community leaders.

1984

October	Gave interview on local radio, together with actress Pamela Manson.
October	Actor John Hurt agreed to take up case of film producer Leonid Elbert.

1986

May	Protest letter and gifts handed to visiting Soviet Trade Organisation at a meeting of Newcastle Chamber of Commerce.

1987

December	Organised Soviet Jewry Shabbat and Chanukkah candle-lighting ceremony.

During the Sharansky campaign, Chairman Melanie Mark spent twenty-four hours in a small cage in the city centre.

In addition to the many groups listed above, there were other groups whose work was no less valuable to the campaign for being on a smaller scale.

CARDIFF AND SWANSEA

The following is a sample of their activities:

1. Cllr Olson wrote to the Foreign Office about the plight of Yakov Kandinov.
2. Together with George Thomas MP (later Viscount Tonypandy, former Speaker of the House of Commons), 35s boarded a vessel in Cardiff Docks on behalf of Raiza Palatnik.
3. Were involved in lobbying the Royal College of Psychiatrists to expel Russia from the World Congress of Psychiatry re Gluzman. Sylvia Aron made a personal approach to Professors Lynford Rees and Kenneth Rawnsley.

NOTTINGHAM

1975

August   Confronted Russian oarsmen at the opening of the second half of the World Rowing Championships with "FREER MOVEMENT OF JEWISH PEOPLE AND IDEAS" banners.

1983

November   Staged protests during the visit of the Soviet State Symphony Orchestra.

READING

1980

April   New 35s group formed.

SHEFFIELD

1983

January   During a visit of forty Donetsk *(twinned with Sheffield)* citizens, 35ers from different groups staged demonstrations.

SOUTHPORT AND ST ANNE'S

1978

January   Planted a tree to publicise the plight of Soviet Jewry.
February   Held a fund-raising and publicity coffee morning.
April   Held a proxy Bar-Mitzvah twinning with Sasha Kremen.

WEST SUSSEX

1979

July   Letter of protest and a bouquet of flowers handed to the Soviet Music Ensemble in Crawley.
Talks given to women's church groups.
Visited Moscow and met refuseniks.
Adopted Lev Roitburd.
Letter-writing campaign for Alexsei Murzhenko and Vaisman.

SOUTHAMPTON

1973

December   Demonstration outside dock gates as passengers boarded the Russian liner *Fedor Shalyapin*.

1977

Spring   (Together with Bournemouth and Essex), demonstration at Torquay outside the venue of Bilderberg Conference, for Sharansky.

ST ALBANS

1979

November Bombarded Soviet Embassy with telephone calls to discover the plight of Riva Feldman, a fifty-year old widow with twin sons who was refused an exit visa and lost her job.

1989

January Sold cards to send to their refuseniks, from a table in front of St Albans Town Hall.

OVERSEAS

BELGIUM (BRUSSELS AND ANTWERP)

1979

June May Day demonstration for all refuseniks.

1980

January Demonstration to mark International Solidarity Week, outside Palais Des Beaux Arts at the first night of the Berezka Moscow Dance Group. Five hundred leaflets with detachable postcards to be sent to the Soviet Ambassador handed out by 35ers asking him to intervene for prisoners Fedorov, Marchenko (non-Jews) and Mendelevich. Displayed banner "FREE THE PRISONERS OF CONSCIENCE".

May Avital Sharansky met Belgian Foreign Minister; she broadcast on local radio and TV.

1983

November Chanukkah service held outside Aeroflot Office.

1984

December Chanukkah ceremony and cultural evening held in Liberal Synagogue.

1985

November Press conference held prior to the Reagan/Gorbachev summit in Geneva.

1986

December   Demonstration outside the Soviet Embassy on behalf of the Begun family. Spoke to officials inside the Embassy.

CANADA

The Canadian 35s had an extremely active programme. The following resume is taken from *Count Us In*, by Wendy Eisen.

"A nucleus of women in each of the four cities (Montreal, Toronto, Ottawa and Winnipeg) met regularly to discuss how best to publicise the plight of refuseniks and prisoners. The moment that news of an arrest of a refusenik reached Canada, the 35s were on the streets in protest. They became proficient at co-ordinating demonstrations on short notice, stencilling and painting signs, writing press releases and securing police permits.

"Most demonstrations in Ottawa were held on the street across from the Soviet Embassy, and in Montreal outside the Soviet Consulate. In Toronto and Winnipeg, cities with no Soviet presence, the women gathered at civic locations such as public parks, government buildings. Like their international counterparts, the Canadian 35s demonstrated in black and their motto was: WE SPEAK OUT FOR THOSE WHO CANNOT SPEAK OUT FOR THEMSELVES.

"The 35s tried to find a gimmick to enable the media to report Soviet news through local protest. When Dr Mikhail Shtern, an endocrinologist from Vinnitsa was sentenced to eight years hard labour for accepting bribes of chicken and eggs from some of his patients, the 35s gathered outside the Soviet Embassy. They carried baskets of eggs and dead chickens strung on a wooden rod to mock the charges."

ISRAEL

The Israeli branch of the 35s was started in 1978 by Doreen Gainsford shortly after her move to Israel. Little was done, however, until after its formal launching in 1983 by (Sir) Martin Gilbert, held at the home of former Israeli Foreign Minister, Abba Eban.

An important aspect of its wrok was in the lobbying of Israeli government ministers, visiting dignitaries and heads of state, on behalf of individual refuseniks. Equally important was the briefing of lawyers sent to Russia in order to aid prisoners before and after their trials. Together with visits by travellers much moral and practical support was given.

For details of the current work of this group, see pages 153 and 184.

LUXEMBOURG
(founded in 1978 by Mrs Lindsay Wittenberg-Mindel)

1979

March   Attempted to hand in a petition to the Soviet Embassy on behalf of Ida Nudel and six other women.

1979

June   On Ida Nudel Day, 35ers stood in main square to obtain signatures for a petition to be sent to President Brezhnev. Signatories included the Minister of Finance and other parliamentarians and two Deputy Mayors. Many members of the public sent postcards to Nudel. There was good media coverage.

1980

November   35s instigated articles in the press on behalf of Ida Nudel and the Hess family. They also delivered a letter to the Commission on Human Rights.

November   Bouquets and a telegram asking them to spare a thought for those Soviet Jews who cannot leave the USSR, sent to visiting Soviet musicians during their recital.

Signatures were collected on a petition for Abe Stollar, Evgeny Levin and Vladimir Raiz[137].

---

[137] Eliane Karaguilla, former secretary and current Chairman of Luxembourg 35s writes: "When we organised the giant petition for Lein, Raiz and Stollar, the Luxembourg Secretary of Foreign Affairs suggested that we gave the petition to a member of his staff who was going to Moscow the next day. We, of course, agreed, and the following day, Mr Goebbels, the Foreign Affairs Secretary, informed us that Lein and Stolar were granted exit visas".

1981

January   Open letter sent to Spartak, the Moscow football team during their visit.

1982

November   Telegram sent to the Prime Minister asking him to intercede on behalf of Sharansky.

November   Flowers and letters presented to Russian Folk Ensemble regarding prisoners.

1983

March   Partook in International Day of Support for Iosif Begun.

1984

January   Delegation of MPs and clergy took a giant birthday card for Sharansky to the Soviet Embassy.

April   Instigated articles in the press and on radio on the anniversary of Sharansky's arrest.

May   Wrote to the President of the European Parliament protesting about the extolling of the virtues of the Soviet Union displayed in an exhibition during the session of the European Parliament in Strasbourg.

1985

February   Launched a letter campaign for Iosif Berenshtein and a telegram campaign for visas for Zunshine, Sharansky, Levin, Begun and Kholmiansky. There was good press coverage.

October   During visit of the Bolshoi Ballet 35ers picketed the theatre with banners and leaflets. They handed a leaflet about Sharansky to Soviet Ambassador Oudoumian.

1986

December   Started press campaign for Nudel, Begun, Volvovsky and Edelshtein.

December   Held a demonstration outside the Soviet Embassy on behalf of the Begun family.

1987

October   Joyce Simson was the guest speaker at the Annual Dinner.

NEW ZEALAND (AUCKLAND)

1978

April   Silent vigil in downtown Auckland.

April   Demonstration at Auckland International Airport to greet a Soviet Trade Delegation.

April   Airfreighted a parcel of fish tied with black ribbon bearing the message "FISHING RIGHTS FOR SOVIET UNION – HUMAN RIGHTS FOR SOVIET JEWS".

1984

December   Demonstration at visit of the Moscow State Circus.

1985

March   Organised national petition for Sharansky.

March   Telegram sent to United Nations Secretary General re persecution of Soviet Jews.

March   Petition sent to MPs.

PROVINCIAL LIST, MAY 1976
(Some of these Groups were affiliates)

Birmingham, Bournemouth, Brighton and Hove, Cambridge, Cardiff, Dublin (and Belfast), Edinburgh, Glasgow, Grimsby, Hull, Leeds, Liverpool, Manchester, Maidstone and Medway towns, Newcastle, Nottingham, Oxford, St Anne's-on-Sea, Sheffield, Southampton, Southport, Sunderland.

LONDON AND OUTER LONDON, JUNE 1988

Brent, Bushey, Edgware, Elstree, Essex, Pinner, South London, Croydon.

Appendix 3
The A-Z of Demonstrating

A.............art exhibition
B.............brooms, sweeping
C.............coffins
D.............diet, prison
E.............Eisteddfod
F.............flowers
G.............graveyard
H.............hearts, broken
I.............ice rink
J.............jog for justice
K.............keys
L.............launch, motor
M...........musical instruments
N.............nappies, babies'
O.............Oliviers, Laurence and Vivien
P.............parachute
Q.............questions, in parliament
R.............royalty
S.............shofarim
T.............trees
U.............umbrellas
V.............Valentine's Day
W...........workmen, dressed as
X.............crement, horse manure
Y.............year – Year of the Child booklet
Z.............Zeal

Index